A HISTOR▐▐▐▐ ▐HE WALLASEY CORPORATION MOTOR BUS UNDERTAKING 1920-1969

Late T.B. Maund FCILT

THE OMNIBUS SOCIETY
www.omnibus-society.org

PROVINCIAL HISTORICAL RESEARCH GROUP

Front Cover: Evocative of the Wallasey fleet as older enthusiasts will remember it and with very contrasting styles of Metro-Cammell bodywork and Leyland chassis. Although of 1948 construction, PD2 No. 25 was delivered with 54-seat bodywork designed over 15 years earlier in contrast to the Atlantean's 77-seater capacity of 1958. (T.B. Maund Collection)

Published by
THE OMNIBUS SOCIETY
Provincial Historical Research Group

Registered Office
100 Sandwell Street
Walsall
WS1 3EB

Printed by Henry Ling Ltd, The Dorset Press, Dorchester DT1 1HD
Design and production: Trevor Preece: trevor@trpub.net

ISBN   978-1-909091-11-5

PHRG

CONTENTS

PHRG

The author enjoys an ice cream in North Wales, August 2012.

A selection from a prodigious output.

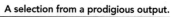

THE AUTHOR – A TRIBUTE

Thomas Bruce Jones Maund, 1924-2013, former bus company manager, author of some of the most authoritative works on transport history and a member of the *Omnibus Society* from 1943 was born in Wallasey on 10 August 1924 and died there on 1 October, 2013.

His professional career started as a junior railway clerk in a local goods office, but after WW2 army service in Africa he began work in the bus industry in 1948 with Basil William's Hants & Sussex. The following year he obtained a position with Ribble Motor Services where with that company and its Standerwick subsidiary for 18 years he was to be known as 'Tom'. He was latterly District Traffic Superintendent in Blackpool. In 1966 he was seconded to the Merseyside Area Land Use/Transport Study (MALTS) and then in 1970 took the opportunity to move abroad to take up a position with United Transport in Kenya, moving on to Western Greyhound in South Africa in 1976. He retired in 1991 and he and his wife Kathleen ('Kay') – née Skelton – whom he had married in 1951 – made their home in Prenton, Wirral. They joked that the first time they met they spent the night together – on an overnight coach en-route to an OS event! Kay was a staunch supporter of her husband's interests and regularly accompanied him at OS Presidential Weekends, etc.

He traced his interest in transport to the late 1920s, having memories of the introduction of double-deck buses in his home town and its tram system, which closed in 1933. His family accepted his interest but, in his own words, *"All attempts to wean me off my 'mania' failed"*. His adventurous nature took him on a solo trip to Liverpool via the ferry at the age of six. The Ribble terminus there provided a ready source of tickets, such that by the age of ten he could be described as a 'serious ticket collector'. The reward of a bicycle for passing the grammar school scholarship widened his horizons and he undertook ambitious trips as far afield as Greater Manchester and the Potteries.

Until then Bruce had been unaware of the existence of any other bus enthusiasts apart from a small set of contacts with whom he corresponded in connection with his ticket collection. One of these was tramway expert W.H. Bett, who lived in Birmingham and who persuaded him to join the Light Railway Transport League. Through its Merseyside representative he met (1941) Peter Hardy, who had been researching Liverpool bus routes, this awakening a serious interest in road passenger transport history as well as a lifelong friendship that only ended with Peter's death in 1986. Through Peter he met a wide range of enthusiasts, including the Omnibus Society, North Western Branch founder Jack Baker. He was to act as the Branch Visits Secretary for a time, helping organise summer trips that reached in that pre-motorway era as far as Darlington and Northampton. In the winter he was involved in arranging a programme of meetings with guest speakers.

Alongside his professional career, Bruce developed a reputation as a thorough researcher of transport history and as a prolific author of his findings. His first published piece was an article about Bere Regis & District for *Modern Transport* while based at Salisbury during the latter years of the war. He followed this up with a piece on Kenya buses when posted there by the army in 1945-7. Deciding to concentrate on the area he knew best, Merseyside, he began work in the early 1950s on what was to emerge as the five-volume Liverpool series, jointly authored with John Horne. He revelled in making new discoveries from minute books and other records and in de-bunking some oft-repeated inaccurate statements. His first publication, *Local Transport in Birkenhead & District*, was a booklet in 1959 for the Omnibus Society, followed soon after by *Transport in Rochdale & District*, using material left to the Society by a deceased member. These were to be followed over the years by a number of texts based on his research.

His introduction to co-author John Horne had come through the Liverpool photographer and enthusiast Norman Forbes, who was doing similar research in Liverpool. The Horne-Maund partnership produced the first volume of *Liverpool Transport* in 1975 and the lavish set of five books stands as perhaps the most thorough piece of published transport research for any UK city. It is all the more remarkable for the fact that for most of the period Bruce was living in South Africa and much of his research was conducted on trips back to the UK where he and Kay would work as a team at the Public Record Office and local archives.

Following his return to the UK in retirement, Bruce's output averaged almost a book a year, with detailed studies on Crosville, Ribble and St Helens (the latter jointly with Mervyn Ashton) and a series of illustrated soft-back books for a Wirral based publisher of local interest titles. His researches expanded to cover titles on tramways (a Birkenhead and Wallasey title with Martin Jenkins in 1987), two volumes on Mersey Ferries (the second again with Martin Jenkins) and three railway titles. He also undertook editing work for publishers such as Venture Publications and NBC Books and was often asked to provide text verification for other transport titles. This prodigious volume of published work was displayed at his funeral on 9 October 2013 as a fitting legacy to a man who devoted a large part of his life to his researches and, importantly, ensured it reached a wide public.

Although at times appearing austere – and with what might have been described as having unreconstructed opinions forged in different times – Bruce was a loyal to his friends and colleagues and a devoted family man. His wife Kay pre-deceased him in 2002 but he is survived by his two sons (Derek and Phillip), one grand-daughter and one great-grand-daughter.

ABOUT THIS BOOK

In 2005-7 the Omnibus Society PHRG had produced three limited print-run items on Merseyside coach operators of the 1920s and 30s written by Bruce (P7/8/9). It was known that he had also written up a number of his other researches as limited circulation items that remained otherwise unpublished. During this same period he was persuaded by the late Derek Giles to allow that on the *History of the Birkenhead Municipal Bus Undertaking* to be published for a wider audience and this eventually appeared in 2008. It would appear that Wallasey was being considered as a companion volume, but Bruce had earlier unearthed new material in the form of hand-written minutes by the General Manager which revealed details of many aspects of the working of the undertaking which were hitherto unknown. These included activities of the department during the 1939-45 war years which would have been regarded as secret at the time and therefore were never published. Proposals which never reached fruition are also dealt with and consequently he wanted to rewrite that item, which was produced as an updated and unpublished version c.2006. That project was therefore put on the back burner and instead the PHRG went ahead with *Pioneer Bus Services in South West Lancashire* (2011). Discussions with Bruce as to reviving plans to publish the *Wallasey* manuscript were ongoing at the time of his death and with the co-operation of son (Derek) we are now enabled to offer this final T.B. Maund title as a tribute.

ACKNOWLEDGEMENTS

The early history of the Wallasey passenger transport undertaking had been set down in *The Tramways of Birkenhead and Wallasey* (Light Rail Transit Association 1987) by the author and Martin Jenkins. Aspects of the relationship between Wallasey Corporation and Crosville Motor Services were also dealt with in *Crosville on Merseyside*, again by the author (Transport Publishing Co. Ltd 1992). A brief history of the Wallasey transport undertaking was published by the Omnibus Society in 1969 but this must now be considered out of date as much additional information came to light subsequently. A pictorial survey of the Wallasey bus fleet was published in 1995 as the author's *The Wallasey Bus* (Ian and Marilyn Boumphrey). Much of the material came to light during the research for the above mentioned volumes and in research by Martin Jenkins. The personal recollections of long-serving Corporation employees, also other Wallasey residents, were acknowledged and thanks extended to the officers of Wirral Borough Libraries who, over a period of many years, gave the author every assistance. The archives of the Omnibus Society Library provided much information and the author recorded his gratitude to Messrs J. N. Barlow, J.E. Eaton, R.S. Griffiths, M. Jenkins, A. Lewis, G. Lumb, K.W. Swallow, T.G. Turner and M. Wallas who had been valuable sources of information. Additionally in this post-humous edition the PHRG Editor further acknowledges the considerable help of Ken Swallow in liasion with Derek Maund. Ted Jones is thanked for sourcing and captioning the illustrations and in turn acknowledges Charles Roberts & Martin Jenkins of the OnLine Transport Archive, Alan Oxley of the OS Photo Archive and Ted Gray.

INTRODUCTION

Before the Industrial Revolution, the Wirral peninsula was a thinly populated area given over to farming and fishing. The main centre was Neston which, with its neighbour Parkgate, enjoyed some prosperity in the late 17th and early 18th centuries as a port for Ireland. However, as the River Dee silted up, navigation moved closer to the estuary and eventually to the Mersey. Second in size and importance was Tranmere. In 1801 the population of the whole of the Hundred of Wirral was only 9,500 but in the next 40 years it had more than tripled to 32,000. The population continued to increase for the next hundred years, settlement being mainly in the north-eastern corner where the old parishes grew together to form the towns of Birkenhead and Wallasey. Following the adoption of steam power on the ferries, improvements in embarkation facilities on both sides of the river resulted in much higher standards of safety and reliability. Timid passengers, and especially ladies, were encouraged to cross and a sail on the river became an acceptable part of the work journey. Many well-to-do people forsook the cramped, unhealthy environment of Liverpool and built houses on cheap land on the Cheshire side of the river. Wallasey was the result of the intergrowth of several separate villages in the very sparsely populated north-east tip of the peninsula. From 1830, when the population was about 2,500, fine family houses were built in Egremont and New Brighton under the stimulus of developers, some of whom had interests in the ferries which were established nearby. From the 1840s Seacombe and Poulton, formerly fishing villages, became the homes of workers employed in developing a system of docks from the Wallasey Pool, the natural inlet which separated Wallasey from Birkenhead. The population grew rapidly to 6,261 in 1841, 8,348 in 1851, to 53,000 by the turn of the century. Town Commissioners were appointed in 1845 and in 1895 an Urban District Council was elected. The town was incorporated as a municipal borough in 1910 and attained county borough status in 1913. Leasowe, Moreton and part of Bidston had been added in 1928 and Saughall Massie in 1933, and by the outbreak of war in 1939 the population had reached almost 100,000.

As the town spread, the need for internal transport increased and the first horse-drawn omnibuses started running in 1861 following the municipalisation of the three ferries at Seacombe, Egremont and New Brighton on 1 August of that year. They remained middle-class conveyances throughout the Victorian years as the customary minimum fares of 2d, 3d and sometimes 6d were quite beyond the pocket of the working man. A horse tramway was laid between Seacombe ferry and Upper Brighton in 1879 and all the trams and buses were brought under common ownership in 1891. The Wallasey United Tramway & Omnibus Co. Ltd was taken over by the Urban District Council on 31 March 1901 and electric tramway operations commenced on 17 March 1902. Bus services started in April 1920 and tramways were abandoned in favour of buses between 1929 and 1933. Both tram and bus services were closely co-ordinated with sailings between

Seacombe ferry and Liverpool. The 1939-45 war placed a great strain on the bus services, particularly in towns like Wallasey where there was considerable damage and disruption by enemy air raids. The post-war years brought bus patronage to its zenith, economic constraints, short-sighted government policies and social change contributing to a gradual decline in the industry's fortunes. Whereas in pre-war days 44% of the working population looked to Liverpool for employment, the post-war years brought greater labour mobility and a changing transport pattern. As private transport ownership in Wallasey was above the average of the Merseyside region, the fortunes of the local bus and ferry services declined at a much faster rate and both became a substantial charge on the rate fund. The resultant merger of the three Merseyside municipal transport undertakings from 1 December 1969 and the closer integration of company services brought palliatives which a government of a different complexion considered to be too demanding on public funds. The subsequent deregulation of the industry from 26 October 1986 radically changed the face of the bus service network. Some of the places mentioned in this book have changed beyond recognition in urban redevelopment schemes. The northern end of Liscard Road has been pedestrianised and two of the three ferries have disappeared without trace; the survivor, Seacombe ferry, has declined almost to the status of a landing place on a pleasure cruise. The decline of New Brighton as a holiday resort has led to the disappearance of the two open-air bathing pools and the Tower Grounds amusement park, all of which generated so much traffic for public transport services in the past.

MONEY

The British coinage was changed on 15 February 1971 from pounds, shillings and pence (£. s. d.) to pounds and new pence. One new penny equals 2.4 old pence. All references to fares are in the old currency as it is impossible to translate the value of money into the new currency. The 3d horse bus fare has to be compared with the contemporary manual worker's wage of perhaps 16 shillings (80p) per week. As a guide, a bus driver's wage on 1939 rates was about £3.15s.0d (£3.75) per week.

CHAPTER 1
1899-1933

In 1899 the Wallasey UDC obtained powers to operate electric tramways and, as in Birkenhead, the sale did not include the omnibus services. After a legal wrangle, they took possession of the existing horse tramways and Wallasey United Tramway and Omnibus Co. in liquidation, and co-operated in the formation of the Seacombe and New Brighton Omnibus Co. Ltd to take over the running of the bus services. The omnibus business was valued at £2,100 for the freehold land and stables in Egerton Street, New Brighton and £2,838 for 78 horses, 14 omnibuses, one waggonette and various items of harness, etc. During 1902 three electric tram routes were opened, all running between Seacombe ferry and New Brighton ferry: (1) via Seabank Road, (2) via Wheatland Lane and Rake Lane, and (3) via Church Street, Seaview Road and Warren Drive. The Seabank Road route had been the main source of revenue for the horse buses and after experimenting with one or two back-street routes it is not surprising that the Wallasey buses ceased running in April 1902, even before those in Birkenhead.

The Council promoted a Bill in 1906 seeking additional tramway powers and also authority to run motor omnibuses 'in connection with the tramways of the Council when the running of carriages thereon is impracticable or during the construction, re-construction, alteration or repair thereof or in extension of any such tramway or also for testing the amount of traffic on any route or between any particular point...' The inclusion of this clause may have been influenced by the Wirral Railway's quest for motor bus powers but the Bill was thrown out because of opposition to the laying of a tramway along Breck Road between Poulton and Wallasey Village. There was no great enthusiasm about buses and the clause was not included in several subsequent Acts of Parliament. A tramway extension to Poulton and Wallasey Village using other roads was opened in 1910-11 and there were no more extensions, though the fleet was expanded until 1920 when there were 77 passenger cars in stock.

With Birkenhead already running buses and keen to cross the docks into Wallasey, the latter promoted a further Bill in 1919 seeking powers to run buses within the borough and on four routes which were then outside. These were from the boundary in Leasowe Road to (1) Leasowe Common, (2) along Reeds Lane and Hoylake Road (later known as Fender Lane) to the Birkenhead boundary at Bidston, (3) Church Road, Upton and (4) Bridge Road, West Kirby. Because of objections from Hoylake Urban District Council (who had ambitions of running their own buses), the Wirral Railway and the road authorities, the powers granted by the Wallasey Corporation Act 1920 were cut down to permit operation within the borough only. The permission of the Dock Board was needed to run buses on any of the dock roads, the Minister of Transport being the arbiter in the event of dispute.

The Council was so confident that Parliament would grant them motor bus powers that an order was placed late in 1919 with A.E.C. Ltd for six Model YC chassis with Tylor engines and with E. & A. Hora Ltd. of London for six 32-seat bodies. At that stage no decision had been reached about the routes to be operated, a report being placed before the Tramways Committee on 14 January 1920 (see Appendix 1). The main needs in Wallasey were the provision of east-west travel facilities as the four tram routes all ran from south to north, and communication with Birkenhead, for which the Act had made no provision. Whilst the general policy was to avoid competition with the trams, the provision of an express service over the Seabank Road tram route, which was handicapped by considerable stretches of single track with loops, was also considered as it was felt that a premium fare could be charged. A route from Manor Road (Seabank Road) to the western end of St. John's Road in Wallasey Village was considered and, after lengthy discussion, the western terminus was altered to Harrison Drive and, despite the fact that buses would follow the trams all the way, it was decided to extend the route to Seacombe ferry as a ferry connection was felt to be essential to the commercial success of the venture.

In the summer, services were proposed from Gorsey Lane or St. Lukes Church to Harrison Drive via Breck Road and Wallasey Village; from New Brighton or Wallasey Village to Leasowe Common and to Hoylake and West Kirby. The latter two were ruled out by the decision of Parliament to restrict operations to within the borough though this was slow to sink in and councillors continued to make suggestions to run outside for some considerable time.

The First Motor Bus Service

The first bus arrived on 12 February and driver training started immediately. Solid tyres, wooden seats and indifferent roads ensured a very uncomfortable ride. On 3 April 1920 all six assembled at Seacombe ferry and buses Nos. 1 and 2 took a party of councillors and officials on a jaunt to Moreton, Hoylake and West Kirby, perhaps a defiant gesture in view of the Hoylake council's opposition. The first service bus left Seacombe at 8.0am, driven by Sid Smith and conducted by Norman Porter who, in the excitement, issued all the passengers with 1½d tickets instead of the new 6d ones for the through journey. The timetable was adjusted from 10 May to improve boat connections as follows:

Seacombe dep.   8.30am, every 15 mins to 10.0am then every half hour to 12.30pm & every 15 mins to 10.30pm.

Harrison Drive dep. 8.16am, 8.36, 8.46, 9.6, 9.16, 9.36, 9.46, 10.6 then every half hour to 12.46pm and at 6, 16, 36 & 46 mins. past each hour to 10.36pm.

The irregular departures from Harrison Drive were timed to connect with the 10-minute ferry service at Seacombe. The journey time was 20 minutes so the maximum requirement was three buses which approached and departed from Seacombe ferry via King Street, Brighton Street and Church Road. Originally there were short 1d stages, e.g. between Harrison Drive and the Cheshire Cheese. However, fares were revised from 10th May 1920 as shown in Table A on page 14.

These relatively high fares were typical of motor bus fares of the period. The through fare was double the tram fare between the same points while the Seacombe-Liscard fare was 50% above the tram fare. It is not difficult to see that, by rebooking at Liscard Village or Manor Road, one could save 1d on the expensive 6d through fare!

Other Services

During June, the buses were used to augment the trams between Seacombe and Holland Road on the Seabank Road route, and Seacombe and St Luke's Church on the Poulton route. The Holland Road service continued into July, during which month a breakdown of the tramway generating plant saw buses running between Seacombe and New Brighton via Seabank Road and between Harrison Drive and New Brighton. The Poulton-Harrison Drive via Breck Road service was tried out in August with disastrous results. Ninety-five passengers were carried on 38 return journeys for a revenue of £3.3.11½d. Breck Road was then little more than a country lane and was largely unpopulated. There was a perfectly good tram service between the terminal points, albeit by a slightly longer route though the difference was only 0.35 miles. Buses were again used to provide emergency services for five days from 25 October 1920 when a coal strike cut ferry sailings from New Brighton and buses provided a feeder service to and from Egremont. After the boats had been restored, the service was continued experimentally for one week to see if a feeder to the ferry would be supported but it was not. On 22 November 1920 there was a breakdown at the generating station and trams were stranded for six hours all across the system. A single bus was allocated to each of the Rake Lane, Warren Drive and Poulton tram routes and two to Seabank Road, the sixth bus remaining on the regular bus route. During October and November the buses carried 8,118 passengers on the Seabank Road tram route.

If ever there was any question about a need for the east-west facility, the response from the public left no room for doubt. Many new bus services took many weeks to build up but in its first month this service carried an average of 2,087 passengers per day, increasing to 2,378 in the second month and 2,876 in the peak summer month of August. Table B shows the variable nature of the traffic, a proportion of which was influenced by the season and weather conditions. In the first full year of operation, the six buses carried 811,135 passengers at a gross loss of £2,368 which was charged to the tramway account.

But this was the only year in which the tramways stood a loss; the following year £1,228 was repaid and the balance of £1,140 in 1927-28.

Cross Docks Services

The horse bus service, which had run between Seacombe ferry and Charing Cross via the Four Bridges since 1903, had been sold to Birkenhead Motor Works (proprietor Vincent Christiansen) in 1919; the new owners provided motor buses (one source says there were five including the former Crosville Dennis, The Alma but the service had been withdrawn by the end of 1919. There were various exchanges between Birkenhead and Wallasey Corporations and the Dock Board had given permission for their private roads to be used by buses. Sub-committees from the two boroughs met at Birkenhead Town Hall on 1 March 1921 and agreed to provide a joint bus service between Seacombe ferry and Charing Cross via Dock Road, Duke Street Bridge, Park Station, Conway Street.

Table A Revised Fares from 10 May 1920
Seacombe Ferry

1½	Egremont Ferry					
2	2	Manor Road (Seabank Road)				
3	2	1½	Liscard Village			
4	3	1½	1½	Marlowe Road		
4	3	3	1½	1½	Leasowe Road	
6	4	3	2	1½	1½	Harrison Drive

Table B Motor Bus Results 1920-21
Seacombe-Harrison Drive Service

1920	Mileage	Passengers Receipts	
April	9,695	58,449	£ 651. 3. 4d
May	10,985	73,732	834. 9. 4d
June	10,447	71,693	836. 7. 2d
July	10,765	73,894	817. 1 10½d
August	11,626	89,173	1,066. 14. 5d
Sept.	10,948	68,928	751. 7. 2½d
October	9,906	61,800	634.11. 10½.d
Nov.	8,265	54,347	493. 16. 3½d
Dec.	7,860	52,246	517. 5. 6½d
1921			
January	8,047	59,774	593.16. 7½«d
February	7,346	52,318	520. 10. 5d
March	8,088	62,116	624. 5. 3½d

Table C Results of Joint Bus Service
Seacombe-Charing Cross service

1921	Mileage	Passengers	Receipts
March	1,598	10,528	£171. 5s. 0d
April	3,644	26,106	431. 0s. 2d
May	3,558	32,310	526. 4s. 4d
June	3,742	31,840	521. 10s. 0d
July	3,700	31,100	510. 17s. 6d
August	3,658	30,360	497. 5s. 10d

Table D Harrison Drive-Foreshore Service
Initial Results

1924	Mileage	Passengers	Revenue
July	197	4,696	£20. 3s. 8d
August	376	13,272	56. 1s. 4½d
Sept.	24	539	2. 8s. 11½d

and Exmouth Street with a through fare of 5d and a minimum fare of 2d. Each operator was to provide an equal number of buses but as only one bus was needed to run a 40-minute service, the day was divided into two shifts which were worked alternately by each town's bus. Operations commenced on 19 March 1921.

The new service was well supported from the start and estimated revenue for the first few months, based on doubling the Wallasey receipts, was as shown in Table C.

An hourly summer service from Charing Cross to Harrison Drive was started on 26 June 1921. This followed the same route as the Seacombe bus to Duke Street Bridge, then turned left along the Dock Road, up Poulton Bridge Road to Poulton and then via Breck Road and Wallasey Village at a through fare of 7d. This ran in the 1922 and 1923 summer seasons and the working arrangements are not known, though both operators participated. It is almost certain that, initially, the same alternating shift system as applied to the Seacombe route was adopted. The withdrawal of the Harrison Drive service at the end of the first season stimulated a demand for a bus service between Birkenhead and Poulton all the year round so the Charing Cross and Liscard service started in October 1921 running hourly from 10.30am to 9.30pm. It followed the same route as the Harrison Drive bus to Poulton, then via Mill Lane, St Albans Road and Wallasey Road. Gorsey Lane was not used until April 1924 when it was made suitable for buses, and Torrington Road replaced St Albans Road two years later, following the widening of the road by the Boot Inn. The working arrangements were now altered so that each Corporation ran the whole of the Seacombe or Liscard route on alternate weeks. The Liscard route was more popular than Harrison Drive and the latter service was taken off before the end of the

1923 season. Cheap railway fares were also a factor as there was a frequent train service from Park to Wallasey station. The legal position as far as Birkenhead was concerned was put right by inserting a clause in the Birkenhead Corporation Act 1923, giving the general right to make agreements about bus services. Wallasey's position was not regularised until the passing of the Wallasey Corporation Act 1927 which authorised the making of agreements with other authorities.

Changes to the Original Route

A proposal to curtail the Harrison Drive service to run from Trafalgar Road to avoid duplicating the trams was rejected as it was felt that the through traffic to and from the ferry would be adversely affected. From 1 December 1923, some journeys were curtailed at the top of Leasowe Road and others were diverted down Leasowe Road to St Nicholas Road. A full service to Harrison Drive was run over the Easter weekend and then a very limited service T until 9 June 1924 when the diversion to St Nicholas Road was restricted to 8.0-9.30am, 12noon-1.30pm and 5.30-7.0pm, all buses running to Harrison Drive at other times. However, depressed economic conditions and the sheer discomfort of riding on the wooden-seated buses over the deplorable roads of the time limited the patronage of the buses. In August, the manager recommended the withdrawal of the service altogether before 1.0pm on weekdays and this was done from 1 September 1924, the Sunday morning service being withdrawn altogether in November. Meanwhile, the Council agreed to do something about the roads and in December the service was further curtailed while Manor Road was reconstructed, 70% of trips running only between Liscard Village and either Harrison Drive or St Nicholas Road; later, during the resurfacing of Wallasey Road and St Hilary Brow, a single bus ran between Liscard Village and the Cheshire Cheese Inn via St Alban's Road, Mill Lane and Breck Road. Normal services were restored on 13 April 1925 but not to St. Nicholas Road as, from the same day, Crosville buses were extended from their former terminus at the top of Leasowe Road to the Queen's Arms Hotel, Liscard Village. By October 1926, the Corporation service was running half-hourly in the morning and every 20 minutes in the afternoon and evening, augmented to every 10 minutes between 5.0 and 7.20pm. On Saturdays, a 10-minute service ran from 12 noon and on Sundays there was a quarter-hourly service. A year later, the early service ran only from Leasowe Road, the first bus from Harrison Drive being at 9.50am then 10.20. Thereafter there was a 20-minute service until 12.20pm after which the buses ran every 10 minutes. On Sundays, the service started quarter-hourly, increasing to every 10 minutes in the afternoons.

From the weekend of 12/13 July 1924, one bus was employed in the summer on a half-mile long route along the length of Harrison Drive which, at that time, ran almost directly on to the beach. The trip cost 1d and had sufficient support to justify a permanent place on a seasonal basis. The results for the first season were:

Table D Harrison Drive-Foreshore Service
Initial Results

1924	Mileage	Passengers	Revenue
July	197	4,626	£20. 3. 8d
August	376	13,272	56. 1. 4½
September	24	539	2. 4. 11½

In 1926 a Leyland Leveret demonstrator, designed for one-man operation, was tried on this route and it also ran along the Promenade at New Brighton between the Pier and Marine Park where the roadway ended until the first part of Kings Parade was opened in 1933. A specially designed Karrier semi-toastrack bus was purchased for the Foreshore service in 1927. There was no attempt to run buses through from Seacombe ferry to the Foreshore until after the 1939-45 war. The service was dependent upon weather conditions and demand, and it was operationally simpler to keep it separate.

During the General Strike in May 1926, Wallasey was the scene of unusual violence during attempts to maintain some sort of public transport service. The windows of nine buses were protected by wire netting and on the afternoon of the first day, Tuesday 4 May, an attempt was made to put a few buses on the road. In Liscard Road one bus was stopped by about 30 men who drove up in a waggonette. The volunteer driver was forcibly ejected and his clothing badly torn; three windows were smashed and the engine put out of action. Another bus was stopped in Brighton Street, a plank being used to break a window and remove the driver.

The eve of the strike coincided with the annual parade and inspection of tramwaymen and the Mayor, Alderman J W Holdsworth, made an impassioned but unsuccessful appeal to the men to remain at work. He was later criticised for his actions in signing a formal proclamation and endeavouring to get a service running on the first day of the strike; he issued the following statement to the press:

> "I desire to deny certain rumours that I have been seriously injured on the occasion of the attempt to turn out the Corporation's motor buses on Tuesday last and I also deny the rumour that the Chief Constable advised me not to allow the buses to turn out. There is no truth whatsoever that I gave any instructions whatsoever in regard to running the buses nor did I order the driver to run into the crowds if the latter did not disperse. On the contrary, I was instrumental in preventing two men from being knocked down and for doing so I was subject to abuse which I would not have taken had it not been for the fact that I was Mayor of the borough and, of course, respect the office I hold. The proclamation of Tuesday's date was signed by me by virtue of my office as Mayor and, as it was an official communication, it could be signed by no one except myself or my deputy.

Therefore no question of my personal responsibility for the proclamation arises and it is unfair to attribute to me solely the responsibility for the proclamation which was made with the authority of the Emergency Committee."

Two men were sentenced to a month's hard labour and another fined £10 or 11 days' imprisonment for sabotaging buses. One man was caught with a notebook containing instructions on disabling buses. 'To stop cars, two men mount car, one with wire cutters to cut wire by switch'. Despite more violence, a skeleton bus service was run from 4.0pm on the 11th, three buses being in service fitted with wire mesh to protect drivers; policemen or special constables rode on the step. On Friday 14th, when the strike was virtually over, eight trams and all nine buses were in service.

The Corporation took a hard line with the strikers, all of whom were deemed to have terminated their employment. The following ultimatum was issued on Saturday 15th:

Terms of Settlement in respect of Wallasey Ex-Tramway Employees: 15 May 1926

1. Ex-Tramway Employees wishing re-engagement with the Corporation Tramways shall apply for service at Tramways Head Office on or before 12 noon on Monday and those of such men who are accepted shall be notified by post or otherwise and be re-engaged at their former hourly rate of pay and bonus. The office will be opened for this purpose today (Saturday) from 4pm to 8pm, tomorrow (Sunday) from 2pm to 6pm and on Monday from 9am to 12 noon.

2. Men applying and not immediately engaged will receive consideration as and when vacancies occur.
3. There will be no alteration in hours.
4. Tramway employees and voluntary workers who worked during the Strike shall be retained if suitable and shall perform such duties as may be allocated to them by the General Manager.
5. Ex-Tramway employees returning to duty shall perform the duties allocated to them by the General Manager.
6. Any re-engagement is made without prejudice to the legal right of the Corporation to claim damages arising out of the Strike from strikers and others responsible.

On 13 July 1927, the Corporation agreed to recognise the Transport and General Workers Union on the same terms as before the strike and to observe all the agreements and decisions of the National Joint Industrial Council for the Tramway industry.

Sunday Morning Services

A churchgoers' service, employing two buses, was operated experimentally every 20 minutes between Lloyd's Corner (the junction of Wheatland Lane and Poulton Road) and Harrison Drive between 10.15 and 11.55am on Sunday mornings in September 1925 but support for this venture was insufficient to justify its retention. Sunday morning tram services, commencing at about 10.15am instead of the normal 12.15pm, were run for the first time in the summer of 1926 operating from 1 August to 31 October; they were reinstated for the months of June to September in 1927. Sunday morning bus services on the cross-docks services, which also started in June 1927, were discontinued after less than three months. There was a limited but consistent demand for these facilities, particularly by churchgoers who, for personal reasons, chose to worship at churches at some distance from their homes. Railway excursions from Liverpool stations also provided traffic in the summer months. The tram services were expensive to provide as the power station and breakdown services had to be fully manned and road staff were paid at premium rates yet normal fares were charged and few passengers were carried. Following public protests at the withdrawal of the trams, it was decided to run special buses from 30 October 1927, passengers being charged at the higher bus fare scale. There were three routes, more or less covering the tram routes every 15 minutes from about 10.00am and employing six buses. They ran from Seacombe to Hose Side Road via Borough Road, Liscard Road and Seaview Road; to Molyneux Drive via Seabank Road and to Harrison Drive via the Poulton tram route to Wallasey Road then via St Hilary Brow and Wallasey Village. In February 1928, the Seabank Road bus was extended down to New Brighton, the first bus service to reach the resort.

The Harrison Drive service was withdrawn after operation on 25 March 1928 as a half-hourly service from 10.0am was to be provided on the new Seacombe-Moreton service which was to start on 1 April. Although this used Breck Road and not Marlowe Road it was considered satisfactory. The Hose Side Road service also ran for the last time on 27 May as it was not resumed after the summer Sunday morning tram service ceased at the end of September. The Seabank Road service was resumed, being absorbed into the ordinary service in January 1929 when buses replaced trams on that service.

New Buses and Lower Fares

The first new Leyland Lion buses were placed in service in March 1926. With pneumatic tyres, upholstered seats and a much lower floor, they were attractive to passengers and the fortunes of the undertaking began to improve, with a small net surplus in the year ending 31 March 1926 increasing annually for some years. Ten Lions were obtained followed by three Karrier single-deckers of which two had three axles and seated 40 passengers. The new buses were originally fitted with doors which opened outwards but these were removed following complaints from the Watch Committee. Two of them had entrances at the front but the last four reverted to the rear entrance arrangement.

On the initiative of Birkenhead Corporation, the cross-docks fares were reduced from 8 March 1926, the through fares to Charing Cross becoming 4d from Liscard and 3½d from Seacombe, the latter being a 35% reduction in five years. Increased patronage enabled bus fares to be reduced generally from 1 April 1928.

New Services

With a population about two-thirds that of Birkenhead, Wallasey nevertheless had a larger tram fleet, the extra cars being required to deal with the very large holiday traffic which was attracted to New Brighton and Harrison Drive during the summer. The tramway network was unique in that all four routes ran between the same two points, Seacombe Ferry and New Brighton, though the longer westerly route through Poulton and Wallasey Village ran beyond Grove Road only on summer Sundays and at other times of peak holiday traffic. The local transport at Wallasey was co-ordinated with the ferry sailings between Seacombe and Liverpool to a much greater extent than applied at Woodside in Birkenhead. The boats and the trams ran at 10-minute intervals and both undertakings took great pride in maintaining regularity. In the late 'twenties, enamel plates bearing two clock faces were fixed on the tram platforms to inform passengers of the times of the boats from Seacombe (and Egremont if applicable) with which the car connected. These 'ferry clocks' were later placed on the rear platform of double-deck buses also and remained in use for many years. In foggy or very windy weather, the northern ferries were frequently disrupted and the public was informed by the flying of flags from the trolley ropes of the trams. Later the same message was conveyed by a roller blind in the front nearside of the buses. It was in two parts, blue for 'New Brighton Ferry Closed' and red for 'Egremont Ferry Closed'. If only New Brighton ferry was closed, the blind was taken only half way down.

Wallasey's tramway policy was not unlike that of Birkenhead and much track was renewed in the 1920s, but by 1927 technical advances in bus design were sufficiently impressive for the Corporation to reconsider their policy and in that year a Trams versus Buses Sub-committee was appointed to make recommendations on future strategy. The year 1927 also saw the passing of the important Wallasey Corporation Act which extended the borough boundary to include Leasowe and Moreton, authorised the construction of a two-mile promenade and sea wall between New Brighton and Wallasey Beach, and granted powers for the operation of trolleybuses.

An experimental limited stop bus peak hour service was inaugurated between Seacombe

two proposals to extend the buses the short distance from the Hotel Victoria to New Brighton Station were rejected by the Corporation and the Mount Road residents had to put up with the service the Corporation thought was good for them, with no service to New Brighton proper nor the growing shopping centre at Liscard until 1944.

Garages

The original buses were housed in a building which stood within the perimeter of the generating station, access being behind the tram depot. The fleet soon outgrew it and some buses were kept in the tram depot. As the fleet expanded, it was obvious that purpose-built accommodation was needed and a new garage to hold 55 buses was planned on land between the tram depot and Seaview Road at an estimated cost of £24,000. The steel-framed brick building had an unobstructed floor area of 18,000sq.ft with supporting lattice girders with a span of 127ft. The repair shop area was 3,820sq.ft and three large fuel tanks with a capacity of 10,000 gallons were installed beneath the building, eight hydrants being provided for use in case of fire. The new buildings were built by Walter E. Hughes of Birkenhead at a cost of £19,244 (garage), £4,525 (paint shop) and £1,521 (waiting room). It was officially opened on 2 May 1929 but parts were probably in use before then. There was a cost overrun of £2,282.18s.7d. The old paint shop was converted to traffic offices. A further sum of £2,267 was spent on paving on the tram depot approach road.

When the tram replacement programme got underway, more garage accommodation was needed and the rear portion of the tram depot was converted. This involved filling in and concreting over the pits in the original tram shed, making new entrances in the rear wall and laying a concrete apron for manoeuvring buses behind the building. In the 1907 extension, which was retained as a tram shed until the final withdrawal, a 30ft concrete runway was laid on both sides and iron gratings were fitted over the pits to facilitate its use as a garage in due course. The dividing walls between some of the arched entrances were broken down to provide wider doors in the façade. The work was done in stages and was completed by mid-1932 at a cost of £10,170.

The First Tramway Abandonment

The recommendation of the Trams vs. Buses Sub-committee was that trams should be replaced by buses as tracks and other equipment needed renewing. The most intensive route, the direct line between Seacombe and New Brighton via Seabank Road, had several single-track sections with loops and the track was very worn. It was decided to substitute with buses, the changeover being effected in the winter months when traffic was lighter. The last tram ran at midnight on Saturday 19 January 1929 and new Titans took over on the Sunday morning. The bus journey time was 16 minutes against the trams' 19 minutes. Six 66-seat three-axle Karrier double-deck buses were also used on the service. The track along Seabank Road was speedily lifted and the road entirely reconstructed, the buses being diverted via Steel Avenue and Penkett Road while this was being done. The buses were popular and, despite having only 51 seats compared with the 66 of the trams, they absorbed the summer holiday traffic without difficulty.

The conversion of the Seabank Road tram route marked the coming of age of the motor bus undertaking. At the busiest times of the day buses ran every four minutes between Seacombe and New Brighton and every two minutes between Seacombe and Molyneux Drive with additional unadvertised short workings between Holland Road or Trafalgar Road and Seacombe. All buses now approached Seacombe via Demesne Street and the lower part of Borough Road and left via Church Road and Brighton Street, the reverse of the tram route. Tram fares were charged on the replacement buses and there were workmen's fares at 2d single and 4d return issued before 7.0am. 1d fare stages were introduced on all bus routes at the time of the changeover thus enabling the Harrison Drive buses to carry passengers on the same terms as the Seabank Road buses between Seacombe and the foot of Manor Road. Inevitably, there were public demands for workmen's facilities on all the bus routes and a new scale was introduced from 1 December 1930 (see Chapter 7).

At this time all suitable employees were given the opportunity to learn bus driving so as to provide a source of drivers for future expansion and to minimise redundancy problems as the tramway system ran down. At this stage there were no such problems as Seabank Road tram drivers unable to learn to drive buses could transfer to the other three tram routes.

Cross Docks Extensions

A service which attracted a steady regular patronage with enormous holiday peaks was inaugurated, jointly with Birkenhead Corporation, in October 1929. This was the New Ferry and New Brighton route which was unusual in starting at the northern edge of Wallasey, passing right through the borough and through the neighbouring borough of Birkenhead to terminate in the Urban District of Bebington. For the first three months of its existence, it was an extension at both ends of the Liscard-Charing Cross route. From Liscard to New Brighton it followed the Rake Lane tram route and from Charing Cross it ran via Borough Road, Central Station, Argyle Street South, Old Chester Road and Rock Ferry station. The mileage in Birkenhead's area was 4.462 (59.26%) and in Wallasey 3.068 (40.74%) and it was agreed that receipts should be pooled. Each operator would take out 10d per mile for running expenses and divide the balance in the same proportions as the mileage.

Buses of both authorities worked on this route simultaneously. The basic frequency was initially half-hourly, though a 20-minute service soon became necessary; the through fare was 7d and, with the first buses running after 9.0am, there was obviously no attempt made to cater for workmen. At some time both Charing Cross services were rerouted in Birkenhead via Park Road East and Claughton Road in lieu of Conway Street and Exmouth Street. This may have been as late as 1931 but no confirmation has been found.

Late in 1929, there were suggestions from the public that the New Ferry service should be diverted via Haymarket, Hamilton Street and Cleveland Street and from January 1930 it ran along Argyle Street and Cleveland Street, providing an evening and Sunday service along the latter thoroughfare where the trams ran only on weekdays and made their last journeys before 8.0pm. A convenient link with the docks was also established. From the summer of 1930, great crowds were carried to New Brighton and many Wallasey people used the service in the other direction to reach the Crosville buses which ran from New Ferry to Chester and North Wales. After the latter were extended to Woodside, they still used the service, alighting at Hamilton Square and walking down to the ferry approach. On busy Sundays there were extra buses from St. Paul's Road, Rock Ferry and Central Station to New Brighton where long queues formed in the evenings.

There was an interesting feature about the destination displays on the Wallasey buses on this service. At the time, Lever Bros. allowed parties to tour their soap factory at Port Sunlight, up to 40,000 visitors a year being attracted. Wallasey considered this to be a traffic generator and displayed 'For Port Sunlight' in the lower aperture when travelling towards New Ferry. Unfortunately there never was a direct service between New Ferry and the works, the best place to change buses for Port Sunlight being Charing Cross, making the display more appropriate to the other joint routes. Nevertheless, it continued to be used until sometime during the 1939-45 War when it was replaced by 'via Woodside', a display which had languished unused on the blinds since 1933.

Trolleybus Powers

Councillor C.F. Rymer was not only a bus and coach operator but a motor dealer with a franchise which included trolleybuses. In November 1923 he persuaded members of the Tramways Committee to attend a demonstration at St Helens where the Corporation had already obtained the necessary statutory powers to run these hybrid vehicles. This was followed up by a further demonstration in Brighton Street on 28 December when an AEC trolleybus ran a short distance using the tramway overhead and a negative skate dragging in the track. A section was then inserted in the Wallasey Corporation Bill of 1924 but this was thrown out by a Town's Meeting because of opposition to the incorporation of Leasowe and Moreton in the borough. The subject lay dormant for three years when a further Bill was prepared, the principal purposes of which were to incorporate Leasowe and Moreton in the borough and build the new promenade between New Brighton and a point west of Harrison Drive. Powers for trolleybuses were secured for the following routes:

1. From New Brighton, along the Promenade, (largely unbuilt) Harrison Drive, Wallasey Village, Perrin Road, Broadway & Broadway Avenue to the depot.

2. From Liscard Village via Wallasey Road , Belvidere Road, Rolleston Drive, Sea Road to the Promenade.

The Bill became the Wallasey Corporation Act 1927, which received the Royal Assent on 27 December 1927.

Although the first tramway conversion had been effected with motor buses, the idea of using trolleybuses was not discarded and, in November 1929, the Council asked the General Manager to prepare a report. The limited powers granted by the 1927 Act had envisaged a trolleybus system which was auxiliary to the tramways whereas the 1930 report saw trolleybuses as a means of replacing tramways and, to some extent, buses. The advantages claimed for the trolleybus were the use of existing electrical equipment, suitably modified, the retention of the transport department as the largest customer of the municipal electricity undertaking, and the authorisation of a longer loan repayment period (10 years for trolleybuses and 20 years for overhead equipment compared with 8 years for motor buses). Following consideration of the report, it was decided to apply for the necessary additional powers and, in accordance with statutory requirements, notices were posted on the tramway standards announcing the Corporation's intentions. This was done so thoroughly that residents almost expected the trolleybuses to appear any day.

The additional powers granted by the Wallasey Corporation (Trolley Vehicles) Order 1931 covered almost the whole of the tramway routes (including Seabank Road but omitting Grove Road) and a number of connecting links. The Corporation was empowered to borrow £154,000 to purchase trolleybuses and £26,103 for equipment of various kinds.

The tramway standards were left in position on the Seabank Road route and on subsequent conversions, being used for gas street lighting, but eventually the General Manager persuaded the Council that a mixed motor bus and trolleybus fleet would lack the flexibility needed in a town where there were great fluctuations in the traffic. Although the Council set great store by quiet running buses, as witness their objections to diesel engines, there were no further serious attempts to introduce the trolleybus to Wallasey.

Route Numbers

During 1930, both Wallasey and Birkenhead Corporations decided to adopt route numbers. Birkenhead had an earlier scheme whereby, since 1926, numbers had been carried on the rear of certain buses. Under this scheme the cross-docks routes had been numbered 8 (Charing Cross-Seacombe), 9 (Charing Cross-Liscard) and 13 (New Ferry-New Brighton). Wallasey's numbers were shown in timetables during 1929-30 but not carried on the buses immediately. The initial allocation was as follows:

1 Seacombe-New Brighton via Seabank Road
2 Seacombe-Harrison Drive via Liscard
3 Seacombe-Harrison Drive via Poulton & Breck Road
4 Seacombe-Moreton (Bermuda Road)
5 Seacombe-Albion Street via Mount Road
6 Egremont Ferry-Albion Street via Mount Road
7 Seacombe-Charing Cross
8 New Brighton-Moreton (Bermuda Road) via Liscard
9 Liscard-Charing Cross
10 New Brighton-New Ferry
11 New Brighton-Moreton (Bermuda Road) via Grove Road

Both Wallasey and Birkenhead planned to start displaying numbers from 1st January 1931 and, in the meantime, Birkenhead adopted a revised scheme using numbers between 10 and 91, allocated on a district basis and giving separate numbers to regular part-way buses. Under this scheme, the cross-docks services were to be numbered 10, 11 and 12 and Wallasey agreed to fall into line. Other changes resulted in the January 1931 allocation being changed as shown below:

1-5, 8, 10 as above
6 Reserved for Seacombe-New Brighton via Belvidere Road
7 Egremont Ferry-Albion Street via Mount Road
9 New Brighton-Moreton (Bermuda Road) via Grove Road
11 Liscard-Charing Cross
12 Seacombe-Charing Cross

Tramway Abandonment Strategy

In 1930 the Council approved a plan to abandon the remaining tramways. By 1 April 1931 parts of the Warren Drive route were to be withdrawn and the remainder joined with the Poulton route to form a circular between Seacombe and Grove Road. The Rake Lane route was to go by 1 April 1932 and the Circular a year later. The replacing buses in the first stage were to give a service to the Belvidere Road area for which there had been agitation for several years. As stated above, trolleybuses had been proposed in 1927 and, in 1929, the diversion of the Seacombe-Harrison Drive via Liscard service to run via Belvidere Road, Broadway Avenue and Broadway had been considered. At this time, residential development was scanty and the roads needed strengthening to take the weight of buses.

The new proposal was for a bus service between Seacombe and New Brighton, following the Warren Drive tram route to Mill Lane then via Rullerton Road, Belvidere Road, Rolleston Drive to Grove Road. At this point it would rejoin the tram route and replace it thence to New Brighton. Church Street was to be used in both directions, the inward line via Falkland Road being abandoned. The changeover date was fixed for 5 January 1931 but road works in Belvidere Road were not finished so it was postponed until 29 March.

The new bus route, which ran every 10 minutes, was never remunerative and was destined to undergo several changes over the years. The Warren Drive tram route was diverted via Wheatland Lane so that two trams ran together every 10 minutes between Seacombe and Liscard Village; on arrival at Grove Road, cars continued over the Poulton route back to Seacombe, and vice versa. To improve direct facilities between New Brighton and Harrison Drive, one bus without a route number ran a shuttle service between these points during the high summer of 1931 but patronage was low and it is not certain that it ran in 1932 or 1933.

The Rake Lane Tramway Conversion

The conversion of the Rake Lane tram route threw up a difficult staff problem and there was a controversial decision which led to much public dissatisfaction. The tram route was exceptionally slow with a journey time of 26 minutes for the 3.25-mile journey, an average speed of only 7.5mph despite the fact that there was double track on most of the route. The proposed journey time for the buses was 18 minutes, at an average speed of 10.8mph. Thus six trams would be replaced by four buses. The peak hour partway service between Seacombe and Liscard Village required three trams but only two buses. 15 drivers and 15 conductors were employed on the trams and, as the Committee proposed to run the Rake Lane bus service through only for part of the day with a New Brighton-Liscard service off-peak, connecting with the Circle trams, the number of bus men required was six of each. The general manager recommended that, irrespective of the duplicate mileage, the service should be run through all day and that the Seacombe-Moreton service should be increased from half-hourly to every 20 minutes, requiring a further six men (three drivers and three conductors). Whilst the Moreton suggestion was accepted, the Committee would not agree to the through service on the Rake Lane route all day and this resulted in a surplus of 12 permanent men.

The problems were compounded by issues of seniority. From the time before the conversion of the Seabank Road tram route in 1929, all tram drivers had been offered free training as bus drivers but many had refused. Less senior men had been trained and, although junior in length of service, they were senior in the drivers' list. The old hands who had refused bus driver training now sought to regain their seniority. Furthermore there were 19 'temporary' men who were guaranteed only 32 hours' pay a week, to cover holidays, sickness and other contingencies. In practice, men received 48 hours most of the time, four or five years' service on the permanent list were entitled to 48 hours and were threatened with demotion to temporary 32-hour status, and this was complicated by the fact that most were in the superannuation scheme. Finally, there were tram drivers, mostly over 50 years of age, who were physically unable to pass the medical examination required by the Ministry of Transport in order to acquire a PSV driving licence or who lacked the aptitude to pass the test. Some of these were retired on pension early, others became conductors and work was found for some in the garage.

The plan to replace the Rake Lane trams from January 1933 was frustrated by the backlog of applications for road service licences and the changeover was eventually made from 5 February 1933. The need to change between tram and bus at Liscard Village brought forth an avalanche of complaints, not just because of the inconvenience of the change but also because there were no through tickets and an additional cost of ½d or 1d was involved. Passengers moved to the Seabank Road and Albion Street bus routes causing overcrowding on those services. The Committee saw the error of their ways but, because an application to the Traffic Commissioners was necessary, it was not until 14 May that the through all-day service could be introduced. This inevitably drained traffic from the Circle tram route but the days of the trams were numbered anyway.

The severity of the staff problem was ameliorated by these developments, the jobs of only five temporary conductors being in jeopardy but the problem was to arise again with the final tramway conversion later in the year.

Moreton Shore & Saughall Massie

Leasowe Road was extended to meet Pasture Road at Leasowe Common in 1931 and, from 1 April 1931, a service was provided from Seacombe in accordance with the demand. The terminus was described on the buses as 'Moreton Shore' or 'Moreton Foreshore' but as 'Leasowe Common (Pasture Road)' in timetables. Birkenhead Corporation had built up a substantial summer traffic between Liverpool and Moreton Shore via Woodside, and Wallasey hoped to cream some of this off with its shorter and more scenic route via Seacombe. Buses at first showed No. 4, but 4A was used from 1933. A licence was also granted for a shuttle service between Leasowe Castle and the Shore but there is no evidence of such a service ever operating. There was also a pipedream of extending the service to Bermuda Road by making up the road to the lighthouse as a further extension of Leasowe Road, then by a new road across the railway, but neither of these was ever built.

A second service between New Brighton and Moreton, Bermuda Road was inaugurated on 3 February 1930, running via Warren Drive, Grove Road, Wallasey Village and then as the other Moreton services. The normal frequency was hourly, requiring just one bus, and a single decker was often used. From 1 April 1933, Saughall Massie was incorporated into the County Borough of Wallasey. It was then a sparsely populated district with poor roads but, in April 1932, the Corporation had applied to the Traffic Commissioners to extend the New Brighton-Bermuda Road service to Saughall Massie Hotel via Saughall Road. This was strongly opposed by Crosville, who served the hamlet with a West Kirby-Birkenhead Park Station service and the licence was refused. The general manager suggested improving Arrowe Lane (later renamed Acton Lane) which joined Hoylake Road opposite the Bermuda Road terminus. The use of this road would have been difficult for Crosville to oppose but there was no real demand and 13 years were to go by before Wallasey's buses served the district regularly.

The undertaking's first buses were six AEC 'Y'- type chassis of 1920 on solid tyres, with 32-seat bodies built in London by E.&A. Hora. Four similar buses were acquired in 1922, but as second-hand purchases from Liverpool Corporation. (T.G. Turner collection)

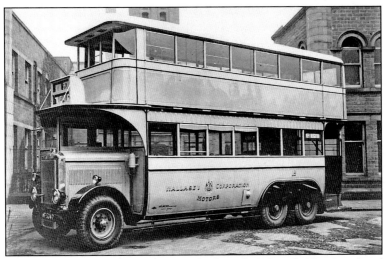

One of the unfortunate Karrier DD six-wheelers of 1928, with 66-seat enclosed staircase Hall Lewis bodies. Fate decided they were to give Wallasey only three years' service and they operated longer in Essex. (Omnibus Society / Brady collection)

Having bought ten nippy Leyland Lions in 1926-7, Wallasey inexplicably then augmented the fleet with three more-ponderous Karrier saloons bodied by Hall Lewis, although No.11 above was a hybrid 31-seat version with folding nearside panels. The other two were conventional 40-seat Dorman-engined six-wheelers, which suffered the same fate as the double-deckers. All three had dual passenger doors. (Ominibus Society / D. Randell)

The initial 36 Leyland Titan TD1s purchased in 19278-9 had 51-seat open-staircase bodywork, and were given dual route and destination indicators when built. Provision for route numbers came later, . (© Omnibus Society / C. Carter)

This 1931 Titan TD1 had bodywork by Eastwood & Kenning, successors to Davidson of Trafford Park, Manchester. Perpetuating the dual doorway and staircase layout of previous deliveries from Davidson, it displays an uncomfortable compromise between piano-front and smooth-profile styling. (© Omnibus Society/ Roy Marshall collection)

CHAPTER 2
1933-39
Plans for the Final Tramway Abandonment

The date for the withdrawal of the remaining trams was fixed for 30 September 1933 and plans were discussed by the Committee in May. The general manager's original proposals were as follows:

1. Route No. 6 to run between Seacombe and New Brighton via Borough Road, Poulton Road, Oxton Road, Torrington Road, Belvidere Road and Warren Drive (instead of via Brighton Street, Church Street, Mill Lane etc).

2. The Circular Route between Seacombe and Grove Road to be retained but to run via Brighton Street and Church Street instead of Wheatland Lane and Mainwaring Road and via Oxton Road and Woodstock Road in lieu of the western end of Poulton Road and Mill Lane.

He recommended running the Poulton route via Claremount Road instead of St George's Road and urged the extension of Sandy Lane through to Claremount Road so that this could be done.

The current winter peak vehicle requirement of 60 vehicles would be increased to 66, and to 79 in the summer. The fleet of 77 buses was proposed to be increased to 88.

At a special meeting on 18 July 1933, variations on these proposals were put forward. Plan 1 was for the restoration of the Church Street and Seaview Road route through to New Brighton, as had been worked by trams until 1931, with the Poulton route terminating at the Grove Road (Warren Drive) junction. This would have resulted in the Belvidere Road and Church Street/Seaview Road buses running together between Grove Road and New Brighton. Plan 2 proposed that the Church Street/Seaview Road buses should continue along Grove Road to Harrison Drive, and the Poulton service should run through to New Brighton. This would have given a five-minute service between Grove Road (Warren Drive) and New Brighton by the Belvidere Road and Poulton buses. Another proposal was for the Belvidere Road buses to run via Brougham Road instead of Borough Road to give a service between Poulton and a point near the Town Hall.

The Committee came out in favour of a compromise which amounted to the restoration of the tram facilities as they had existed until March 1931, modified as to the Oxton Road diversion, plus the proposed rerouting of the No. 6 service via Brougham Road and Poulton. The No. 6 and new Poulton services were to run through to New Brighton between June and September but terminate at Grove Road in the winter, except on Saturdays.

However certain councillors were anxious to see additional facilities within the borough so that direct journeys were possible between as many districts as possible. They were also unhappy about the lower part of Mill Lane being unserved. The difficulty of reaching Poulton from Egremont by public transport was seen as a serious weakness in the network, although there was no evidence of any sustained demand for such a facility. This was at a time when people were accustomed to walking such distances and the fact remained that the walking distance between the two districts, across Central Park, was somewhat shorter than any possible bus journey. Nevertheless, against the advice of the general manager, plans were made to remedy this perceived lack of facilities. The Committee had failed to take into consideration the need to await the Traffic Commissioners' pleasure and the tramway abandonment had to be delayed by two months to 30 November while the necessary road service licences were obtained.

Staff problems now needed attention; in June 1933 a potential bus driver shortage was threatened as there were no more men within the undertaking suitable for training. The number of men capable of driving buses was 125, of whom 103 had been trained internally. Seventeen tram drivers were unsuitable for any sort of work on buses and five were capable of conducting. The future of tramwaymen who could not be employed on the buses now had to be addressed as there was no longer an option to transfer men to another tram service. A list of 23 men to be given 'special consideration' was drawn up. Several tram drivers were considered unfit to drive buses because of age or being too short in the leg; three had failed the driving test, five were refused conductors' licences by the Traffic Commissioners, and others were failed on various medical grounds. Two subsequently obtained PSV drivers' licences. The men concerned were treated sympathetically as several had over 30 years' service. Several were retired early, with their wages made up until they were 65, and some were found day cleaning or labouring work in the garage. A few temporary employees were declared redundant in order to make way for displaced tram drivers to take up conducting duties.

The New Bus Network

From 1 December 1933 the new services came into operation, the route via Church Street and Seaview Road being numbered 16 and that via Poulton Road, Oxton Road and Wallasey Village becoming No. 17. A new circular route was created by extending route No. 13 from its terminus at Serpentine Road via Martins Lane, Liscard Road, Mill Lane, Poulton Road and Borough Road back to Seacombe. This former peak hour service now ran all day on weekdays only with a 20-minute service off-peak and a 10-minute peak frequency. In the opposite direction it was numbered 15. Bus fares on all routes were reduced from the same day but were still higher than tram fares over short stages.

The service along Poulton Road was now excessive. At off-peak times, a tram every 10 minutes and a bus every 20 minutes were replaced by three buses every ten minutes – a 6, a 4 or a 15 (13 inwards) and a 17. At peak hours, two trams and two buses were replaced by six buses every 10 minutes – a 4 to Moreton, a 4 to Leasowe Road (or a 3 to Harrison Drive), a 6 to Grove Road, a 6 to Broadway Avenue, a 15, and a 17 to Grove Road or New Brighton. This was costly and insupportable and steps were soon taken to make some economies, the Circular being abandoned from 18 March 1934 when route 13 was cut back to its original role as a peak hour service between Seacombe and Martins Lane (Serpentine Road). During the winter timetable, the 15 continued to run between Seacombe and St. Luke's Church every 10 minutes during the peak and every 20 minutes off-peak, alternating with the Moreton buses. On Saturday afternoon between 1.50 and 4.50, when the 4 ran every 10 minutes, it was suspended. On the summer timetable, it ran until about noon when the 4A Moreton Shore buses took up the service. It had the distinction of being the only Wallasey short working to have had a separate route number. This arrangement saved two buses off-peak and four during the peak. On the same date, route 6 was diverted to run via Borough Road instead of Brougham Road. The 6 and 17 were interworked at Grove Road until about 1.30pm, after which they both ran through to New Brighton. From 1 July 1934, the rush hour No. 3 between Seacombe and Harrison Drive via Poulton was replaced by duplicates on route 4 between Seacombe and Leasowe Road (Wallasey Village), a measure which saved only a few miles a week as the same number of buses were still needed.

In June, the Committee had met to consider further changes to the network. Talks with Birkenhead Corporation regarding the diversion of the No.10 service via Woodside and its extension to Eastham Ferry in summer were discussed, but the main proposal was the reintroduction of the former tramway Circular route during the winter months only, by curtailing the 16 and 17 routes at Grove Road, the Warren Drive service being taken over by extending the 6 to New Brighton. However, this was rejected and the following changes were made from 1 October, bringing the services into the form which they took for many years. Route 13 and 15 were withdrawn completely, the numbers falling into disuse. The former was replaced by a rerouting of the 6 via King Street, Trafalgar Road, Martins Lane, Mill Lane, Rullerton Road and Belvidere Road while the 17 was diverted via Poulton Road and Mill Lane as the trams had run for so many years. Peak hour short workings on the 17 were provided between Seacombe and Marlowe Road (Wallasey Road), requiring three buses. The 17 now ran through to and from New Brighton daily in the summer from about 8.00am and on Saturday afternoons in winter while the 6 ran through only on Saturdays and Sundays after about 2.00pm in the summer and not at all in the winter.

Promenade Services

In 1930, the Bathing Station was opened west of Harrison Drive; this provided facilities for bathers to change clothes and was used by those who did not rent chalets or bring tents to the beach. A narrow road was built leading from the foot of the Drive, parallel to the beach, and several passing places with large 'No Parking' notices were built for the buses. The Grove Road-Foreshore service was diverted, 1½d being charged for the longer journey. A special semi-toastrack Karrier bus, delivered in 1927, was normally sufficient, though up to five other single-deckers could often be seen on busy Sundays until the Promenade extension was built. The widened roadway at the Bathing Station terminus had such a steep camber that double-decker buses could not be safely used until improvements were made in 1949.

The first section of the New Brighton promenade extension (King's Parade), from Marine Park to the Red Noses (great sandstone rocks now almost obscured by changes in levels of the surrounding land), was opened towards the end of 1933 and a weekend promenade service started in June 1934. At first the starting point was at the Tower Grounds but during the high season it became extremely difficult to reverse buses into Egerton Street so the terminus was moved to the Victoria Gardens. Some years later, when crowds made it dangerous to turn round by the pier, buses ran along Waterloo Road and Virginia Road on the inward journey. The road service licence authorised a 12-minute service in accordance with traffic requirements and it was usually run by one single-decker bus at a through fare of 2d. From 1935, two 20-seat Leyland Cubs with canvas roofs were used for this work.

In 1936 route numbers 18 (Bathing Station) and 19 (Promenade) were allocated; the same numbers were used in the 1937-38 season for Football Specials to New Brighton FC Ground (then in Rake Lane near Penkett Road), No. 18 via Liscard and No. 19 via Penkett Road but this does not seem to have been done in subsequent seasons. The opening of New Brighton Bathing Pool in 1934 seriously affected traffic to and from the Derby Bathing Pool.

The King's Parade extension to a point about 200 yards west of Harrison Drive was completed in 1939 and opened with due ceremony on 20 May. The No. 19 service was extended through to the end of the promenade where there was at that time a continuous road so that buses returned by a part of the inner carriageway and the lower section of Harrison Drive. The terminus was styled 'Wallasey Beach' and four more Leyland Cubs with luxury bodies were placed in service. As the normal limit for one-man buses was 20 passengers, special dispensation was granted for these 25-seaters, initially for one year. Occasionally double-decker buses appeared on the Promenade, the first occasion being the maiden voyage of the SS Mauretania when the top decks were full of people watching the new liner leaving the Mersey. At the beginning of the 1939 summer season, a new board was fixed at the stopping place at the top of Harrison Drive announcing the No. 18 service to the Bathing Station and also No. 20 to the Promenade end. However, there is no evidence that the No. 20 service ever ran in pre-war days.

Terminal Arrangements

The old terminus at Seacombe ferry had a clockwise tramway loop with sidings on each side of Victoria Place. Buses had been allotted particular places as stands, though these were not marked in any way and there were no queuing facilities. A line of cabs stood on the east-west axis, facing the ferry terminal buildings; to the south of them, facing the other way, stood the No. 12, 6, 4 and 2 buses. In the south-east corner there was a pavement island where the 1 and 5 buses stood. The construction of the new ferry approach and terminal buildings in 1932-33 caused some disruption but, when completed, the place was transformed. Passengers were set down outside the terminal building as before and the buses then ran round to reverse into position, herringbone fashion, on the south side, passengers approaching by means of a covered colonnade. The various services were indicated by signboards and queue rails were erected after a time. Later, white lines and large route numbers painted on the roadway guided drivers into position; the paint was later replaced by metal studs some of which could still be seen in position 60 years later. The original allocation of stands from east to west was 1, 1, 2, 14, 14, 5, 5, 6, 6, 13, 15, 16, 16, 17, 3, 4, 12. From October 1934 this was altered to 1, 1, 2, 14, 14, 16, 16, 5, 5, 6, 6, 17, 17, 4, 4, 12. In fact. the 12 never occupied its stand as buses parked on the corner facing into Birkenhead Road. However, there is photographic evidence suggesting that, for a short time during off-peak times, the stands were concentrated at the end nearest to the ferry terminal as 1, 2, 14, 16, 17, 5, 6 and 4. After the arrival of each boat and as soon as the buses were loaded, the inspector blew his whistle and the convoy of buses set off – up to 15 of them at peak hours.

At New Brighton, all buses both approached and left New Brighton ferry terminus via Victoria Road up to 1930, unlike the trams which always arrived via Rowson Street and Virginia Road and left via Victoria Road. At weekends during the summer of 1930, the Victoria Road end of Virginia Road was used as a terminus, buses approaching via Belmont Road and Balmoral Road and leaving via Victoria Road. For the 1931 season the tram route was followed, queue barriers being erected for some distance along Virginia Road. From 1933, Virginia Road was used daily in summer though, up to 10.00am, all buses approached and departed via Victoria Road and turned at the pier for the convenience of ferry passengers, although the ferry was closed in winter from 1936. The permanent adoption of Virginia Road as a year-round terminus did not come until 27 May 1943.

At Harrison Drive, buses terminated by reversing into Groveland Road and stood there. This arrangement continued, despite complaints of congestion, until 24 December 1934 when the stop was transferred to Wallasey Village. At Liscard Village, buses on route 11 unloaded outside the Capitol cinema and turned round the small island in the centre of the junction which had originally borne the 'Monkey House' and was now host to a noisome underground toilet and a Bundy clock where the conductors inserted their keys to record their times. Until a widening scheme in 1937-38, which involved the erection of a new Wellington Hotel and Coronation Buildings, Wallasey Road was very narrow but buses loaded near the later Electricity Showrooms and outside the Capitol cinema. A traffic roundabout was built at the crossroads, necessitating the relocation of some bus stops. The No. 10 stop to New Brighton was moved to what was then an embayment opposite Manor Road, causing many complaints.

Moreton Services Expand

The Moreton services continued to make losses, the problems being the popularity of the much faster and more frequent Crosville service from Liscard and the long stretch of Leasowe Road with a very low population. The No. 8 service from New Brighton continued to run hourly in winter, with one additional trip from New Brighton at 4.15pm to cater for schools traffic, and half-hourly in summer until 1936 when the summer service was increased to three buses an hour after 2.00pm on Saturdays and Sundays, giving a combined 15-minute service from New Brighton with route 9. As Moreton's population grew, Wallasey Corporation attempted to develop branch routes away from the main road. The first of these was the diversion of the No. 9 along Borrowdale Road to Burrell Drive from 11 July 1937. The original plan had envisaged a loop continuing from Burrell Drive via Cartmel Drive, Seaforth Drive and Upton Road but the Corporation stood back from any potential confrontation with Birkenhead over encroachment on their service along Upton Road. From 7 February 1938, the No. 8 route was experimentally diverted along Joan Avenue and Douglas Drive instead of following Hoylake Road throughout. This was unlicensed and brought forth many protests from residents and so the diversion was abandoned after four weeks. It was licensed soon afterwards but the roads were then found to be unsuitable structurally and the project was abandoned. The same service was extended along Bermuda Road to Hardie Avenue on 1 November 1938, the extension, for which no additional running time was allowed, having been delayed for several months awaiting the resiting of a Birkenhead Corporation shelter which obstructed the junction. The No. 9 was essentially a single-decker route and, from 1935, a 20-seat Leyland Cub was often used. The two original Cubs had been equipped with stand-model TIM machines and were operated as one-man buses. Their use on route 9 was criticised as ticket issue was slow and passengers complained of having to queue in the rain.

From 1 October 1936 a supplementary service was run on route 4 between Seacombe ferry and Birket Avenue between 12.00 noon and 7.00pm on Saturdays and 4.30 to 11.30pm on Mondays to Fridays, giving a 10-minute service over this section, but this was withdrawn in February 1937 due to lack of support. There were fears that traffic on the Moreton services would be seriously affected by the electrification of the Wirral railway

have granted the application if the Wallasey terminus had been elsewhere. Poulton Bridge was subsequently used by route 11 whenever Duke Street bridge was closed to traffic. Hitherto, all three joint services had been diverted over the Four Bridges on such occasions.

The Service Pattern

As buses took over from trams at the end of 1933, a pattern of service emerged which persisted until the outbreak of war in 1939. The timetable for August 1932 shows eight bus routes serving Seacombe ferry, Nos 1, 2, 3, 4, 5, 6, 12 and 13. Of these, No. 1, the former 'S' tram route, was the most frequent with a five- or six-minute frequency throughout the day. The first bus left Victoria Road (Rowson Street) at 5.12am and no bus ventured as far as New Brighton terminus until the 7.40am from Seacombe, the whole of the timetabled early morning peak hour service being from Victoria Road or Molyneux Drive with unadvertised short workings from Holland Road and Trafalgar Road. The early buses turned by running down Rowson Street, turning into Wellington Road and then reaching Victoria Road via Waterloo Road. The afternoon peak was longer than on the other services but was confined to Molyneux Drive extras. The last bus for New Brighton left Seacombe at 11.57pm on weekdays and half an hour earlier on Sundays. Sunday services commenced at about 9.00am. At very busy holiday times it was customary to run a supplementary service between Brougham Road and New Brighton for the benefit of local residents, who were liable to be crowded out by visitors filling the buses at Seacombe ferry. During the 1938 summer season at least, such a service was run every Wednesday evening when traffic was heavy because of half-day closing of the shops. These buses turned by using Vienna Street, a short street connecting Demesne Street with Brighton Street, which has since disappeared under Riverside school extensions.

The No. 2 route between Seacombe and Harrison Drive was a late starter, with no service before about 7.30am on weekdays and about 9.30am on Sundays. A 10-minute service operated throughout most of the day, but there was no peak hour augmentation except for buses off other services using the Manor Road route between the depot and Seacombe. The peak hour short workings between Seacombe ferry and Liscard on route 14 returned to Seacombe by route 2 as there was no convenient way of turning. Summer holiday augmentation normally covered the whole route but there were very occasional workings from Brougham Road.

By 1932 the No. 3 Harrison Drive via Poulton route had been completely overshadowed by the No. 4, Moreton, route. Two buses were needed in the morning and one in the evening (or Saturday noon). Departures were at 8.25, 8.42 and 8.55am from Harrison Drive and at 5.20, 5.50 and 6.20pm from Seacombe (1.05 and 1.35pm on Saturdays). However, the service was withdrawn after 30 June 1934, being replaced by additional duplicates on route 4 to and from the top of Leasowe Road. The No. 4 service grew as the population of Leasowe and Moreton expanded. In 1932, even in summer, the No. 4 service supported only a half-hourly service until 12.00 noon, the first departure from Bermuda Road being at 7.00am. From noon there was a combined 10-minute service as far as Leasowe Castle, made up of a half-hourly Moreton Shore service and an irregular service to Bermuda Road. The first advertised departures on Sundays were at 10.00am from both ends but on fine Bank Holidays and summer Sundays, there was a more or less continuous service to and from the Shore. The last departure for Bermuda Road daily was at 11.27pm and this made a last journey at 11.57 on route 8 to Liscard.

From about 1932, short distance passengers tended to crowd out passengers for Leasowe and Moreton at peak hours and duplication was provided between Seacombe and Cliff Road, involving what would now be regarded as a dangerous reversing movement from Breck Road into steep Fox Hey Road. However, this arrangement was short-lived as, by 1933, the duplicates ran to the top of Leasowe Road every 10 minutes except when there was a No. 3. By 1934 the early morning service had greatly improved with departures for the ferry from the top of Leasowe Road at 5.15 and 6.15am and then quite frequently. The first departure from Moreton left at 6.30am and the growth of Leasowe as a residential suburb gave rise to some trips between Birket Avenue and Seacombe. By 1938 one very early journey ran via Wheatland Lane instead of Borough Road and the 6.15am from Leasowe Road had been extended back to start from Leasowe Castle at 6.09am. The normal through service ran every 20 minutes off-peak and 10 minutes in the peak with a 20-minute summer service to the Shore (by then numbered 4A) from 12.10pm on weekdays and 10.10am on Sundays.

The No. 5 service between Seacombe and Albion Street, like the No. 2, was a late starter and, additionally, it never ran on Sundays. Four buses provided a 10-minute peak hour service starting at 7.50am (later 7.40am) from the Hotel Victoria and this continued until 9.40am after which two buses provided a 20-minute service until 4.20pm from Seacombe. The last bus from Seacombe ran at 11.00pm and there was an unusual depot working from Albion Street to Liscard via Penkett Road and Manor Road. From about 1932, peak-hour duplicates ran between Seacombe and Kirkway (Mount Pleasant Road). In addition, it was augmented by the No. 7 route to and from Egremont ferry on which traffic gradually diminished. In 1934 there had been five morning trips from Albion Street to Egremont at 8.00am and every 20 minutes until 9.20am, and nine afternoon trips between 4.30 and 7.10pm (Saturdays 12.05 to 2.30pm). One bus sufficed to provide a service on which the journey time was tight at 10 minutes with no layover, almost two minutes being needed for the steep climb up Tobin Street in bottom gear. By 1938, the service was being worked by a Lion or 20-seat Leyland Cub with three trips in the morning and four in the evening. When fog or rough weather stopped the Egremont boats, the No. 7

buses became No. 5's and ran through to Seacombe, but from 1936 the New Brighton and Egremont ferries lost their winter services and the No. 7 became just a summer service. It was withdrawn in August 1938 and the ferry itself closed on the outbreak of war in September 1939.

As already described, the No. 6 Belvidere Road service suffered more changes of route than any other; it was never profitable but always had a 10-minute service and ran until midnight. From quite early in its history, peak hour duplication was provided between Seacombe and Broadway Avenue. Originally, the No. 6 ran through to New Brighton daily, having replaced the 'WD' tram beyond Grove Road (Warren Drive) but, after the final tramway abandonment, the No. 16 took over this duty and extension of No. 6 became a summer afternoon and evening phenomenon. By the end of the decade, New Brighton was reached only at summer weekends. A proposal to reduce losses by running only a 20-minute service off-peak was strongly opposed in July 1939.

The early morning service on the No. 14 Rake Lane route was, as in tram days, a combined 14/16 between Grove Road or Grasmere Drive and Seacombe via Wheatland Lane, showing No. 16 and the 14 proper started at 7.20am from New Brighton. On Sundays there was no service until 12.10pm. From 9 March 1935, the service frequency was increased from 10 to 5 minutes between noon and 6.30pm, but this was excessive and reverted to 10 minutes after an experimental period, except on busy Saturday afternoons, though only a 10-minute service was advertised. At holiday times it was customary to operate a supplementary service between Lloyd's Corner (corner of Wheatland Lane and Poulton Road) for the benefit of residents. These buses turned by using the lower part of Liscard Road and Poulton Road; apart from a Sunday morning service in 1927-28, this was the only occasion when buses used this part of Liscard Road when carrying passengers. Peak hour duplication ran between Seacombe and Liscard Village, and in the mornings there were some trips from Martins Lane. Special buses operated to Earlston Road for football matches at the old 'Rakers' ground.

The combined 14/16 service started at 5.15am on weekdays and ran until 7.00am after which the 16 proper via Church Street commenced from Grove Road; the first bus from New Brighton ran only at 7.55am. As in tramway days, the peak hour duplication ran between Seacombe and Hose Side Road (Mount Pleasant Road end). As a 10-minute service was provided at most times of the day, augmentation was never required, the extra passengers at holiday times merely filling up what was normally unused accommodation. This service ran up to midnight on weekdays and from 9.30am to 11.30pm on Sundays.

The 17 service via Poulton started early, soon after 5.00am from Grove Road with the odd trip from St Luke's Church only. When running through to New Brighton in the summer and on weekday evenings throughout the year, it combined with the 16 to give an even 5-minute service between Grove Road and New Brighton. Peak hour duplication ran between Seacombe and Marlowe Road (Wallasey Road) with some St. Luke's Church trips. There may also have been some inward morning trips from Clifford Road from the late 1930s. At busy holiday times, extra buses ran between Lloyds Corner and New Brighton for the benefit of residents as the buses from Seacombe tended to share the Harrison Drive holiday traffic with route No. 2.

The afternoon peak was short, the full duplication on all routes operating only on five departures, 5.20 to 6.00pm. Most buses ran 'live' in both directions even though bus requirements could perhaps have been reduced slightly by running empty against the traffic flow. An exception was Kirkway where the buses returned empty to Seacombe to avoid the necessity for a third bus.

Of the routes not serving Seacombe, routes 8 and 9 between New Brighton and Moreton provided basic hourly services on each route combining to give a half-hourly frequency from common points. In the afternoon, the 8 increased to half-hourly and there was a 75-minute gap on the 9 to move the departure time between the two No. 8s. From about 1934, the summer Saturday and Sunday afternoon and evening services on No. 8 were increased to three departures at 0, 15 and 45 minutes past the hour from New Brighton, the 9 slotting in at 32 past. Some of the early and late journeys on the 8 were really part of the No. 4 service workings. In 1932, the first departure from Bermuda Road to New Brighton was at 8.15am but, by 1934, this had advanced to 6.57am. There was little augmentation necessary. Secondary school pupils resident in Moreton used the Crosville buses as cheap half-fare contracts were available and the service was faster, even allowing some of them to go home for lunch.

Following poor financial results in 1936-37, winter services were reduced in 1937. The Saturday extension of No. 6 to New Brighton was cancelled and the No. 17 ran through to New Brighton only from 12.30pm on Saturdays and 6.30pm on Sundays. The question of through buses to New Brighton was also controversial and there was constant agitation for all the buses on routes 6, 16 and 17 to run through. The 16 was the shortest route between Seacombe and Grove Road and, as the influential Warren Drive residents had more political clout, these buses always ran through as had the trams before them. As the buses all left Seacombe ferry together, and the 16 was the shortest route, it was impossible to arrange immediate connections at Grove Road as the 6 and 17 arrived there three and five minutes after the 16 had gone. In those days, a wait of seven or even five minutes was considered to be intolerable.

One suggestion was that, in the winter, the 16 and 17 services should be linked as a circular, a reversion to something like the situation that existed during the last two years of the tramways, the through service to New Brighton being provided by route 6. However this was abandoned when it was realised that, because of ferry connections, there would still need to be layover at Grove Road.

Bus Allocations

With such a mixed fleet, it is surprising that no attempt was made to allocate specific types to particular duties. The underpowered Daimlers were often found on the 16 but, apart from that, all types of double-decker buses were allocated indiscriminately. By 1933, all regular duties were covered by double-decker buses except route 9 which needed one single-decker bus, and the Bathing Station shuttle which was the particular preserve of Karrier No. 11. This left nine Leyland Lions spare and several were delicensed for the winter. An exception was the winter of 1933-34 when the remodelling of services after the tramway abandonment taxed the fleet resources to the limit and, even though the changeover was made in mid-winter, the Lions came back into daily service for a time. Three were required for the off-peak circular service 13/15 and one for route 9, though Karrier No. 11 made a rare winter appearance at this time on this route. At peak hours 13/15 needed six buses and other Lions were used as duplicates on routes 5 and 6 respectively to Kirkway and Broadway Avenue and occasionally on 16 to Hose Side Road. When the Circle was cut back after less than four months' operation, each part needed only two buses and the position was further eased by the arrival of the balance of the TD3 order.

From 1934, a Lion would be allocated to the Promenade service which originally ran daily, but from 1936 this was the preserve of the Cubs Nos. 12-13. From that time on there were only seven single-decker buses in stock and every available one would be in service at busy summer weekends on Harrison Drive and the Promenade. If there was a spare Lion available it would be used on a lightly-trafficked route such as No. 6 or, on a Sunday evening, between Molyneux Drive and Seacombe on route 1 to give residents a chance as all the buses coming through from New Brighton were full. From late 1935, one of the Cubs ran on route 9 and this duty involved some early morning journeys on 8. Occasionally, one would turn up in the most unlikely place such as on the 14 in the morning peak on a wet morning when it was customary to put out four extra buses. During the 1937-38 summer seasons, a double-decker bus was used on 9, the Cub thus released working the 7 in the death throes of this route in 1938.

Wallasey buses had relatively low patronage during the off-peak, much lower than in Birkenhead whose buses averaged 10% more mileage. Several routes always ran at a loss but were maintained as a civic service. Attempts to reduce services to curb the losses were always hotly contested by councillors and the public in general. The following table shows the position in the mid-1930s:

ROUTE PROFITABILITY ANALYSIS

Route	Profit / (loss) £		
	1934-35	1935-36	1936-37
1	9616	7879	6097
2	4768	3850	3124
3	(3)		
4	(3779)	(3517)	(5326)
5	(992)	(683)	(310)
6	(721)	(1069)	(1237)
7	(296)	(243)	(208)
8	(1420)	(1443)	(1875)
9	(1995)	(2025)	(2144)
10	3112	2152	1542
11	1603	1676	1235
12	(154)	47	26
13	(208)		
14	5334	4662	4548
16	2502	1466	687
17	(1565)	(1932)	(2780)
18	230	199	43
19	(50)	(36)	(52)
Spl buses	114	110	61
Spl tickets	1063	1139	1080
Sundries	155	152	101
Misc	19278	13750	5232
	1672	1625	1955
Total	20950	15375	7187

Cross-subsidisation of the weak routes by the strong was an accepted policy. The finances of the undertaking were very healthy and contributions to the General Rate Fund (in effect, a dividend to the shareholders) amounted to £5,000 per annum for each of the years ended 31 March 1934 to 1939 inclusive. However, there were many who believed that the profits should go to the users in the form of reduced fares rather than to the ratepayers and there was a concerted effort to get fares further reduced in 1937-38. This led to a review of the bus undertaking by the Borough Treasurer, who reported to the Council on 8 July 1938.

The Treasurer agreed with the general manager's view that fares should not be reduced, particularly as petrol tax had just been increased from 8d to 9d per gallon. He advocated the continuation of the Reserve Fund, retaining sufficient funds to meet the annual debt on loan charges and that over-optimistic forecasts should be avoided in view of the very serious effect that fluctuating weather could have on the revenue.

The electrification of the Wirral section of the LMS railway from 14 March 1938, with through services between New Brighton/Moreton and Liverpool in less than half the time it took by bus and ferry, initially took its toll at the rate of £20 per day but this was soon regained in other ways. New Brighton and Wallasey people working in Liverpool city centre could go home to lunch by train, and the buses and ferries could not compete with that.

The Borough Treasurer's recommendations were those of a doctrinaire accountant with only a passing knowledge of the economics of a bus undertaking. He suggested the replacement of 12 buses annually in order to equalise future loan charges, a reduction in the number of buses and more intensive utilisation of the fleet. The latter was apparently a reference to the lower bus usage obtaining in Wallasey compared with Birkenhead.

In his reply, the manager pointed out that batches of 18 and 24 vehicles had been taken into stock during the past two years; the 24 were all steel (a relatively recent technical development) and it was not known if they would last the eight-year life then used for accounting purposes. No policy change could therefore be implemented before 1946. The following particulars of bus usage were quoted:

	Double deck	Single deck
No. of buses in stock	89	7
Peak requirements a.m.	78	1
Holiday etc. requirements	4	
Overhaul		2
Body Shop	2	
Paint Shop	2	
Accident Repairs	1	

In 1937-38 the annual double-decker usage had been 34,296 miles (94 miles per day) compared with Birkenhead's 37,780 (103.5 miles per day). Only one Leyland Lion was licensed throughout the year, the other four being licensed only from May to September and rarely used. The record for bus No. 7 in 1937 was May 6 days, June 9, July 0, August 12 and September 3 days. However, the loan charges on these buses had long been repaid so they cost little more than the running expenses.

Posting Boxes

Posting boxes enabling members of the public to post letters after the normal collection times, and were introduced on tramcars in April 1927. The small rectangular boxes were hung from the front dash. When the Seabank Road tram route was converted to bus operation on 20 January 1929, the facility was continued on the buses but boxes were hung on a bracket fitted to the rear panel. Only certain buses had this fitment so care had to be taken that one of the correct buses was allocated to the duty concerned. The facility was extended to the No. 6 bus when the Warren Drive and Poulton routes were partially converted in March 1931, to the Moreton-Seacombe route in September 1932, to the Albion Street route upon abandonment of the Rake Lane trams and to the 16 and 17 routes when trams finished on 30 November 1933. In 1934 the boxes were carried by buses leaving the outer terminus between 9.30 and 9.42pm. Their contents were collected by a postman at Seacombe ferry and taken over to Liverpool where, together with collections from Birkenhead, they were taken to the Head Post Office in Victoria Street. The Corporation received £4 per box per annum and the boxes are believed to have been stored at the bus inspector's office at Seacombe. The facility was discontinued on 4 September 1936 when 9.30pm collections were provided from selected post boxes throughout the town.

What might have been! An impressive line-up of new AEC buses at Seacombe Ferry, portraying Nos.99, 98, 100 and 101, all 1934 deliveries with bodywork by Roe, except for one English Electric (No.98). Nos 101-2 were a pair of AEC 'Q's, a model years ahead of its time which, whilst prone to skidding because of the short rear overhang, gave nine years' service on the sett-surfaced roads in the town and docks areas. (Omnibus Society / Norris collection)

CHAPTER 3
THE 1939-45 WAR

Reduced Services

In July 1939 the Traffic Commissioners had already told all operators to have contingency plans ready, reductions of 40% being anticipated as necessary to reduce the consumption of petroleum products, all of which had to be imported at that time. This was soon shown to be impossible as workers' services had to be maintained and, very soon, increased as war production accelerated. The original plan submitted by the Corporation was rejected as it reduced mileage only by 15.17% and a further scheme was prepared with a 35% reduction compared with 1938. Operators were expected to have their contingency plans in operation within three weeks of the declaration of war. Wallasey made some reductions, including the total suspension of routes 8 and 9, from the day after war was declared – 4 September – but the main emergency timetable came into operation on 24 September together with those of Birkenhead Corporation and Crosville. An early war casualty was the all-day 10-minute frequency on both Woodside and Seacombe ferries in favour of quarter-hourly sailings, although the peak hour 10-minute frequency was retained.

The following services were withdrawn altogether:

4A	Seacombe – Moreton Shore
8	New Brighton – Moreton (Hardie Avenue) via Liscard
9	New Brighton – Moreton (Borrowdale Road) via Grove Road
18	Harrison Drive – Derby Bathing Pool
19	New Brighton – Wallasey Beach via Promenade

To replace route 8, transfer tickets were introduced between routes 2 and 4 at Leasowe Road (Wallasey Village), and the Crosville buses between West Kirby, Moreton and Liscard were also available. However, some hardship was proved, particularly at school times, and an hourly service on weekdays between 8.15am and 6.15pm was restored from 2 January 1940 between New Brighton and Bermuda Road (Hoylake Road), the Hardie Avenue extension being temporarily withdrawn. The service was subsequently diverted to Borrowdale Road (Burrell Drive) from 1 June 1941.

The Blackout

Interior lights were reduced by fitting low-powered bulbs, and masking or removing some bulbs altogether. Wallasey provided more light by applying a blue, gelatinous substance to the upper half of the saloon windows and the route number glasses. However this produced a most depressing effect during the daylight hours and there was much caustic comment in the local press about 'the Wallasey blues'. The route numbers, though just about visible at night, could scarcely be seen in daytime. Criticism was so vociferous that the 'blues' had been replaced by an interior lighting scheme as used at Manchester by May 1940. Mudguards, platform edges and handrails of buses were painted white as were kerbs and the bases of street lights, pillar boxes and other street furniture. Of course, there was little other traffic on the roads but working in these conditions can only be described as nerve-wracking and led to neuroses and other ailments. Extra running time had to be allowed for night driving.

Petrol and diesel rationing came into force on 23 September 1939 and, to the dismay of the management, permits for only 50% of the 1938 consumption were received. There were few people about in the blackout as all places of public entertainment were closed at first and the elimination of late buses, for which there was a very limited demand, was an effective way of saving fuel for essential purposes. In the light of experience, further adjustments were made in February 1940, mainly to late buses, which in general finished at about 10.30-11.0pm. Off-peak services were generally 15-20 minutes instead of 10 minutes and the frequency of the No. 12 Seacombe-Charing Cross service was reduced to 40 minutes, requiring only one bus.

The department was inundated with applications from military units for free travel facilities for Territorial soldiers. One unit was using 400 free tickets per week and, with limited accommodation available, these privileges were soon withdrawn.

Wartime problems were exacerbated by exceptional weather, with heavy snowfalls from 27 January to 4 February 1940, 2,234 miles (4.47%) being lost during the nine days. Most routes were clear although roads were narrowed by piles of snow at the sides. The No. 5 route was curtailed at Kirkway as Mount Road, being hilly, was impassable for much of the time. Considerable damage was caused, no fewer than 37 roof lights in the depot being cracked or broken due to the weight of snow. Forty-six of the 71 vehicles licensed required special attention because of broken springs, radiator problems, electrical defects caused by snow and ice, and even a broken axle and damaged differential caused by running over deeply rutted frozen snow. Nineteen buses were involved in collisions caused mainly by road conditions. Fog was also a greater danger in the blackout than in normal times. Thick, almost impenetrable fogs, exacerbated by hundreds of domestic chimneys, were common in winter and the disruption caused on 30 and 31 December 1939 was typical. On the first date a service was maintained on routes 1, 2, 5, 6, 11, 16 and 17, but 4, 10 and 14 were suspended from 9.0pm for 1-1½ hours resulting in a loss of 600 miles (8.9%). On the second night, a Sunday, a service was given on routes 1, 2, 14, 16 and 17, but 4, 6 and 10 were suspended for periods of 1-3 hours from 6.45pm with a loss of 430 miles (17.4%). A fog service often meant the conductor walking in front of the bus with a torch.

As the 'phoney war' continued and nothing much happened, some restrictions were relaxed. Cinemas reopened and, in the summer of 1940, there was sufficient fuel available for some holiday services to be operated including the Derby Bathing Pool and Promenade services. During May, the Virginia Road terminus was used on Saturdays and Sundays and from 1 June to 30 September daily from 10.00am. Whit Monday was cancelled as a bank holiday but some augmentation was provided on routes 1, 4, 8, 10, 14, 16 and 17. However, complacency was shattered when the first bombs fell on Wallasey on 10 August 1940 and, although the early raids were relatively small-scale affairs, they were sufficient to cause some disruption of bus services. One of the first 'incidents' was at Stroud's Corner, at the junction of Rake Lane and Mount Pleasant Road. Strangely, although most other bomb scars have long since been eliminated, the gap in this row of buildings has remained there, over 60 years later. The tendency at that time was to close long sections of roadway either side of incidents and buses on routes 8, 10 and 14 were diverted via Penkett Road, Steel Avenue, Seabank Road and Magazine Lane. This amounted to an extra 94 miles per day and the diversion was still in force on 17 September, the additional mileage run between 10 August and 15 September being 3,204, playing havoc with the fuel ration. The damage attracted crowds of sightseers from all over Wallasey and Birkenhead and the restricted bus services had difficulty in catering for this unexpected additional traffic. Little did these sightseers realise how familiar this kind of destruction was soon to become. The next memorable incident occurred on 31 August 1940 when bombs straddled the Town Hall, one exploding outside in Brighton Street. A long stretch of Brighton Street was closed, routes 1, 2, 5, 6 and 16 being diverted via Brougham Road and Liscard Road, 1, 2 and 5 regaining their normal routes via Church Street while route 6 ran via Serpentine Road to Martins Lane, omitting King Street and Trafalgar Road altogether.

Late services were curtailed from 10 October, saving 3,475 miles per week, and from 5 December 1940 the services on routes 2, 14, 16 and 17 were augmented to every 10 minutes between 12 noon and 4.00pm and on route 4 to 15 minutes between 2.00 and 4.00pm. To do this within the existing fuel ration, evening services were further reduced to half-hourly with last buses at 10.00pm. From 18 November, the afternoon peak 10-minute service was run from Seacombe between 4.00pm and 6.30pm instead of from 4.30pm to 7.00pm as a result of a move towards earlier finishing times to enable people to reach their homes before darkness fell.

The Air Raids

The first large-scale air raids started on 20 December 1940 when, during three nights, far more casualties were caused and damage done than in all the previous attacks. These raids were eclipsed by the devastation of 12-14 March during which 10,000 people were rendered homeless, 174 were killed and 158 seriously injured in Wallasey alone. No part of the town was left unscathed and the bus services continued to serve the depleted population as best they could under well-nigh impossible conditions. Many strange diversions were adopted at this time and perhaps the most lengthy was that followed by Birkenhead Corporation buses working route 12 between Seacombe and Charing Cross. There were bomb craters in Dock Road, Gorsedale Road and Poulton Road so buses ran via St Paul's Road, Wheatland Lane, Mainwaring Road, Liscard Road, Parkside, Hampstead Road, Poulton Road, Gorsey Lane, rejoining the normal route at Duke Street Bridge though there were further diversions in Birkenhead. Routes 4 and 17 also used part of this diversion. As a bomb had fallen in Brighton Street, near Leopold Street, buses ran in and out via Demesne Street while the bombing of Earlston Road near the library caused route 5 to divert via Zigzag Road, Rake Lane, Edinburgh Road, Seaview Road, Earlston Road to Kirkway. Many normally unserved thoroughfares found they had bus services for a time, including Hawarden Avenue, Rappart Road, Falkland Road, Gloucester Road, Vernon Avenue and Lucerne Road, to mention but a few. Between 21 December and 11 January 1941 extra mileage caused by diversions totalled 1,844 miles.

Censorship of the press ensured that none of this was published, and what information has been recorded is based on personal observations at the time. However, the *Wallasey News* of 12 October 1940 carried an official notice to the effect that, in the event of Seacombe ferry being temporarily closed, routes 4 and 17 would divert on the inward journey at St Luke's Church to Birkenhead North station and a shuttle service would be run between Seacombe and St. Luke's Church. Extra buses would run on routes 11 and 12 to Birkenhead Park Station and these would be augmented at peak hours by special buses from Hose Side Road and Broadway Avenue to Park Station. Other services would run to and from Seacombe as normal. The ferry service had been suspended on 13 September when buses had run to Park Station between 5.30am and 12.30pm; ten buses were run during the peak and three from 10.00am, incurring 334 miles. On 2 November 1940 the advertised scheme was amended for buses to run to Rendel Street tunnel entrance via Park Station; agreement had been reached for buses to run through the tunnel to Liverpool but this would have been impossible from Rendel Street as the branch tunnel was too low for double-decker buses.

Whether any of this was subsequently put into operation is unknown as, so far as is known, it was 13 March 1941 before Seacombe ferry was again put out of action, not because of damage to the infrastructure but because of the presence of mines in the river. It is believed that in the morning peak buses ran to Hamilton Square station as Park station had been destroyed and North station damaged during the night; in the afternoon it is certain that they did, as all the buses normally running from Seacombe were seen reversed into the kerb in the lower section of Hamilton Street, beside the Mersey Railway power station. Unfortunately, the Four Bridges route was also closed as there was a mine in Wallasey Dock and each convoy had to run via Cleveland Street,

Livingstone Street, Corporation Road and Duke Street bridge, resuming their normal routes as best they could. During the day, a shuttle bus service labelled 'Woodside' ran across the Four Bridges between Seacombe ferry and Hamilton Square station. There was also a shuttle service at certain times through the main tunnel which, as now, could accommodate double-decker buses in the outside lanes. This was run on behalf of the Mersey Tunnel Joint Committee at a flat fare of 5d and ran only between the main tunnel entrances; it is not known whether Wallasey buses took part but it seems likely that they did as there is a record of a meeting on the subject on 12 August 1941 and subsequent correspondence with the general manager of Liverpool Corporation Passenger Transport in November.

A further hazard was the erection of concrete road blocks obstructing over half the road at various places. Between July and September 1940 three buses were damaged by colliding with these obstructions during the blackout in Earlston Road, St George's Road and Seabank Road. Birkenhead Corporation's Laird Street bus depot received a direct hit in the December 1940 and March 1941 air raids and several buses were destroyed or very seriously damaged. On 13 March there was a direct hit on the Water Department premises adjoining the Seaview Road depot resulting in extensive damage to the former tram depot and several buses, many of which had to go into service in a damaged state. As recorded in Chapter 6, ten buses were sent to body-builders for repairs. The depot received much damage, particularly to the glass roofs of both garages. The lighting plant was also put out of action in the March 1941 attacks.

An eight-night 'blitz' from 1 to 8 May mainly affected the Liverpool side of the river and aerial activity thereafter continued sporadically until 10 January 1942, after which the enemy concentrated its efforts elsewhere.

The air raids caused a migration from the borough and fewer passengers were travelling. From 22 May 1941, the principal services to and from Seacombe were run every 15 instead of every 10 minutes throughout the day, resulting in a saving of four buses. There was now a considerable surplus of buses in the fleet. When an offer came from Kingston-upon-Hull Corporation Transport to purchase six Leyland TD2s at £300 each and three Daimlers at £350, the general manager contacted the Regional Transport Commissioner who initially opposed the sale of the buses outside the North West Region. He suggested three operators who might be willing to hire surplus buses, Liverpool and Birkenhead Corporations and Crosville Motor Services Ltd. Birkenhead was not interested but Liverpool hired four buses with drivers to operate an emergency service between Pier Head and Dingle for the damaged Liverpool Overhead Railway between 6.30am and 8.30pm which ran until 31 October 1941.

Negotiations with Crosville resulted in thirty buses being hired to them, at first to help on their Liverpool area services and then mainly at Wrexham (though three were at Crewe) where they remained for some years, not only on the ROF services for which they were intended but also on such long routes as Chester-Wrexham-Llangollen which had hitherto been single-decker routes but now needed double-deckers. The hire charge was £1 per bus per day with Crosville covering all expenses including road tax and insurance. Seven returned after a few months and then another two, but twenty-one remained until 1945-46.

All eight Daimlers (including Nos. 81-85 which had not been replaced) were sold to Kingston-upon-Hull Corporation to replace similar vehicles lost in air raids there. The remaining Daimler spares were sold to Hull, Coventry, Luton and Stockton-on-Tees Corporations and back to Daimler.

To avoid a catastrophe in the event of a direct hit on the depot, it was decided, in June 1941, that thirty-one buses should be dispersed overnight at the following sites:

Rake Lane recreation ground	6
Warren Park	5
High School Playing field, Mount Pleasant Road	6
Belvidere Road playing fields	5
Rugby ground, Reeds Lane	14
TOTAL	31

This created all sorts of problems, not the least of which was ensuring that every bus was cleaned and fuelled. Buses at Reeds Lane were vandalised and fire extinguishers stolen, and it was decided to use night cleaners as firewatchers and watchmen, engaging temporary women cleaners to replace them. It is interesting to note that within 24 hours of the vandalism being reported to the police, the youths responsible were found, being subsequently taken to court and fined.

Further Fuel Economy

The restricted services led to many complaints of inadequacy, sometimes related to buses on unspecified contract services running empty past waiting queues; these buses often had no conductors so could not be used on service, though the clamour became so loud that eventually conductors were sent to meet them so that they could work their way home on route 10. Other complaints arose from the constantly shifting demand with people migrating in and out of the borough as air raids intensified or subsided, and changes in work patterns of which the Motor Bus Department was frequently not notified.

There were also labour shortages which, because of the depletion of the fleet during the war, were less serious than in many other undertakings. From 22 April 1941, a 2d minimum fare was authorised on through buses leaving Seacombe on route 4 in the evening peak hours and in December 1941 this was extended to route 17, a single-decker bus being put on between Seacombe and St Luke's Church in addition to the regular duplicates to Marlowe Road (Wallasey Road) during the evening peak. There was a proposal to curtail the latter at the Mill Lane end of Marlowe Road so that they could then return to Seacombe via Woodstock Road and Oxton Road, thus achieving a quicker turnround and eliminating the need for a dangerous reversing manoeuvre in the blackout. However, traffic requirements were such that this was impracticable.

The department managed to increase services slightly during the summer in 1941 and 1942 and, although there is no conclusive evidence, it seems likely that, during the winter, fuel was conserved by reducing mileage beyond that required by rationing. The tyre shortage was very serious and a new scheme in 1942 outlawed discounts and imposed regulations whereby new tyres and tubes were supplied only on the surrender of old casings and tubes. In October 1942 the Regional Transport Commissioner called a meeting of all general managers in the region, requesting a further 10% reduction in view of the shortage of both fuel and rubber. At the time the average weekly mileage was 33,725, which was reduced by 2,025 miles on 5 November and a further 1,334 miles on 4 February 1943. This was achieved mainly by altering Saturday evening services from 15- to 30-minute frequencies, running last buses at 9.30pm and reducing all Sunday services to half-hourly. The Commissioner wanted even earlier last buses, at 9.15pm on weekdays and 9.0pm on Sundays. A priority system for war workers with permits was introduced. At Easter 1943 the Commissioner directed that no additional services were to be run and fuel saved by suspension of works services over the holiday was not to be used for augmentation purposes.

The issue of transfer tickets from route 17 to route 16 was discontinued on Sundays to deter travel because no guarantee of accommodation on the No. 16 bus at Grove Road (Warren Drive) could be given. A suggestion for minimum fares on the last buses from both ends on route 10 was not supported by Birkenhead Corporation. The abolition of ½d children's fares from 4 July 1943 to persuade them to walk short distances brought forth loud complaints from parents whose children used the buses for school trips.

Other measures included the elimination of many request stops which saved wear on tyres and brake linings, the rule being a minimum 440 yards between stops. Many stops had been inherited from the trams and were very close together; they were never reinstated after the war. In May, the Regional Transport Commissioner, in support of the government's 'Holidays at Home' scheme, proposed to allocate fuel for an additional 4,000 miles spread over three months. This was considered hopelessly inadequate but there was no more available and eventually it was agreed, in conjunction with Birkenhead, to use it to run a 10-minute Sunday service on route 10 in July and August as the occasion demanded.

Late workers complained about the lack of facilities to get home and, from 11 September 1944, a special bus showing route No. 3 left Seacombe ferry at 11.00pm on weekdays, travelling via Wheatland Lane, Poulton Road, Oxton Road, Torrington Road, Belvidere Road, Grove Road, Mount Pleasant Road, Rake Lane and Liscard Village to the depot. This continued until normal services were restored after the war. With an improvement in the fortunes of war, additional late departures and augmented Saturday and Sunday services were permitted from 20 November 1944.

Special Wartime Services

In addition to the emergency services mentioned earlier, Wallasey buses were used on many special duties during the war. From 27 September to 22 November 1940, six buses were provided for the morning and afternoon peak to augment Birkenhead Corporation vehicles, providing a service for the Mersey Railway to bridge the gap between Birkenhead Park and Hamilton Square stations. This was remunerative to the Corporation, 222,994 passengers being carried over 14,058 miles for £1,214. The basis of charging was a 5s.0d call-out fee, 1s.6d per mile, and 7s.6d per hour waiting time, the 'withdrawn' TD2s 69-77 being used. From November, three buses (old 69-70 and 80) went on hire to Liverpool Corporation who manned and serviced them, old Nos. 71, 75 and 76 following in December and 72, 73 and 74 (Daimlers) and 77 in January 1941. These were mainly, if not entirely, used to run between Kirkdale or Bankhall stations and Liverpool (Exchange) following the bombing of the electric railway lines. The charge for the hire was £1 per day. Eight buses were returned on 23 February 1941 and the other two soon after.

Between 20 and 22 December 1940, two buses were engaged on conveying homeless people whose houses had been bombed to various Rest Centres. From 26 December to 1 January two further buses were employed, morning and evening, to convey military working parties from Liverpool to assist Air Raid Precautions people to clear up after the air raids. Wallasey buses provided several special workers' and contract services to war factories which were kept secret, and details of some of them have only recently come to light. It is suspected that there were others about which nothing is yet known. The first, which commenced on 18 April 1940, were run in connection with the building of an RAF Camp in West Kirby Road, beyond Saughall Massie. Two morning trips were run on route 4 from Seacombe and two on route 8 from Liscard, extending beyond Bermuda Road via Hoylake Road, Saughall Road and West Kirby Road to convey building workers and there were similar return services in the afternoon. The terminus was near the present-day

Oldfield Lane. The extra distance was 1.61 miles and the through fare from Seacombe was fixed at 7d, 2d more than to Bermuda Road. The buses were well patronised, the results for the initial period between 18 April and 7 May being as follows:

	Total	No. of Journeys	Average Passengers Per journey	Average receipts per journey
From				
Seacombe	1,377	2	41	19s 6d
Liscard	1,813	2	53	19s 0d
To				
Seacombe	1,162	2	46	4s 10d
Liscard	1,835	2	57	3s 6d

The revenue per bus mile was 18.03d (Seacombe) and 20.75d (Liscard); this compared with 16.74d for all services during the same period. The camp lay in the territory of Crosville Motor Services but they had never run on the roads concerned. Crosville told Wallasey that, whilst they had no objection to these services running during the construction period, they would expect to operate any recreational services when the camp was occupied. The general manager passed this letter to the Regional Traffic Commissioner, whose comment was that any application would be treated on its merits. Crosville objected unsuccessfully to the Liscard service being extended to and from New Brighton late in June 1940, and some time late in the year both services were suspended for a time, resuming on 11 January 1941. It was curtailed at the corner of Saughall Road and Hoylake Road from 30 January because of the poor state of the road beyond; presumably the workers were conveyed by lorries. The service was restored after road repairs had been made and the date of its final withdrawal has not been discovered. When the camp was fully occupied by service personnel, facilities were provided by Crosville, to and from West Kirby or Meols station.

There were many special journeys including an arrangement for taking Local Defence Volunteers to and from their posts; volunteer drivers were used for this and by mid-1940 the supply was drying up and there was dissatisfaction as the LDV (by this time renamed Home Guard), were not adhering to the agreed routes, incurring additional mileage for which there was no fuel. This facility was withdrawn on 14 July but there were still random calls for buses. One was called for on Saturday 7 September 1940, leaving the depot at 11.50pm, and did not return until 3.55pm on Sunday having run 19 miles and conveyed only 13 passengers. The wage cost alone was £1.6s.8d. One single-decker bus was used to take civil servants to their billets on 28 June and 1 July 1940 and in September it was decided to license one of the Cubs for use on Home Guard work. There seems to have been a certain amount of local initiative exercised in these matters and in mid-1941 the military and the Regional Transport Commissioner collaborated to prevent abuses and waste of fuel. From July five single-decker buses were to be earmarked for Home Guard use in case of an emergency, two at Barnston, one at Little Sutton and two at Bebington. This superseded the arrangement for keeping one bus on call.

Lion No. 7 was converted back from an ambulance to a bus in June 1941 and was used for a time on a contract between Wallasey and Morgan Crucibles at Neston. Another job, worked by a double-decker bus, was to the Inland Sorting Depot at Simonswood, near Kirkby. Bus No. 17 hit a bridge at Kirkby on one occasion whilst working this. There was another contract to Martin Hearn's factory at Hooton Park Aerodrome at least part of which involved the use of a single-decker bus, the driver of which was stopped for speeding on New Chester Road on one occasion. Following the May 1941 air raids which did considerable damage to the Liverpool docks it was necessary to divert dock labour to berths which were available and from 8 May to 3 June 1941 buses were in use carrying Liverpool dockers to Birkenhead. No fewer than 6,391 passengers were carried over 3,623 miles for £312.8s.0d, charges being raised on the same basis as for the earlier Mersey Railway hire. From 15 July from two to six buses daily were carrying dock labour, mainly to Garston Dock and Bromborough Port. This work continued until after the war.

Two Daimlers were hired to Lancaster Corporation for a short time in July or August 1941. From October 1941 special buses were run daily between the main Tunnel Entrance, Birkenhead and Gladstone Dock, Bootle on behalf of Cammell Lairds whose workers were engaged on ship repair work. This was still running in 1943. The position in January 1942 was that the morning run-out required 41 buses for normal services and 16 for special operations.

The Staff in Wartime

The war had a profound effect on the staff of the undertaking. As already mentioned, the strain of driving in blackout conditions took its toll on the health of the road staff and sickness rates and requests for transfer to light duties increased markedly. Nine men who were on the reserve were called up before war broke out and by the end of September 38 had gone. This had increased to 51 by November and there were complaints that several men had not handed in their uniforms and some conductors had not returned the 3s.6d. lent to them for change. These early staff losses presented no great difficulty as reduced services required fewer men. Before long, inflation caused by wartime conditions resulted in war bonuses being granted by the various conciliation bodies which governed pay to various grades. As in the 1914-18 war these were intended to be temporary increases as it was expected that costs would fall again after the cessation of hostilities. Scale wages and salaries did not increase, pay being expressed as 'plus war bonus'. The initial award for unskilled workers (which included drivers and conductors) in 1940 was 4s.0d per week.

Numerous employees resigned to take advantage of new employment opportunities in the armaments industry and staff shortages loomed. In Wallasey the road staff comprised drivers, conductor/drivers and conductors, the latter being divided into 48-hour men and 32-hour men. Conductor/drivers were graded as conductors but employed on driving duties, at driver rates, as required. The grade had been devised to meet the increased driver requirement for summer services, temporary conductors being engaged to replace them. Turnover was so low before 1939 that men could serve as temporary conductors for five years or more before there was a permanent vacancy.

By spring 1940 so many conductor/drivers were working as drivers that there was a conductor shortage and it was decided to recruit women. The first conductress started work on 5 July 1940 and 11 more followed more or less immediately, the total eventually employed being 35. They received 90% of the men's rate but worked a 40-hour week compared with the normal 48 hours. Later three women, trained to drive double-decker buses, were the first to be licensed in the North West Traffic Area. It is not known to what extent they were used as it was announced in June 1944 that they would be used only when men were not available. Women were also recruited for cleaning and clerical duties. The Essential Works Order theoretically prevented staff in reserved occupations from resigning, nevertheless there was a constant trickle of labour out of the department and very few replacements. Bus driving was a reserved occupation which meant that drivers could not resign. Many drivers sought a way to do this as there was more amenable and better paid work available but this was always resisted. In March 1941 there were 32 spare drivers on the payroll, ie drivers not allocated to rostered duties. Of these seven were required to cover for sickness, 15 for holidays and 10 for special services. Soon after, it was noted that four drivers had left despite their resignations not being accepted and they were reported to the Regional Transport Commissioner and the Ministry of Labour.

In June 1941 the Ministry of Labour placed the undertaking on the Register of Protected Establishments, the effect of which was to apply reserved occupation status to registered individuals at a lower age than usual and the management immediately registered fourteen drivers, two fitters and two clerical staff. There were several cases of drivers refusing to work one-man buses or conductor/drivers refusing to drive; the emergency legislation provided for such men to be suspended without pay for three days and this was rigorously enforced by the department, who usually refused applications by men who wanted to leave the job.

These conditions created an atmosphere of resentment, one manifestation of which was lack of co-operation in difficult conditions such as fog. On 30 December 1941 at 6.30am, a driver who had recently been appointed as chairman of the local T&GWU branch refused to take his bus out in fog and was followed by several other drivers, though many went out normally. 395 miles were lost and another 300 later in the day. On 7 January 1942 three drivers on Cammell Laird specials and one on service stopped their buses in Gorsey Lane near the gas works and refused to go further. During the time they were there, thirty-four Wallasey buses and several Birkenhead buses passed them. All received disciplinary action.

Several of the older drivers, after medical examination, were declared unfit for driving duties and most were found some sort of less demanding work in the depot, irrespective of the existence of a vacancy on the establishment. This was at a time when long and loyal service was appreciated by the councillors and management and there was no question of casting these men aside. Those who became unfit for any kind of work were permitted to retire on pension prematurely.

Wartime conditions demanded some changes to working practices. Because of interruptions during air raids, scheduled work was not being completed by the night shift and six night cleaners were transferred to day work in October 1940. This resulted in a reduction in pay as day cleaners were paid £3.4s.4d for a 47-hour week while night men received £3.8s.6d for 48 hours. As reduced services did not require the services of a full-time timekeeper at New Brighton, the office was closed and the inspectors concerned redeployed on ticket checking duties. A time recording clock was moved from the depot to the corner of Victoria Road and Rowson Street.

By 1942, the mechanical condition of some of the buses was serious and a number of Leyland and AEC engines were sent to the Burtonwood Motor Engineering Co. for reconditioning. Torque converters, of which Wallasey had a very large number, were sent to Leyland Motors for repair and reconditioning. The Ministry of War Transport had some Vehicle Repair Advisers who held public meetings at which advice was given to operators about making the best of the very limited resources available in wartime. There was cross-fertilisation of ideas and experiences between operators, and the Rolling Stock Superintendent went to Bolton to observe some make-and-mend remedy they had devised to deal with oil seals on torque converters.

It was Birkenhead Corporation's practice to allocate separate route numbers to regular part-way workings and, during the war, they used No. 9 for short journeys on the joint route 10, usually between Liscard and Central station. Wallasey would have nothing to do with part-way numbers but Birkenhead continued the practice until 1949 when Wallasey used the number for a completely different route.

A New Manager

In November 1942, Mr W.R. Goodier, from H.V. Burlingham Ltd, body-builders of Blackpool, was appointed deputy general manager and on 30 September 1943 Mr H.H. Lincoln, who had been general manager since 1923, retired. Mr Goodier was appointed Acting General Manager and was retrospectively confirmed in the position from 1 April 1944. A fresh mind brought a number of service alterations from 1 April 1944. Route 5 was, at long last, extended the short distance from the Hotel Victoria to New Brighton station, route 8 was increased to every 40-minutes and rerouted along Seaview Road and Mount Pleasant Road instead of Liscard Village and Rake Lane (which was already served by routes 10 and 14), while route 17 was taken off Broadway, St George's Road and the lower part of Sandy Lane and diverted along Claremount Road, the upper part of Sandy Lane and the northern part of St. George's Road. The last diversion was not entirely popular as buses no longer passed the top of Harrison Drive or Wallasey station and, from 1 January 1946, the buses came off St George's Road and reverted to using the lower part of Sandy Lane and Wallasey Village. As mentioned in Chapter 2, Virginia Road was adopted as the permanent New Brighton terminus from 27 May 1943 and the following year the Committee agreed in principle to the provision of a new inspectors' office to replace that at the foot of Victoria Road.

The war was now drawing to a close; as a morale booster the chimes and strike of Seacombe ferry clock had been restored between 7.00am and 11.00pm in June 1943. Extra evening running time on route 4 during the winter months, agreed in October 1943, was short-lived as the blackout was partially lifted by the introduction of 'starlight' on the principal thoroughfares. A 'dim-out', allowing peace-time curtains, came into force in September 1944 and restrictions on vehicle lighting were partially lifted in January 1945 thus alleviating the lot of bus drivers. Thoughts turned towards a return to peacetime operations but few realised to what extent the conditions of 1939 had gone, never to return.

Financial Effect of the War

Although costs rose steeply during the war, the reduction in mileage and the elimination of loss-making services resulted in a much higher utilisation of the available accommo-dation and no increase in fares could be justified. The average number of passengers per mile run increased from 8.55 in 1938-39 to 12.67 in 1944-45. Fewer passengers during the air raid period resulted in a loss of £2,003 being incurred in 1940-41 and an application was made to increase workmen's fares, Birkenhead and Crosville having agreed to fall into line over common sections of route. However, the Regional Transport Commissioner, in accordance with general wartime policy, refused to grant the application, a justifiable decision as, the following year, the undertaking broke even with

One of six Leyland Cubs operated by the undertaking, No.2 was from a quartet of 1939 KP4 diesel models with Burlingham 25-seat bodies, only able to serve one season on their intended duties due to the outbreak of WW2. (Omnibus Society / Norris collection)

a surplus of just £122. In the year 1942-43, operations benefited from the government's Holidays at Home campaign, producing a surplus of £7,049, almost equal to that of 1938-39. However, passenger journeys decreased sharply, reflecting the depopulation of the town, whereas in Birkenhead, whose buses served more of the Wirral hinterland, there was a 12% increase over the war period. Despite some depopulation, Birkenhead benefited from an increase in employment with a consequent rise in short work trips. The average fare paid in Birkenhead was slightly lower than that in Wallasey even though some of the routes were longer.

Roe bodied a Leyland TD3c for Wallasey in 1934, as well as the AECs. Appearance had matured to standards common for the next 24 years and more (apart from the centre-entrance). This bus alone had torque-convertor transmission. More TD3s came from Roe with rear platforms that year (© Omnibus Society / R. Marshall collection)

Dual-sourcing brought the final AEC chassis into the fleet in 1939, six arriving with the characteristic Metro-Cammell 54-seat bodies. All remained in service until 1952. Note the unusual refinement of a windscreen wiper on the nearside bulkhead window of No.66 ! (© Omnibus Society / R. Marshall collection)

The poor quality of this illustration is excused by its rarity in showing one of the centre-entrance Roe-bodied AECs of 1934 sold to Salford Corporation during their fleet crisis of 1946-7. It is accompanied by one of Salford's own late-1930s Leylands with almost identical bodies to Wallasey's 'standards' from the same builder. (© Edward Gray)

Not recorded in the text was the hiring of several 1946 Wallasey Leyland Titan PD1s by Bolton Corporation in 1956, accompanied by other Titans from Warrington, Wigan, and Rawtenstall. This is No.83, which went back to its home town for a few more years of service. (© Ted Jones)

CHAPTER 4
THE POST-WAR YEARS 1945-53

The change back to peacetime conditions was slow as many wartime measures remained in force. Fuel was not immediately freed from rationing and there were many shortages of materials and labour. Many men had had their personal horizons widened during the war and, on demobilisation from the forces, declined to return to their former employment. There was a new militancy in the ranks of labour, perhaps a reaction to strict discipline in the forces and also a consequence of the election of a Labour government in July 1945.

From 6 August 1945, route 6 was diverted to the Promenade via Sandcliffe Road at weekends for a few weeks, turning at the end of Sandcliffe Road. This had been agreed by the Committee in September 1944, replacing a plan to use Sea Road which the low railway bridge made impossible. Late buses up to about 10.30pm were restored from 19 November 1945 though some routes such as 5 and 6 ceased at 7.0pm on Mondays to Fridays and 8.0pm on Saturdays, and route 8 was improved only to the extent of a 40-minute frequency, ceasing at 8.20pm instead of the wartime hourly service. The busy joint No. 10 service fared best with a 10-minute service in the early morning and from about 1.00pm to 7.00pm. There were more improvements from 3 June 1946. The trunk routes, 1, 2, 4/4B, 11, 14, 16 and 17, ran until about 11.15pm, 10 until 11.36pm, and 5, 6, 8 and 12 until about 10.20pm. The special journey numbered 3 between Seacombe ferry and the depot at 11.15pm was withdrawn. The very late pre-war departures from Seacombe ferry up to 11.57pm were never restored.

Seaside Services

From Easter Monday, 1 April 1946, route 6 was further extended on Saturday and Sunday afternoons as required to New Brighton Bathing Pool via Sandcliffe Road and the Promenade. However, this was not a success as people expected to find their buses in Virginia Road and, for the 1947-49 seasons, it ran through to that point via Waterloo Road, returning via the Promenade. From 1946, route 4A to Moreton Shore was run in accordance with traffic requirements. Some journeys on route 2 were extended to the Promenade at the bottom of Harrison Drive and other trips on routes 1 and 2 were linked as a Circular along the Promenade between New Brighton and Harrison Drive. A special circular fare of 8d was charged for a round trip but there was no fixed timetable and uncertainty as to whether the service was running or not did nothing to aid its success. It was not repeated in 1947.

There was a tremendous demand for holiday travel facilities, which was difficult to meet with the limited resources available. Another permanent war casualty was the 10-minute off-peak ferry service from Seacombe and the steamers and connecting buses continued to run every 15 minutes, augmented to 10 minutes only at the rush hours. The delivery of new buses and the removal of fuel restrictions enabled summer services to be considerably augmented for the 1947 season when the weather was exceptionally fine.

Several minor changes were implemented during this period. The diversion of route 17 along the northern part of St George's Road, thus missing out the important Harrison Drive stop, was ended from 1st January 1946 when buses travelled along the full length of Sandy Lane to Wallasey Village. In June 1946, route 8 was rerouted along Seabank Road and Magazine Lane instead of Rowson Street, Upper Brighton, taking the buses close to the Seabank Road shops and nearer to Vale Park. In response to a request for early workmen's facilities to the east end of the dock estate, some of the early Wheatland Lane journeys on route 16 were diverted via Kelvin Road and Birkenhead Road instead of St Paul's Road from 2nd December 1946. However, patronage was so poor that after two months' trial, all but the 5.15am trip from Grasmere Drive followed the normal route.

There was some criticism of the need to change buses at the top of Harrison Drive in order to reach the Embankment and Derby Bathing Pool. This added to the length and cost of the journey. The problem was the severe camber of the road at the Derby Bathing Pool terminus and this was extensively rebuilt during the winter of 1949-50, enabling double-decker buses to be used for the first time. For the 1950-51 seasons, the summer weekend extension of route 6 was to Derby Bathing Pool via Grove Road and Harrison Drive (not Sandcliffe Road) and at busy times, extra buses on route 2, also ran through. The shuttle was also run with double-deckers at times, a conductor's nightmare if the bus was full as there was so little time to get the fares in. Route 6 also experienced a permanent rerouting in the town centre from 20 December 1947 when it was diverted via Grosvenor Street and Westminster Road in lieu of Liscard Road. This was done to eliminate the sharp right-angle turn from Liscard Road into Mill Lane.

Another unsuccessful summer Sunday experiment was the introduction, following public pressure, of a summer service on route 5 between Seacombe and New Brighton station, a service which had always been 'weekdays only'. It started only on 3 August 1947 and, on reintroduction on 16 May 1948, it ran through to Virginia Road via Atherton Street and Wellington Road on a hard-to-remember 45-minute frequency but the results were so poor that it was permanently withdrawn on Sundays from 3 October that year.

Moreton Services

Much of Wallasey's post-war housing drive was concentrated on Moreton as there was little land available in the older part of the town and building efforts were mainly directed to replacement of properties destroyed in the air raids. The long-suffering residents of

Saughall Massie, still without facilities after being part of Wallasey for 12 years, were demanding some attention. During the war they had no buses at all as the infrequent Crosville West Kirby-Park station service, which ran along Garden Hey Road, had been cut back to Overchurch Road. Housing developments in Moreton were initially on the north side in the area which was to grow into the Town Meadow Lane estate so, from 19 November 1945, route 4 was extended in two directions. Route 4 buses ran via Acton Lane and Saughall Road to Saughall Massie Hotel while a new 4B revived the pre-war extension down Bermuda Road to Hardie Avenue but attached to a Seacombe rather than a New Brighton route. Each ran half-hourly (20-minutes in the peak).

From 19 July 1947, Saughall Massie gained a new facility in the form of route 8A from New Brighton which ran on summer Saturdays and Sundays only. From reinstatement on 15 May 1948, it ran on Saturdays throughout the year and on Sundays during the summer. From 20 June 1948, routes 4 and 4B were rerouted via Brougham Road and Demesne Street (inward), Church Road, Brighton Street (outward), echoing the short-lived diversion of route 6 in 1933-34. The police did not like buses on narrow Borough Road, though the purpose of the diversion was said to be the provision of better facilities between Moreton, Leasowe and the Town Hall. All the peak hour part-way buses and the Moreton Shore buses continued to use Borough Road, though on the outward journey they left Seacombe via Church Road instead of the lower part of Borough Road, in order to observe the stopping place in Church Road used by the Brougham Road buses.

In 1947, expansion of the Moreton services was again under consideration and Wallasey wanted to include a route along Pasture Road so that there would be a regular all-day service to Moreton Shore, not only from Wallasey proper but also from Saughall Massie and points west of Moreton Cross. Pasture Road, which of course had been entirely within the County Borough of Wallasey since 1928, had been served by Birkenhead's buses since 1927 and Birkenhead's view was that a service of Wallasey buses along Pasture Road was unnecessary. In a letter to Goodier on 5 December 1947, George Cherry, the Birkenhead manager, said that Birkenhead ran up to 40 buses an hour to Moreton Shore at busy times though this argument was rather weak as, if such heavy duplication was necessary, it implied that there would be no room for local passengers in any case. Discussions dragged on and, in October 1948, Birkenhead suggested a restriction on the Wallasey buses, no passenger to be both picked up and set down between Moreton Schools and Leasowe Children's Hospital. A conference between representatives of the two councils followed in which Wallasey agreed not to carry local passengers between Moreton Cross and the Shore and also allowed Birkenhead access to the housing estates at Danger Lane and Town Meadow Lane for workmen's traffic. This was a rare, probably unique, example of one municipal operator giving protection within its own boundary to another municipal operator. In the meantime, in 1948 the peak hour frequencies to and from Seacombe had been stepped up to 10 minutes, the half-hourly Saughall Massie and Hardie Avenue buses by a half-hourly service to Bermuda Road (Hoylake Road). This applied also on Saturdays from 2.00pm and Sundays from 11.00am.

From 30 May 1949, the Moreton services were completely recast and increased. Three half-hourly services were run from Seacombe, giving a 10-minute combined service which did not give direct connections with the boats at off-peak times. These were as follows:

4   Seacombe-Moreton (Borrowdale Road) via Castleway North & Birket Avenue.
4A   Seacombe-Saughall Massie Hotel via Pasture Road
4B   Seacombe-Moreton (Hardie Avenue) via Leasowe Castle & Reeds Lane (unchanged)

The new 4 gave some cover to the new Leasowe Estate, which was gradually being extended. The special unscheduled summer weekend service to Moreton Shore was given the strange number 4S and a new queue barrier was erected in Birkenhead Road near the Marine Hotel on the corner of Church Road. Three bays at the main terminus at Seacombe were now allocated to the 4 group.

The 8A New Brighton-Saughall Massie weekend buses were also diverted via Pasture Road and a new hourly weekend service 9 was introduced, running from New Brighton along the Promenade, Harrison Drive, Bayswater Road, Leasowe Road, Castleway North and Birket Avenue to Moreton Cross. This was licensed to run on Saturdays throughout the year and on Sundays in summer but it was a failure, being withdrawn permanently on 24 September 1949. The following year a new weekend 9 appeared, running from New Brighton by the 14 route to Liscard, the 2 route to Harrison Drive, then via Harrison Drive, Bayswater Road, Leasowe Road and Reeds Lane to Birket Avenue. This was even less successful than its predecessor; it did not even see the season out, being withdrawn on 27 August 1950.

Following improvement of the road, routes 4A and 8A were diverted via Hoylake Road and Saughall Road instead of Acton Lane from 1 August 1949. The completion of adequate roads enabled the Town Meadow estate to be served from 16 October 1950 when route 4B was extended from Hardie Avenue over a loop via Town Meadow Lane, Maryland Lane and Pasture Road back to Moreton Cross, then by the normal route to Seacombe. The loop was served in the opposite direction by route 4 which was taken off Borrowdale Road without replacement. At weekends route 8A also served the loop clockwise; it was taken away from Saughall Massie (again, without replacement) and rerouted via Reeds Lane instead of Pasture Road. This arrangement did not last long as, from 10 February 1951, it was renumbered 7, diverted via Danger Lane and Pasture

Avenue, and followed the Town Meadow Lane loop anti-clockwise. The staking of a claim on Pasture Avenue seems to have been triggered by Birkenhead's application for a road service licence for a peak hour service (21B) between Market Place South and Bermuda Road (Town Meadow Lane) via Danger Lane, Pasture Avenue and Town Meadow Lane as the *quid pro quo* for Wallasey's Pasture Road facility. It was granted in June 1951 but, although it was listed in the timetable, as far as can be ascertained it was never run. Birkenhead added 'via Pasture Ave.' to post-war bottom and side route blinds but the display was never used.

From 1 April 1951, routes 4, 4A and 4B were renumbered 3, 4 and 5 respectively. It does not seem to have occurred to anyone that 4 could have been left unaltered and just the other two changed! Route 5 between Seacombe and New Brighton station became route 15.

Threat of Nationalisation

Among the many provisions of the Transport Act 1947 was the setting up of Area Schemes which would absorb all local bus services into state-controlled Boards. Somewhat to the surprise of the government, this socialist boon was not welcomed by bus-owning local authorities, even those controlled by Labour councils, as they were reluctant to part with undertakings which, in many cases, made a useful contribution to the rate fund. The Wallasey councils of those days were far from being Labour controlled and they objected very strongly to being deprived of what was still a very profitable municipal enterprise. During the immediate pre-war years, the rates had benefited by £5,000 per annum, increased to £8,500 in 1940-41. These contributions resumed at £5,000 per annum in 1944-45.

Sections 63-64 of the Transport Act forbade undertakings to spend or make contracts for more than one year with a view to preventing operators milking funds if they were to be acquired. However, section 177 of the Wallasey Corporation Act 1927 provided that all money received by the Corporation in any year ending 31 March, on account of the tramways undertaking (which included the motor bus undertaking), should be carried and form part of the revenue for that year of the General Rate Fund and all payments and expenses made and incurred in respect of the undertaking should be paid out of that fund. In the year ending 31 March 1948, £40,000 was transferred to the Rate Fund followed by £15,000 in each of the next two years. The resistance of local authorities and private companies resulted in the first Area Scheme, proposed for the North East in 1949, being abandoned and, with a change of government in 1951, the threat disappeared. The problem of the transfer of reserves was solved by the increase in costs and fall in traffic which prevented the accumulation of funds and no more payments were made to the Rate Fund during the life of the undertaking.

Cross Docks Services

New Brighton was a popular venue for Birkenhead people and heavy duplication was required on the sole direct service, No. 10 from New Ferry via Old Chester Road, Chester Street, Bridge Street and Cleveland Street. The arrangement with Birkenhead Corporation was that Birkenhead would provide the duplication required for traffic to New Brighton and Wallasey would take the people home. In practice, there was usually a mix of the two Corporations' buses, extra trips running to and from St. Paul's Road, Rock Ferry and Central station. In 1946, there were talks with Birkenhead about extending the scope of the cross-docks services to give direct facilities to and from New Brighton from a wider area of Birkenhead and Bebington. Wallasey wanted facilities to get its people into the Wirral countryside and a strategy was sought whereby both objectives could be achieved economically.

From 1 June 1947 two new services commenced daily operations for a three-month trial period. The first was an extension of the existing Charing Cross-Liscard joint service (11) at both ends to run between Higher Tranmere (The Wiend, Thornton Road) via Woodchurch Lane, Half Way House, Woodchurch Road, Oxton Road then over the existing route to Liscard. The extension to New Brighton followed a different route from the No. 10 service, running via Seaview Road, Earlston Road, Kirkway, Mount Pleasant Road, Magazine Lane and Seabank Road. This service ran every 20 minutes and was augmented at busy times by an intermediate service between Charing Cross and Liscard. This new venture was an immediate success, providing not only for New Brighton traffic but giving new internal facilities within each town. Before the three-month experimental period was up, it was decided to run it until the end of October, a decision which was soon changed to daily operation to the same timetable throughout the year.

The second new service (No. 18) ran between New Brighton and Arrowe Park, following the Promenade, Sandcliffe Road, Belvidere Road, Poulton Bridge, St James' Church, Tollemache Road, Ford Hill and Upton to Arrowe Park. The 40-minute frequency, requiring one bus of each Corporation, gave a direct service between Birkenhead's North End housing estates and New Brighton, and enabled Wallasey people to reach the Wirral countryside without a change of bus. A 20-minute service was authorised on Saturdays and Sundays but this was never advertised. This too was a great success, and it was decided to continue it until 31 October and then on Saturdays and Sundays throughout the winter. This was the first regular service to use Poulton Bridge and it is of interest to note that Birkenhead declined to use the number 13, which was the obvious choice, being a vacant number in both operators' series and the number proposed for the abortive Central station-Harrison Drive service planned in 1937. Several Birkenhead buses still had 'via Poulton Bridge 13' on their side destination blinds but Wallasey was put to the trouble of renumbering its existing Derby Bathing Pool route from 18 to 20 in order to appease Birkenhead's superstitions.

The extension of route 11 marked the end of the long-standing arrangement whereby 11 and 12 were worked by each operator on alternate weeks and thereafter buses of both Corporations appeared on each service daily.

In April 1948 further developments to the joint services were proposed including the southward extension of No. 10 from New Ferry to Bromborough Cross and No. 11 to Gorsey Hey, Higher Bebington. It was also proposed to extend route 12 Seacombe-Charing Cross at both ends to form a new service between New Brighton and Bebington station. Wallasey saw an opportunity to eliminate some loss-making mileage on the No. 5 Seacombe-New Brighton station service and proposed that the extension of the 12 from Seacombe to New Brighton should be over this route, via Penkett Road, Mount Road and Albion Street. The territorial divisions on this were as follows:

	Miles	%
New Brighton-Seacombe via route 5	3.011	35.37
Seacombe-Charing Cross	2.653	31.16
Charing Cross-Bebington station	2.850	33.47
Total	8.514	100.00

Revenue was shared equally on the Seacombe-Charing Cross route, the exact proportions being Birkenhead 49.05% / Wallasey 50.95%, and it was proposed that this should continue.

Birkenhead saw the extension of the 12 to New Brighton as an extra means of getting trippers to the seaside and saw through the ruse to prop up Wallasey's ailing route 5. They refused to accept the indirect route, insisting that the extension be made by the direct route along Seabank Road, Wallasey's route 1, and this was eventually conceded.

These extensions came into force on 30 May 1949, alternate buses on route 10 going through to Bromborough Cross. The extended 11 now commenced at 7.40am instead of 10.00am and was slightly diverted in Wallasey via Poulton Road and Mill Lane in order to provide a facility between St Luke's Church and Liscard Village although the short journeys between Liscard and Charing Cross continued to follow the old route via Oxton Road and Woodstock Road.

An amendment to the agreement governing the apportionment of revenue on route 10 was proposed to take effect from 1 April 1949 but was delayed until 1 September. The deduction of 10d per mile for operating costs was abolished and the revenue divided 59% to Birkenhead and 41% to Wallasey.

Bridge Delays

From their inception, the cross-docks services had been disrupted by the raising of Duke Street Bridge to allow the passage of shipping. In the early days when there was no workmen's traffic and people were not always in a hurry, this was not particularly important but during the war and just after, when thousands of workers were being conveyed from Wallasey into Birkenhead, these delays had serious consequences. Wallasey Corporation dealt with the morning peak hour traffic; in 1950, 23 buses were being used, there being 20 peak hour trips to Central station. A bridge delay on the first trip often meant the second trip was not worked at all. In the afternoons, Birkenhead supplied the augmentation except for three Wallasey buses.

These bridge closures were unpredictable and lengthy, closures of up to 40 minutes being commonplace. The warning bells would start ringing, the red stop lights would come on and the gatemen would close the gates across the roadway. The bridge would then roll back upon its bascules to allow shipping to pass. Further delays were caused by railway shunting. The main dock railway crossed Duke Street alongside Corporation Road, 200 yards on the Birkenhead side of the bridge and, even nearer to the bridge, wagons were moved on and off Rea's Jetty by rope and hydraulic capstan.

When the 11 and 12 were relatively short routes, their correction after a delay was a fairly simple matter, usually consisting of missing a complete round trip. On route 10, and ultimately on the extended 11 and 12, the delays were more disruptive and conflicting decisions made with the best intentions by regulators at different locations would often result in irregularities which took hours to sort out. At New Ferry when three buses arrived together it was common practice to load one to Liscard, one non-stop to the Tunnel Entrance via New Chester Road (thus making up about 10 minutes), and allow the third to follow the normal route. From 6 November 1950, Cammell Lairds' finishing time was changed from 5.00 to 4.30pm, spreading the afternoon peak for a time until other firms adopted earlier finishing times.

Following a series of meetings with the Dock Board and British Railways, it was agreed that the bridges would not be opened for barges only between 7.00 and 9.00am and that telephone advice would be given of delays whenever practicable. Wallasey Corporation agreed to station an inspector at the top of Gorsey Lane to divert buses via Poulton Bridge. This was the best arrangement that could be made. Much later, when motor traffic was greatly increased and the congestion created by waiting traffic itself became a problem, automatic warning signs were installed to inform drivers of the state of all three bridge crossings. By that time, use of the Birkenhead docks by large ships had diminished and the bridge delays were less frequent and of shorter duration.

The first signs of retrenchment were apparent late in 1949, and from January 1950 the Bromborough and Gorsey Hey journeys on routes 10 and 11 were confined to weekday peak hours and summer Sundays. At the same time, route 12 reverted to Seacombe-Charing Cross, the Bebington station journeys being run half-hourly only during the summer months, with an additional service between Bebington station and Seacombe from approximately 2.30 on Saturdays or 4.00 on Mondays to Fridays until 6.00pm. After the 1950 summer season, the Sunday service to Gorsey Hey was withdrawn. In June 1951 the short journeys on 11 between Liscard and Charing Cross were replaced by a new joint service 9 between the same points via Mill Lane, Poulton Bridge, Beaufort Road and Park station. The Poulton Bridge suffered fewer delays from bridge closures and shunting so the route was popular on this account. The through journeys on route 11 now reverted to the original route via Oxton Road and Woodstock Road.

With the passing of the post-war boom the New Brighton-Arrowe Park service was withdrawn altogether for the winter of 1951-52 and on its resumption for Easter 1952 it was extended a short distance beyond Arrowe Park to the entrance to the new Woodchurch housing estate at Ackers Road. The frequency now became every 45 minutes and a limited daily service in the afternoons and evenings only was resumed in May. This service was extended through the estate to Orret's Meadow Road in July 1954.

The Gorsedale Road Fiasco

In December 1946, the Corporation applied for a licence for a completely new local service which would have been numbered 3 between Seacombe ferry and Liscard Village via Birkenhead Road, Kelvin Road, Wheatland Lane, Lucerne Road, Gorsedale Road, Norwood Road, Mostyn Street, Poulton Road, Mill Lane and St Alban's Road. It was to run on Mondays to Saturdays every 40 minutes between 7.00am and 6.40pm. One of the objectives was the provision of a link between the lower part of Poulton and Liscard Village. Confident of obtaining a licence, the Corporation erected bus stop poles at various points en route and added 'via Gorsedale Road' to the route blinds of the buses. However, it was opposed by the Chief Constable of Wallasey who pointed out the dangers arising from the presence of hordes of children playing in the roadway, particularly along Gorsedale Road and Mostyn Street. There were other road safety objections such as the danger of crossing Gorsey Lane where the adjacent railway bridge limited visibility and buses, starting from rest on a gradient, would be crossing very slowly. There were some within the motor bus department who had similar reservations to the Chief Constable. In March 1947 it was agreed to substitute Gorsey Lane for Mostyn Street but the problem of emerging into Gorsey Lane in the outward direction still remained. Aerial photographs were taken to demonstrate the density of the area to strengthen the Corporation's case but the Licensing Authority refused the application on 31 May 1947 because of continued police objections. The poles remained as silent witnesses of the struggle between two arms of the local authority and eventually, during the construction of the tunnel approach roads 20 years later, both Gorsedale Road and Norwood Road were stopped up at their Gorsey Lane ends. As described above, the Liscard-Poulton link was achieved first by the partial diversion of route 11 buses and later by the new joint service 9. Small buses came to part of Gorsedale Road in 1962.

The End of the Post-War Boom

The peak of the post-war travel boom was reached in the financial year 1949-50 when 36.6 million passengers were carried over 3.2 million miles. Thereafter traffic started to fall off gradually during the next decade. Increasing costs made it essential to make economies and the limitation of the first fares increase (see chapter 7) added to the department's difficulties. Retrenchment on the cross-docks services has already been mentioned. The midday augmentation of the Seacombe ferry and connecting bus services from a 15- to a 10-minute frequency was abandoned in October 1950 as far fewer people went home to lunch. This relieved the Motor Bus Department of some scheduling difficulties as crews had to be brought in for short periods to man the extra buses. The resultant three-part split duties were very unpopular. Route 5 (later 15) and 6 were reduced to a 40-minute frequency during the evenings from October 1950 and they both lost their Sunday services from 7th October 1951. From 29 October to 16 March 1952, 20-minute frequencies applied between 5.30 and 6.30am on all weekdays, after 8.00pm on Mondays to Fridays and from 10.00am all day on Sundays. This pattern was continued in subsequent years but, when the winter schedule 1953-54 was being discussed, the Motor Bus department wanted 15-minute services on Sunday afternoons and evenings on the 16 and 17 services. This resulted in the Ferries department providing a 15-minute service between 2.30 and 9.30pm, the Motor Bus department being ordered by the Council to pay half the additional cost incurred by the Ferries. A 40-minute Sunday service on route 6 was restored for the summer from 1952 to 1959 but not from 1960 onwards. The summer extension of route 6 to Derby Bathing Pool was not run after 1951.

The operation of three loss-making services between Seacombe and Moreton made it difficult to reduce the basic frequency from 10 to 15 minutes as this would have resulted in an irregular headway of 45 minutes by each route. Such a timetable would almost certainly have led to a further loss of traffic as it would have been difficult for the public to work out the times of buses. The problem was tackled by cancelling route 3 after 8.0pm on Monday to Fridays and all day Sundays from 29 October 1951. Routes 4 and 5 each ran every 40 minutes but, following public clamour, a half-hourly service was substituted, the Sunday afternoon and evening service on route 3 was reinstated from

18 November. At the same time, the frequency of routes 2, 14, 16 and 17 was reduced from 15 to 20 minutes after about 8.00pm on Mondays to Fridays and on Sundays.

The withdrawal of route 3 off-peak on Mondays to Fridays from 31 December 1951 brought forth a further outcry and from 14 January it was reinstated on a part-way basis, between Castleway North (Leasowe Road) and Town Meadow Lane only. This was intended as an experiment for one-man operation and a hired Leyland Olympic 44-seat underfloor-engined single-decker bus was run for a month. However, because of a lack of agreement by the staff, it is believed to have run with a full crew. When the 3 was not running, route 5 continued part of the way round the terminal loop to Lingham Lane (later to Flaxhill), returning via Bermuda Road. Route 3 was fully reinstated from 26 May 1952 though, in subsequent winters, there were reductions in frequencies on all the Moreton services.

Old Buses Kept Going

The exceptionally heavy demands on the undertaking could not have been met within the limits of a normal fleet of 90-odd buses. Wallasey, having placed orders with Leyland early in the war, was luckier than some towns, receiving 24 new buses in the second half of 1946 and a further 24 two years later. A few of the buses returned by Crosville were unfit for further service and were quickly disposed of; others were sold to Salford Corporation who were assembling an assortment of second-hand buses so that it could close down its almost derelict tramway system. Ten pre-war double-deckers were selected for eventual rebodying, four as coaches and six as double-deckers. However, 19 pre-war double-decker buses, dating from 1932-36, were kept in service with 100 added to their fleet numbers until 1948-49, and it was 1952 before the last pre-war buses were withdrawn. Special demands were still experienced and contractors Wimpey hired 12 buses daily in 1953-54 to carry workmen at £63 per day, a profit to the Corporation of £41 per day excluding depreciation.

Vehicle Allocation

When the first new Leyland PD1s (78-101) arrived in 1946, they were allocated to routes 2, 4/4B, 10 & 14 which required 18 or 19 buses. Surprisingly, faced with this influx of new Wallasey buses, Birkenhead continued to allocate 1937-38 Leyland TD5cs to route 10 until 1949 when their first post-war Guy Arabs arrived. The second batch of Leyland PD1s (11-34) arrived from August 1948 enabling all the other Moreton workings and 11, 12 and 17 to be PD1-operated. This left 1, 5, 6 & 16 worked by pre-war buses and this continued throughout 1949-50. All but three of the 1932-36 buses were withdrawn at the end of the 1948 summer season. The second batch of PD1s introduced a new feature – destination blinds on which short working points were printed in red on white to draw attention to

No.54, from the last batch of Leyland Titans with the 'traditional' style of Metro-Cammell bodywork was a PD2 chassis of 1951, seen here on cross-docks service 10 in 1967, having just reached the Birkenhead side of the frequently-opened Duke Street bascule bridge. The background is mostly filled with Blue Funnel Line cargo ships 'at home' in the West Float Dock. The tracks in the roadway were for railway freight traffic. (© Ted Jones)

the fact that the bus was not covering the whole route. This feature was continued for the remainder of the independent life of the undertaking. The first batch of Leyland PD2s entered service between January and March 1951 and swept out many of the TD4c and TD5c buses. PD1s now appeared in increasing numbers on 1, 5, 6 and 16 having been replaced by PD2s on other routes. When the 8ft wide PD2s arrived, the fleet became entirely post-war and both PD1s and PD2s were allocated indiscriminately until 1959.

Wallasey No.102 was formerly Metro-Cammell-bodied No.14, a 1936 Titan TD4c with its new 1949 H V Burlingham body. All six of these 1949 bodies were transferred to new Titan PD2 chassis in 1955. (© K.W. Swallow)

Four of the 1936 TD4c chassis were rebodied by Burlingham as coaches in 1948 and, echoing what happened to the rebodied double deckers, two of these coach bodies were transferred to newer chassis in 1957, paradoxically remounted yet again on double-decker Leyland Titan frames. This shot of No.8 on its prewar chassis was taken at Belle Vue Zoo in Manchester, on a private-hire in 1955. (© Ted Jones)

The final batch of 'Standard' Metro-Cammell bodies could be distinguished by the upper-deck rainwater valances being curtailed above the first side window instead of extending to the rearmost window, and the lower deck windows seeming deeper than before. No.48 was apparently still in fine fettle at Seacombe in July1968. (© Ted Jones)

"There she goes" (or worse) many a tardy passenger off the Seacombe ferry might have said, but they would only have had to wait a short time for the next '16'. This is a rear view of the classic Metro-Cammell 'standard' body in its final form, on No.48 of 1951. (© Ted Jones)

CHAPTER 5
THE YEARS OF DECLINE – 1953-69

The New Brighton-Moreton services were revised from 25 May 1953; route 8 was unchanged but 7 became a daily instead of a weekend service being diverted via Castleway North and Birket Avenue instead of Leasowe Castle and Reeds Lane. The section via Danger Lane and Pasture Avenue was abandoned. No. 7 buses now ran via Bermuda Road and Town Meadow Lane to Flaxhill, returning the same way. Routes 7 and 8 made up a combined 20-minute service (15-minute on Saturdays and Sundays) except on weekday mornings when route 7 did not run but a Liscard Village-Moreton Cross supplementary service on 8 was continued.

The Frankby Cemetery Service

Early in 1953, the Corporation applied for a licence for a weekend service between New Brighton and Frankby Cemetery which the Council had bought many years before but was now coming into general use. It was opposed by Crosville who, before the war, had run a summer service to Heswall by this route but had not resumed it after the war. The Corporation's application was approved with the proviso that buses must run non-stop between Moreton Cross and Frankby thus protecting the Birkenhead Corporation service between Moreton and Upton and both Birkenhead Corporation and Crosville services thence to Frankby. One return journey on Saturdays and Sundays commenced running on 13 June 1953. The Corporation chose route No. 21, an unfortunate choice in view of the presence of the long-established Birkenhead route 21 in Moreton. The Saturday service was found to be unnecessary and was withdrawn for the winter on 14 November, being restored on 29 May 1954 but withdrawn permanently from 31 July. From 29 May 1955, it was curtailed at Liscard and ran virtually unchanged for the next 50 years, and is likely to continue to do so.

Leisure Services

August 1952 saw the inauguration of the Town Tour. Commencing on New Brighton promenade, near the Floral Pavilion, it ran via the Promenade, Harrison Drive, Bayswater Road, Greenleas Road, Leasowe Road, Pasture Road, Hoylake Road, Reeds Lane, Birket Avenue, Castleway North, Leasowe Road, Wallasey Village, Breck Road, Poulton Bridge Road, Dock Road (later via Poulton Bridge to Beaufort Road and back again), Seacombe ferry, Brighton Street, Church Street, Liscard Road, Seaview Road and Warren Drive back to New Brighton. The tour operated as required during the summer season, using Leyland Cubs and coaches in 1952, PD1s 84-85 from 1954 to 1957 then PD1s 20-21 until 1960. In 1961 PD2 No. 58 was fitted with public address equipment so that a commentary could be given.

From 2 June 1963 the Town Tour was replaced by the Wirral Tour which started at the same place and followed the same route to Moreton, then via Upton, Frankby and Lower Caldy Cross Roads to Thurstaston. The route then lay through Irby to Arrowe Park where there was a halt for tea, then via Woodchurch Road and over the No. 11 route to Charing Cross; buses then ran via Park Road South and Tollemache Road to St. James' Church and over the 18 route via Poulton Bridge, Belvidere Road and Sandcliffe Road back to New Brighton. Atlantean No. 3, also fitted with public address equipment, was used and it is not known when this activity ceased but it was advertised for 1967 and probably fell victim to staff shortages.

These tours were run on excursion and tour licences which were strongly opposed by the local coach operators as they considered this type of work to be their exclusive province. However, regular coach excursions from New Brighton Promenade had not been run for some years and the Corporation applications for licences were granted on that basis.

Another rather different initiative took the form of a new Saturday evening shuttle service No. 13 between New Brighton station and the Tower to cater for ballroom dancers. Running via Cressingham Road, Rowson Street and Molyneux Drive, it started on 23 May 1953 and was withdrawn after operation on 27 March 1954. During that time it took only £39 in revenue, running 601 miles, averaging 15.57d per mile, well below the cost of operation. Leyland PD1 No. 21 was used. 'Tower and Tivoli' was also added to its destination blinds suggesting that an extension was considered but not implemented.

The Promenade service, No. 19, was enlivened when PD1 127, now renumbered 84, was fitted with a body similar in outline to the cruise ship Royal Iris in 1964. Its original purpose was to tour the inland towns promoting the Ferries Department cruise programme and the delights of New Brighton as a resort. As it was not required to do this in summer, it was pressed into service on the Promenade from 1966. It seated 22 passengers and eventually went to the Isle of Man where it was repainted to resemble an Isle of Man Steam Packet vessel. It went for preservation in 1973 but its ultimate fate is unknown.

Cross-Docks Developments

There had long been a demand for a service across the Four Bridges, especially at peak hours, and, with the increasing importance of Birkenhead as a workplace for Wallasey residents, there was also a call for direct transport facilities from parts of the borough unserved by the cross-docks network. Both these needs were met by a new joint route 13 which started running at Monday to Friday peak hours between Trafalgar Road, Egremont and Central station, Birkenhead on 17 January 1955 for a six-month trial. It ran every 20 minutes via King Street, Brighton Street, Brougham Road, Wheatland Lane,

Kelvin Road, Four Bridges, Cleveland Street, Bridge Street and Chester Street, both operators supplying buses daily. The objection to a service across the Four Bridges had always been the severe delays caused by bridge closures and shunting, but changes on the docks had reduced these incidents and the service quickly became popular with Wallasey workers. After a year's operation, a Saturday service was also put on but an attempt to popularise Egremont foreshore with Birkenhead people by running an all-day service during the school summer holidays was a failure. From May 1956, the extended journeys on route 11 between The Wiend and Gorsey Hey were permanently withdrawn, reflecting the continued gradual reduction in patronage.

The summer weekend extension of route 12 between New Brighton and Bebington station survived with various timetable changes until 1963 when it was curtailed in Higher Tranmere to terminate at the top of Bebington Road. However it was withdrawn at the end of the 1964 summer season, reverting to daily operation between Seacombe and Charing Cross only, but with one morning trip from Bebington station to Seacombe which ran until 1967. The New Brighton-Arrowe Park-Woodchurch service No. 18 survived at weekends until late in the 1960s when it became a casualty of the staff shortages, no official withdrawal date having ever been announced.

Financial Problems and Experiments

By the late 1950s, the financial state of the Motor Bus Department was giving serious cause for concern and, with similar losses on the ferries, the burden on the ratepayers was growing. Commercial advertisements were displayed on buses from 1952 to raise additional revenue. In those days Councils tended to take up moral stances about advertisements and there was a ban on 'political, moneylending and holiday resort' advertisements. The Suez fuel crisis in the last months of 1956 brought back fuel rationing and all operators were required to reduce mileage by 10%. Cuts introduced from 31 December 1956 included the withdrawal of routes 6 and 15 off-peak (though a storm of protest resulted in their swift reinstatement on a 40-minute frequency), the withdrawal of route 9 between 2.00 and 4.00pm and after 7.00pm on Saturdays, and the curtailment of route 16 at Grove Road at certain times. Other frequencies were reduced from 10 to 15 minutes or 15 to 20. Little hardship was caused and the financial results for 1956-57 were better. Nevertheless, political pressure ensured that all the cuts were restored as soon as the crisis was over in April 1957. However, lessons had been learned and the experience used to good effect when the time was ripe.

In 1958, the department entered a period of experimentation with the twofold objective of increasing revenue and reducing expenditure. Already it was apparent that the traditional pattern of service, wedded to Seacombe ferry sailings, no longer met public needs but the efforts of the management were often thwarted by the Council, which vetoed proposals on purely political grounds. In February 1958, on the same day as the introduction of route 2A (see below), the diversion of routes 7 and 8 over the route of the 15 service between Mount Pleasant Road and New Brighton was announced. Both alterations were announced as three-month experiments but there was so much opposition to the diversion of routes 7 and 8 that it was 'postponed' before it was introduced. The demise of the 15 seems to have been envisaged though there were some strange suggestions. One envisaged it being increased from half-hourly to every 20 minutes, curtailed at Trafalgar Road in the off-peak and extended from New Brighton station to Virginia Road. As mentioned earlier, there was a great need for a link between the Mount Road district and the commercial centre of the town at Liscard as passengers no longer accepted as reasonable the lengthy walk to the 16 route at Warren Drive or the 10 and 14 routes at Rowson Street. However, well-meaning councillors with no depth of bus operating experience failed to appreciate that anyone travelling from Seacombe ferry to places along the 15 route would not accept a change of buses at Trafalgar Road and would use one of the alternative routes even if it entailed a lengthy walk.

In fact, the 7 and 8 were not then diverted and instead of making an economy the department found itself having to run an additional bus on a half-hourly service, No. 22, between Liscard and New Brighton via Seaview Road, Mount Pleasant Road, Mount Road and over the 15 route. This service ran for a six-month trial period between April and October 1958, after which it was withdrawn without a replacement.

The financial state of both bus and ferry undertakings had become serious as traffic was lost to personal transport and television, the latter keeping people at home instead of travelling by bus to the cinema. Furthermore, as fares rose to cover higher costs of operation, rail fares to Liverpool became more attractive. The railway did not just attract traffic from the environs of the stations in the borough – New Brighton, Wallasey (Grove Road), Wallasey Village, Leasowe and Moreton – but also from Birkenhead Park and Hamilton Square in Birkenhead, which could be reached from Wallasey by the cross-docks bus services. After six months of deliberations, the Council tried to stem the flow of lost passengers by introducing through bus and ferry weekly contracts in May 1959 (see Chapter 7), but the losses continued and these were withdrawn in October 1960.

Meanwhile, the Leasowe Estate was growing rapidly and routes 3 and 7 were diverted from part of Leasowe Road and Castleway North to Gardenside and Twickenham Drive from 9 June 1958. The long 'country' section of the Moreton routes, which produced hardly any revenue, had at last disappeared. In May 1960, and the Moreton terminus of route 7 was altered to an anti-clockwise loop via Maryland Lane, Town Meadow Lane and Bermuda Road to eliminate the need to reverse and to even out timings between the various services.

One of the factors contributing to loss of bus traffic was the growing reluctance on the part of the public to walk lengthy distances to a bus stop. The frequent services of earlier years had only been possible by concentrating the traffic into main traffic arteries and people had thought it no hardship to walk a quarter of a mile or even more to catch a bus. This was now changing and, particularly in new housing areas, would-be passengers demanded almost door-to-door service. The satisfaction of these demands often required the operation of additional mileage, to cover the cost of which more revenue was needed. Route extensions were often only a temporary palliative for falling traffic. Route 2 had an hourly off-peak one-way loop added in February 1958, buses running via Green Lane, Greenleas Road, Bayswater Road, Newport Avenue and Groveland Road to Harrison Drive. In the inward direction, passengers boarding on the loop had to sit out the layover at the terminus which did not go down very well. The buses showed No. 2A but, at peak hours, time constraints allowed only the old No. 2 service to be run. A suggestion to divert the service via Marlowe Road, Cliff Road and Breck Road met with no support.

However, the Green Lane loop arrangement lasted for almost five years being replaced in January 1963 by a simple extension from Harrison Drive to Green Lane (Bayswater Road) via Groveland Road at off-peak times on Monday to Friday and Sunday afternoons and evenings, route No. 2B being shown. Route 2A was now run at school times and hourly on Saturdays from 9.45am to 4.45pm, missing out the 11.45 and 1.45 departures. The complexity of the arrangements with 2, 2A and 2B being run at different times and on different days was hardly conducive to encouraging traffic.

The Leyland Atlantean Buses

Wallasey received much publicity towards the end of 1958 as the first municipal operator of the revolutionary rear-engine, front-entrance double-decker Leyland Atlantean. The Wallasey version seated 77 passengers, a 37.5% increase over the latest Leyland PD2s, the first bus entering public service on route 1 on 8 December 1958. Because of its front entrance, it was felt that there might be some danger to passengers when loading at Seacombe where buses reversed into their loading bays, and a device resembling a ship's gangway was for a time placed along the nearside of the bus. After a brief trial, Atlantean No. 1 was withdrawn for modifications and staff training, re-entering service in April or May 1959 on route 8 on which no reversing was necessary. Five more identical buses arrived in September 1959 and routes 2 and 14 were officially converted although traditional rear-entrance buses were also used as more than six buses were needed. Fourteen more Atlanteans were delivered during March 1960 and a further ten in July to September 1961, making a total of thirty. All the Wallasey routes except 6, 15 and 17 were then progressively converted and the stands at Seacombe were rearranged so that buses loaded nose in. Atlanteans started to appear on the cross-docks routes 10 and 13 in April

1960, route 11 in 1961 and 9 in 1962. The seating capacity of these thirty buses (which could of course be utilised fully only at peak periods) was equivalent to that of forty-one of the old rear-entrance buses. This increased capacity enabled peak hour duplication, most of which was provided at overtime rates, to be reduced and some headways to be widened, achieving worthwhile economies. It is believed that the peak hour operation of buses via Borough Road on routes 3, 4 and 5 ceased when Atlanteans were introduced.

More Experiments

On 18 June 1960, Wallasey celebrated the 50th anniversary of its incorporation as a borough and various festivities were arranged to mark the occasion including a procession depicting the development of local transport. As Wallasey had no preserved vehicles, a horse bus was hired from Manchester Corporation and an ex-Bolton Leyland Titan TD1 from Leyland Motors Ltd. The latter was of the enclosed platform and stairs model which had never been operated by Wallasey but it was calculated to fool the layman. Unfortunately, their liveries were quite inappropriate to Wallasey so they were given a coat of water paint before the procession and luckily the weather kept fine. Atlantean 20 and PD2 29 also took part, decorated with bunting.

To provide a link between Marlowe Road (Mill Lane) and Egremont, route 6 was taken off Rullerton Road in May 1960 and rerouted via Mill Lane and Marlowe Road which were wider. Towards the end of the year there were further timetable changes. From 12 September, route 16 was curtailed at off-peak times at Grove Road (Warren Drive) with connections and transfers to route 17 for New Brighton. During peak hours the position was reversed with route 16 running through and 17 turning at Grove Road. This apparently incomprehensible arrangement fitted the vehicle workings economically, bearing in mind the increased peak hour frequencies. The Committee had originally approved the general manager's suggestion for rerouting the 16 via Gerard Road and Rolleston Drive but this was referred back by the Council and reversed, difficulties with the location of stops at Grove Road (Warren Drive) to facilitate transfers being a concern. The relocation of the No. 6 terminal stop in Lyndhurst Road, the buses running thence to Rolleston Drive, was suggested but rejected in the sure knowledge that strong opposition would be forthcoming from residents. The object was to pave the way to a partial withdrawal of route 6. This formula continued until 16th April 1962 when new timetables gave alternate through journeys by both routes except at peak times when the 16 turned at Grove Road. This lasted until the general adoption of the 20-minute frequency all day after which both services ran through all day except the 16 at peak hours. The odd early morning 16 journey via Kelvin Road and Birkenhead Road disappeared during these upheavals which also included the withdrawal of evening services on the 6 and 15 routes. Another suggestion was for the 16 to divert over unsuitable residential roads via Elleray Park Road, Glen Park Road and Mount Road and a one-way circle as a rail feeder from Harrison Drive via St. Hilary Brow, Belvidere Road, Rolleston Drive and Grove Road or to run route 6 to Harrison Drive off-peak.

From 31 October 1960, two new experimental services were introduced. The first, No. 22, followed the now familiar off-peak pattern with a 40-minute frequency between 9.00am and 5.00pm. The route required two buses. It commenced at Holland Road (Haydock Road) and ran via Holland Road (returning via Hertford Drive and Haydock Road), Seabank Road, Trafalgar Road, Martins Lane, Liscard Road, and then as the No. 7 to Moreton Cross and Town Meadow Lane, traversing the loop in the opposite direction to No. 7. The coaches were usually employed on this service and, from December, the 8 wide PD2s, which could display '22' on their two-column number blinds, were used on Fridays and Saturdays.

The second experiment was a 'Line of Docks' service No. 23 between Seacombe ferry and Mill Lane (Woodstock Road) via Birkenhead Road, Dock Road, Poulton Bridge Road and Mill Lane, returning via Oxton Road and Poulton Road. This ran every 20 minutes at peak times and, as the journey time was 11 minutes outwards and 12 minutes back, two buses had to be employed. Special supplementary destination and route boards were carried in the front bulkhead and rearmost nearside windows. However, it was a dismal failure and lasted only until 11 February 1961. It might have been better if it had run to Liscard but it is suspected that Birkenhead Corporation, whilst prepared to accept some extraction of traffic from route 12 along Dock Road, drew the line at competition with routes 10 and 11 to Liscard and threatened to submit an official objection to the Traffic Commissioners. The diversion of some peak hour trips on these services might have served the same purpose much more economically.

The 22 lasted rather longer, continuing in its original form until 9 September 1961 when it was curtailed to operate only between Holland Road and Leasowe Road (Wallasey Village) via Steel Avenue, Penkett Road, Rake Lane, Liscard and St. Hilary's Brow. The simplification of the route enabled one bus to maintain the 40-minute headway but it still failed to attract sufficient traffic and was withdrawn on 31 March 1962.

During 1961, there were experiments designed to make the peak hour services more attractive by speeding some of them up. On 2 January 1961, route 6 duplicate journeys to Broadway Avenue were made 'limited stop', running via Wheatland Lane, Liscard Road and Wallasey Road instead of by the normal route via King Street and Martins Lane. They were restricted to the evening peak in March and withdrawn altogether soon afterwards. In April, limited stop peak hour journeys on 3 and 5 commenced but came off after three months. It was, again, too little too late. Limited stop journeys required a hard core of regular passengers so that they could run full, non-stop for a substantial part of the journey. Too often, the limited stop bus was part-loaded and the service bus was leaving passengers behind en route. A further application was granted by the Traffic Commissioners in November for journeys on route 3. The 8.10am from Town Meadow Lane was to serve all stops to Gardenside (Leasowe Road corner) and then run non-stop to Seacombe with a setting-down stop at Wallasey Village station if required. The approach to Seacombe was to be via Wheatland Lane and St Paul's Road as the police did not want any more buses using Borough Road. The return journey at 5.40pm from Seacombe had the same conditions except that there was no reciprocal pick-up at Wallasey Village station. It is not known how long this service lasted.

The purely leisure services were finding it difficult to survive. The Promenade service 19 was extended from the promenade end at Wallasey Beach to Derby Bathing Pool in August 1961 and the 4S service to Moreton Shore ran for the last time in about 1960. Places like Moreton Shore with its primitive facilities were now out of fashion and the regular service on route 4 was normally quite sufficient for the low demand.

Traffic congestion problems in Birkenhead became severe, mainly because of the conflicting needs of local and tunnel traffic. New control arrangements led to route 10 being rerouted away from the Tunnel entrance in 1961 and the peak hour journeys were retained on Chester Street but terminating at Kings Square as route 10A. Route 13 was similarly treated. In April 1961 there had been suggestions for extending the 13 to Green Lane for Cammell Laird workers and rerouting the 10 to Clatterbridge, both of which were rejected.

A New Manager

The general manager, W.R. Goodier, was due to retire on attaining the age of 65 on 27 March 1960 and it was proposed to form a Passenger Transport Department by amalgamating the motor bus and ferries undertakings, the Committees having been combined in May 1958. A Sub-committee was appointed to give full consideration to this proposal, which was eventually adopted. However, a new Motor Bus manager, G.G. Harding, aged 37, was appointed to succeed Goodier, taking up his duties in March 1961. He had previously been the manager of the Aberdare UDC undertaking in South Wales.

In 1963, the ferries manager retired and a start was made on a gradual amalgamation of the two departments, a process made difficult by trade union practices and inter-departmental jealousies which had taken root during more than half a century. Harding, who had a marine engineering qualification and held the rank of Lieutenant Commander in the RNR, took charge of the whole Passenger Transport Department. He had very serious problems to address as the bus undertaking was now losing passengers at the rate of over one million per year. The decline of New Brighton as a holiday resort and the growth of personal transport reduced the summer demand to the extent that winter losses could no longer be covered by summer profits.

One of Harding's interests was hovercrafts, and when an experimental craft entered service between Moreton and Rhyl in the summer of 1962, two temporary services to and from New Brighton and Moreton Shore, 8A via Kings Parade, Bayswater Road and Greenleas Road and 8B via Liscard were run for two months to convey passengers and spectators.

Harding modernised the livery of the buses and eliminated the old-fashioned 'Wallasey Corporation Motors' title. Wallasey was the last municipality to carry the once common 'Motors' title on its buses but not the last to use it as the official title, as the Rawtenstall undertaking retained this style.

One of the complaints which had been aired over many years was that slavish adherence to ferry connections resulted in buses being bunched over common sections such as Poulton Road and Brighton Street-King Street. In February 1962 a six-month experiment was inaugurated whereby ferry connections were ignored in the off-peak times and timetables arranged to provide more or less even headways over the common sections. However no increase in traffic resulted and ferry passengers complained about missed connections. Layover time was not reduced and there was no integration of workings between services, which might have saved money. The experiment was abandoned after six months.

Stern Measures

The Seacombe night ferry service was withdrawn from 10 September 1962. Birkenhead and Liverpool Corporations had been running a tunnel night bus service since 1956 and it was decided to provide a bus feeder running three trips in the early hours from the main Birkenhead tunnel entrance to Seaview Road depot via Canning Street, Four Bridges, Kelvin Road, Wheatland Lane and Liscard Road. However, this was so little used that it was withdrawn after operation on 20 January 1963.

Traders in Victoria Road, New Brighton complained that the routing of buses to New Brighton via Virginia Road discouraged people from patronising their shops. The use of Victoria Road in both directions during the winter was turned down in 1960, a compromise proposal being the use of Waterloo Road instead of Rowson Street and Wellington Road inwards so that the buses would use a short stretch of Victoria Road with a setting-down stop. However, this was vetoed by the police. The shopkeepers continued their campaign and routes 14 and 17 were rerouted inward via Victoria Road to the pier from 1 October 1962; this was not successful and was withdrawn on 29 March 1963.

Seacombe ferry sailings were reduced to a 20-minute off-peak service on Mondays to Fridays from 10 September 1962 and bus services were adjusted accordingly. The original scheme provided for supplementary services between Liscard and Harrison Drive and an 'Inner Circle' between Brougham Road and Magazine Lane via King Street and Seabank Road, returning via Rake Lane and Liscard Road (and vice versa); these would have provided 10-minute services over the 20-minute 2, 1 and 14 services respectively. However, the Liscard-Harrison Drive buses were withdrawn in favour of retiming routes 7 and 8 to give a 10-minute service with the 2 between Liscard and the top of Leasowe Road, and the 'Inner Circular' was shortened on road safety grounds to run between Molyneux Drive and Queens Arms, Liscard Village via Seabank Road, King Street, Brougham Road and Liscard Road. The 2 was extended from Harrison Drive to Kingsway via Grove Road and Rolleston. Drive to compensate for reductions in route 6 but this lasted only until 9 December. Turning difficulties had been addressed by applying for a loop via Kingsway, Knowsley Road and Bowdon Road. The Molyneux Drive-Queens Arms trips were also withdrawn, probably at the same time.

Not all services were cut to the same extent, a 10-minute combined service being run on 3, 4 and 5 from 12.00 noon to 7.00pm on Mondays to Fridays and all day Saturdays.

Four 31-seat Albion 'Nimbus' vehicles were delivered in November-December 1962. They were equipped for one-man operation and a new hourly off-peak driver-only Monday to Saturday service (No. 23) commenced on 20 November 1962. It penetrated a number of residential areas hitherto unserved, running from Gorsedale Road via Ashville Road, Poulton Road, Hampstead Road, Parkside, Liscard Road, Mill Lane, Cliff Road, Mossdene Road, Mosslands Drive and Leasowe Road to Green Lane (Greenleas Road).

Routes 6 and 15 were converted to one-man operation off-peak from 18 March 1963, again using Albion 'Nimbus' vehicles. Harding believed that worthwhile economies could be achieved by the conversion of all the town routes off-peak, using Atlanteans with the top deck closed off. At that time, one-man operation with double-decker buses had not been legalised. The introduction of a flat fare of 4½d, possibly with the retention of a 3d fare for short rides, was considered, the belief being that, if passenger numbers could be stabilised, this would put the undertaking on its feet. The awkwardness of the 4½d fare was a negative factor but it was believed that the use of Holstimatic equipment coupled with some off-bus fare collection would overcome the problem.

Atlanteans were used in this way on route 14 but not until 23 November 1966, the method being extended to routes 1, 2, 3 and 5 by January 1967.

The First Minibuses

Merseyside's first minibus service started in Wallasey on 13 May 1963. A second-hand Trojan 13-seater was placed in service between Martins Lane (Grosvenor Street) and New Brighton station using some roads unsuitable for full-size buses; hail and ride applied over these sections. After serving Liscard centre, route 22 ran via Urmson Road, Withens Lane, Strathcona Road, Penkett Road, Steel Avenue, Seabank Road, Hertford Drive, Hale Road, Magazine Brow and Lane, Gordon Road, Vaughan Road, Kirkland Road, Dalmorton Road, Rowson Street and Victoria Road. It ran hourly off-peak but not on Wednesday afternoons when many shops were closed. Some of the features of the earlier 22 in the Seabank Road area were covered. At Kirkland Road, the route was very close to the promenade and some of the streets were very steep. Both the 22 and 23 services endured with minor changes for over thirty years, the Gorsedale Road end of the 23 being withdrawn in October 1996, but the other routes are still covered in modified forms. The buses on route 22 were timed to connect with trains at New Brighton station but the demand for such a facility was negligible and from 13 July 1964 the service was cut back to run half-hourly between Liscard Village and Kirkland Road only with a flat fare of 6d.

Proposals which did not come to fruition were the operation of direct hospital visiting buses to Cleaver Hospital, Heswall and Clatterbridge on Thursdays and Sundays. The applications for road service licences were refused by the Traffic Commissioners who upheld objections by Birkenhead Corporation and Crosville.

The most drastic service cuts yet were made from 1 March 1965 with an estimated saving of £17,000 per year in operating costs. Routes 6 and 15 were withdrawn altogether, route 8 being rerouted between Mount Pleasant Road and New Brighton via Mount Road, Hamilton Road, Albion Street and Atherton Street. This gave the Mount Road district its long-awaited connection with Liscard shopping centre. At peak hours, existing duplication was diverted to provide a 10-minute service over parts of the abandoned routes. Molyneux Drive duplicates on route 1 were diverted at Holland Road (as 1A) via Steel Avenue, Penkett Road, Earlston Road, Kirkway and Mount Road to Stoneby Drive, this being chosen as the furthest point to which buses could go to allow of two buses running this service.

It brought forth a storm of protest and, from 28 June, it was extended through to the Hotel Victoria, Albion Street which had been the terminus of the Mount Road route until 1944.

The Belvidere Road district was covered by the operation of route 16A between Seacombe and Grove Road (Warren Drive) via Wheatland Lane, Liscard Road, Seaview

Road, Kingsway and Rolleston Drive. This replaced the Liscard (14) and Hose Side Road (16) duplicates as well as route 6 buses. It was not practicable to show '16A' and buses displayed '16' with a 16A plate in a saloon window.

Route 17, which was duplicated by routes 3, 4 and 5 most of the way between Seacombe and Poulton, was curtailed to run between Balfour Road (at the western end of Poulton Road) and New Brighton. Balfour Road was chosen as a point where a common stop with the connecting services could be sited. This was a most unpopular measure and the through service was restored from 3 July, though route 16 was curtailed at the same time to run between Seacombe and Grove Road only.

Operational Research

The serious contraction in traffic and the consequent financial losses made it essential to examine the network to see what meaningful economies could be made while retaining a level of service to meet the needs of the residents. In 1963 Mr Harding invited the Department of Engineering Production at Birmingham University to make a pilot operational research investigation, and in 1965 a team from Birmingham and Hull universities carried out an origin-and-destination survey to determine travel habits, using borrowed Almex machines. The result was a reduction of thirteen buses and a 3% cut in peak hour services. The pilot survey report contradicted the oft-repeated allegation that bus fares had not kept pace with general price increases. They said that "the price of a bus journey has increased much faster than personal incomes over the last 15 years and, if the rate of increase is allowed to continue, then personal rather than public transport will appear more and more attractive to Wallasey citizens".

Mr Harding was interested in the operational research being carried out by Professor Quarmby at Leeds University, and the Council agreed to the engagement of a firm of consultants, BOR, to continue and expand the work already done and to determine the best network on the basis of optimum journey times. The work was carried out in 1966. It is interesting to note that Ribble Motor Services Ltd carried out a survey of its Carlisle city services at the same time, using the same consultants, and Almex ticket machines belonging to J. Fishwick & Sons of Leyland were used in both surveys.

The Computerised Bus Service

The new network came into effect on Sunday 12 February 1967, which was chosen because the Sunday and Monday were half-term holidays. The old network was based on the tram system established in 1902-11 with subsequent developments, mainly ferry-orientated. The new one recognised the steep decline in ferry traffic and the need to plan equally on the internal needs of the borough. The changes were therefore radical and controversial. A fares increase, previously refused because of the government's Prices and Incomes policy, was brought in simultaneously and while the synchronisation of a major upheaval with a fare increase was administratively convenient, it was psychologically undesirable and this aspect of the change undoubtedly added fuel to the fires of dissent which followed. Fifty-nine buses, including four for Cadbury's biscuit factory at Moreton, were needed at peak hours.

Only one service was completely withdrawn, the 17, successor to the former Poulton tram route, but the frequencies on the other ex-tram routes, 1 and 14, were reduced from 20 to 40 minutes at off-peak times at a time when there was staff to spare. Routes 2/2B, 5 and 14 ran at off-peak times only and 2/2B did not run at all on weekday evenings, Saturdays or Sundays. Route 4 ran at peak hours only on Mondays to Fridays but all day at weekends, but the frequency of 3 was increased to compensate for the loss of the 4 and 5.

A number of new services, six of them circulars, were introduced. A Moreton circular (24, 25) was run off-peak using one-man Albions. Route 24 ran from Saughall Massie over route 4 to Gardenside, then over route 3 to Stavordale Road. Here it broke new ground through Sandbrook estate to Moreton Cross, then via Town Meadow Lane and Bermuda Road to Saughall Massie; the 25 ran in the reverse direction. This was a compromise, following the objections of Birkenhead Corporation to a link between Borrowdale Road and Saughall Massie via Overchurch Road. The other major new service was the 30/31 Liscard-Moreton Circle. From Burrell Drive (the existing terminus of route 8), route 30 proceeded via Moreton Cross and over route 7 to Leasowe Road then via Wallasey Village, Grove Road, Hose Side Road and Seaview Road to Liscard, then as route 7 to Moreton Cross and on to Burrell Drive. Route 31 ran in the opposite direction. This route ran all day every day and was well patronised but it was superimposed on a virtually unaltered 7 and 8, the No. 8 finishing in the early evening on Monday to Friday but illogically continuing until 11.00pm on Sundays. Together with the circular 24/25, processions of buses were to be seen in Leasowe Estate and Borrowdale Road. On Saturdays, three buses were often seen in the latter thoroughfare – one coming, one going, and one standing at the terminus. Yet no attempt was made to serve Danger Lane and Pasture Avenue.

On the Monday morning, with all schools closed, people waited up to 50 minutes for buses in Wallasey Village in the morning peak and there was overloading in Leasowe Road, Breck Road and Wallasey Road. Route 16 was unable to cope between Liscard and Seacombe, as was route 1 from Manor Road inwards. Two spare buses and crews were available to meet any special demands. During the evening peak, probably for the first time ever, the waiting buses failed to clear the passengers from the ferry at Seacombe. The pattern was repeated on the following day when about half the schools had resumed and by Wednesday, when all schools were back, some changes had been made to the peak hour part-way buses though there were still many inadequacies. Within a week the management claimed that an adequate service was being provided but many passengers had already been permanently lost by then.

Public confusion was in no way due to lack of publicity. Comprehensive free booklets and new fare tables were issued and information bureaux were set up in strategic places throughout the borough. The principle of different networks at peak and off-peak times was already established in Wallasey to a limited extent and the new network took it much further. Facilities which had existed for decades were abandoned or disrupted and the new formula was complex in the extreme. The cross-docks services remained unchanged.

The withdrawal of the 17 was to some extent covered by extending the minibus service 22 from Liscard to Harrison Drive where it terminated in the yard of Wallasey (Grove Road) station. It ran via Wallasey Road, Belvidere Road, Rosclare Drive, Claremount Road and Sandy Lane. The route between Liscard and Kirkland Road was also altered to run via Martins Lane, Trafalgar Road, Stringhey Road and Penkett Road instead of Urmson Road and Withens Lane, so some places which had been unserved since the withdrawal of routes 6 and 15 in 1965 were back on the bus map, albeit with only an hourly off-peak service.

New Monday to Friday peak hour services were numbered 26, 32 and 33. The former followed the old 17 route from Seacombe to Poulton Road (Gorsey Lane) then via routes 10 and 11 to Liscard with a 10-minute frequency. The others formed a circle, the 33 following the 26 almost all the way, to Wallasey Road then via Belvidere Road, Rolleston Drive, Grove Road, Hose Side Road, Mount Pleasant Road and over route 1A to Seacombe via Seabank Road and King Street. Route 32 operated in reverse and there was a combined 10-minute service.

An added off-peak facility which was not part of the 'computerised' system was Limited Stop route 28, advertised as 'Liscard Village to Seacombe Ferry in five minutes'. It ran non-stop over route 2 from Seacombe and back over route 14, every 20 minutes off-peak. Obviously there was insufficient through traffic to justify it and, just when a load might have been forthcoming, it stopped running because the bus was needed for a peak hour duty. It ran for about four weeks after which it was replaced by a supplementary service on route 14 between Seacombe and Liscard as the 40-minute 14s were quite inadequate for the demand.

Public Outrage

The public could not be expected to accept with equanimity the disruption of facilities enjoyed for generations. The loudest outcry was against the withdrawal of route 2 during peak hours, evenings and weekends. The demand between Egremont and Liscard was not satisfied by the 19-seater on route 22 and many school children were without facilities. From mid-April, route 22 was kept running in the evenings between Harrison Drive and Trafalgar Road. The total withdrawal of the 17 brought forth fewer complaints but it was unnecessary to leave Marlowe Road unserved, and from 3 April route 26 was diverted from Torrington Road to serve Marlowe Road and Wallasey Road.

The storm of protest became a party political issue and council meetings became rowdy affairs. Local papers were full of complaints about 'the computerised bus service' and between 12 February and 26 April over half a million passengers were lost. Apart from those lost to private transport, many found it quicker to walk than to wait for a bus on a 40-minute frequency. There is no doubt that grave errors of judgement were made in planning these services. The survey results were treated as holy writ instead of being used as a guide. Harding came in for much public criticism. His innovative approach to the financial crisis deserves praise but he lacked a 'feel' for the undertaking and he ignored the pleadings of senior members of his staff, apparently interpreting their objections as resistance to change. It is significant that when Ribble Motor Services received the results of their Carlisle survey by the same consultants, they put them in a cupboard and took no action!

It was obvious that something had to be done but, apart from the changes noted above, it was Sunday 18 June before major changes were effected. Route 2/2B was reintroduced at peak hours, weekday evenings and at weekends with a 20-minute frequency; it was rerouted via Claremount Road and Sandy Lane, compensating for the loss of route 17 over this section, though the few 2A school journeys continued to run via Wallasey Village and St. Hilary Brow. Routes 14 and 16 were fully restored, the former on a 15-minute frequency and the latter every 20 minutes. The alterations were said to be for a three-month trial period but they remained in force beyond that.

The Moreton Circular (24-25) was abandoned in favour of a modified route 24 between Saughall Massie and Fender Lane roundabout via Sandbrook estate. On Saturdays it ran only between Moreton Cross and Fender Lane. The 30/31 Circle was reduced to every 30-40 minutes on Saturdays.

Cross Docks Changes

Unconnected with these events was the conversion of route 12 between Seacombe and Charing Cross to one-man operation on 13 March 1967 and the last extended journey, the 7.40am trip from Bebington station to Seacombe, finally disappeared. As Wallasey had no suitable buses, Birkenhead Corporation undertook the full operation, Wallasey's share of the mileage being run off on other services. There were other events affecting the Birkenhead services in 1967. Traffic flyovers were being built to segregate the tunnel traffic from that of the town and this involved massive demolition of property and stopping up of streets. Peak hour routes 10A and 13 were curtailed at Bridge Street in July 1967 as their St Mary's Gate terminus ceased to exist. Another change was the diversion of alternate journeys on route 11 via Storeton Road and Mount Road, Prenton as 11A in October 1967. Again, this involved Birkenhead Corporation buses only, Wallasey buses running only on the 11 via Woodchurch Lane and Borough Road.

Labour Problems

In common with most undertakings, Wallasey Corporation suffered serious staff shortages as full employment made better-paid jobs with regular hours available. Services became unreliable and thus less attractive. Additionally, the late 1960s were turbulent years on the labour relations front and Wallasey was one of many municipal undertakings hit by a strike late in 1967. The stoppage was over wages and working conditions generally. Wallasey men resumed working on 16 December but some services were still disrupted as Birkenhead men were among the last to resume nationally, going back to work on 28 December. These problems were a great incentive to advance one-man operation but, although it had been legalised, the industry was not yet ready for single manning of double-decker buses. Although the fleet had been reduced to 73 buses, of which about 60 were operational, nearly half of them were of rear-entrance design and thus unsuitable for one-man operation. Further traffic was lost as a result of strikes though Wallasey was not as badly affected as Liverpool where buses were off the road for 11 weeks and 15% of passengers were lost.

The Last Months

The Moreton-Liscard Circle 30/31 was withdrawn from 4 January 1969, with routes 7 and 8 being augmented and kept running later in compensation. In addition, route 2 was revised and extended to operate between Seacombe and Grove Road (Warren Drive) via Green Lane, Bayswater Road, Newport Avenue, Groveland Road and Grove Road, the route number 2B falling into disuse. This covered part of the 30/31. The 24 was extended back to Moreton Cross via Danger Lane and Pasture Avenue at the same time. The last service alteration under Corporation auspices was to route 22 on 14 July 1969; it was diverted via Claremount Road, Broadway, Perrin Road and Wallasey Village instead of Sandy Lane, initially for a three-month experimental period, but it was successful and became permanent. Fares were raised yet again on 26 October 1969.

On 1 December 1969, the Wallasey Corporation Passenger Transport undertaking passed to the Merseyside Passenger Transport Executive, together with those of Birkenhead and Liverpool. The Birkenhead and Wallasey undertakings were joined administratively as the Wirral Division and Seaview Road offices, being much superior to those at Laird Street, Birkenhead, were chosen as the Divisional Headquarters.

Some Latter-Day Demonstrators

At Seacombe in March 1952, RPA 771 was the first Leyland 44-seat Olympic HR44 integral bus built (in 1951), being demonstrated to operators around the country. (© K.W.Swallow)

Approaching its New Brighton terminus, CVC 124C was a Daimler Roadliner SRC6 model which made a brief appearance in July 1965, but fortunately failed to impress as their Cummins engines would later prove unreliable in a bus application. (© K.W. Swallow)

This 1967 Bristol RELL6 (LAE 770E) was the first on the open market, and with a Leyland engine was a more interesting proposition. Its dual doorways reduced seating to 35 plus standee space. (© K.W. Swallow)

The Unloved Minibuses

No.99, a 1967 Bedford J2SZ10 with Duple Midland 19-seat body that remained in the fleet for nine years. Seen on layover at Grove Road Station when new in March 1967. (© K.W. Swallow)

One of four 1962 Albion Nimbus 'midibuses' with Strachans bodies, which were of greater utility in the fleet with their 31 seats. Brand-new No.32 climbs Mossdene Road in Wallasey, in 1962. (Martin Jenkins collection / © Online Transport Archive)

Purchased 1963 from Banstead Coaches, this Trojan 13-seat was found not robust enough and soon discarded. (© Online Transport Archive / R.T. Wilson collection)

CHAPTER 6
THE WALLASEY BUS FLEET

Services were inaugurated in April 1920 with six AEC 'YC' models with bodies by E. & A. Hora of 36-38 Peckham Road, London S E, a company first registered in 1896. Powered by Tylor JB4 4-cylinder engines with 5in. bore and 6in. stroke, as used in AEC military vehicles during the 1914-18 war, they had a capacity of 7.7 litres and developed 45hp at 1,000rpm. By contemporary standards this was a very powerful engine which was useful in tackling the gradients in Manor Road and St Hilary Brow though speed on the level was modest. With a wheelbase of 14ft 2½in., the 32-seat body, with an overall length of about 27ft, overhung almost 11ft behind the rear axle. Entry was from the rear by way of a separate structure rather like a sentry box in which there was a seat for the conductor. The wooden slatted seats included a rear-facing one for five passengers along the front bulkhead and there were three upholstered places on the driver's bench seat, reached by a separate door at the front nearside. Their solid tyres and wooden seats, coupled with the granite setts and poor waterbound macadam roads of the time ensured an uncomfortable ride.

The interior ceiling was of alternate brown and yellow tongue-and-grooved boards with three rows of cut-glass lamps; the roof was of stretched canvas. A partition enabled smokers and non-smokers to be segregated. Eight destination boards were slotted in at waist level, one each on the front and rear and three each side. Fleet numbers were carried inside a ring on each cab door and on the rear.

These buses were numbered 1-6 and registered with the odd numbers HF 589-599. The Wallasey licensing office adopted the unusual system of allocating odd numbers to motor cars and even numbers to motor cycles. When the motor car series eventually reached HF 9999 in October 1934, the motor cycle series had reached only HF 4402 and all vehicles were subsequently given even numbers up to HF 9998.

In 1922, four similar buses were bought from Liverpool Corporation for £425 each. These had been purchased in 1919 to assist the tramways which had become seriously run down during the war but they were no longer required. They were identical to the Wallasey vehicles except that they had a roller blind destination indicator at the front. They were numbered 7-10 and were (strictly illegally) re-registered from KB 1968/73/79/69 to HF 1737-43 (odd numbers).

The AECs were noisy and uncomfortable and their bodies needed constant attention. In November 1925 the Council decided to scrap them and ordered five of the new all-Leyland PLSC1 Lions. AECs Nos. 1, 4, 5, 8 and 9 were withdrawn by March 1926 but 2-3 were renumbered 8-9 and continued in service for a few more months as did 6, 7 and 10.

The original No. 8 and the body of No. 1 were cannibalised for spares. Most became lorries eventually though 2-3 and 6 worked as buses for F & E Beeden, Weedon, as did 10 with Lavington and Devizes Motor Services. The body of 4 and the chassis of 5 were sold in May 1926 for £132 and 2, 3, 6, 7 and 10 were sold in November 1926 for £120 each.

The Leyland Lions

The first of the new buses (Nos. 1-2) were delivered on 8 March 1926 but did not enter service on the Harrison Drive route until 25th, by which time Nos. 3-5 had also arrived. The Leyland Lion was revolutionary in its time as a change in the method of attaching the axles to the chassis frame resulted in the level of the floor being almost a foot lower than on the earlier buses. This not only made boarding and alighting much easier for passengers but improved stability. The first Lions, of the LSC1 model (later designated PLSC1), came on the market in January 1926 and Wallasey took delivery of five in March. They were numbered 1-5 (HF4109-17 odd) and were fitted with standard 31-seat Leyland bodies with rear entrances. The saloon was divided into two compartments and there was a folding door at the top of the steps.

The Lion was powered by a 5.1-litre 4-cylinder petrol engine which transmitted its drive through a single plate clutch and 4-speed sliding mesh gearbox to a double-reduction spiral rear axle and it was the latter which gave the Lion its distinctive whine when in motion. The bodies had a planked arch roof with stretched canvas covering and a destination box, operated from the driver's cab, mounted on top of the roof at the front. Rear destination indicators were not originally fitted to Nos. 1-5 but were later mounted internally in the nearside rear window.

The PLSC1 Lion had a wheelbase of 14ft 6in. and a nominal chassis length of 24ft. The chassis cost £870 and the complete price with Leyland body was £1,270. Late in 1926 a longer version, the PLSC3, was introduced with a 16ft 5in. wheelbase and all Birkenhead Lions were of that model. However, Wallasey stuck to the shorter model and bought another five, which entered service between September 1926 and March 1927. Nos. 6-7 (HF 4531/3) had front entrances and centrally located rear emergency doors while 8-10 (HF 4535/7/9) had rear entrances like the original five; all five had two compartments and roof-mounted destination indicators front and rear. Route number boxes were fitted to all 10 Lions on the front bulkhead under the canopy late in 1933.

Lions 1-6 were withdrawn on 31 December 1935 and sold to J.W. Bell, a coach owner and garage proprietor in Moreton who sold them on. No. 1 became a fairground van but the others all saw further service as buses, mainly in North Wales; some of them used to appear regularly in New Brighton working private hires or excursions for their new owners.

Nos. 7-10 were in regular summer use until 1939 when they were all converted to emergency ambulances in October. No. 7, painted dark green, was reinstated as a public service vehicle in June 1941 and ran on a special contract to Neston for a time, after which it became a towing vehicle until the end of 1946, an ex-army Chevrolet being licensed for that duty on 1 January 1947. It was then used by the shelter cleaning crew and for winter gritting on trade plates 060 HF. No. 8 became a mobile canteen while 9 and 10 became water-carriers for the National Fire Service; 8 then became an Illuminated bus from May 1946 to November 1950 when one of its last duties was in connection with a Civil Defence recruiting campaign. On 8 November it slowly toured the Moreton area, parking at suitable locations with Sousa marches and current hit tunes blaring forth. Parts of its decorations were later incorporated in the next illuminated bus, TD4c No. 53.

In November 1954, both 7 and 8 were sold to Morris and Pulford, building contractors, who left them on the site of the factory they had built. No. 7 was used as a store while 8 was put alongside the factory with a connecting door and was used as a canteen. No. 7 was acquired by R.S. Griffiths with a view to preservation but was eventually broken up in 1961. No. 8 remained at the factory until the 1970s when it was exchanged for a Bedford OB/Beadle bus by Hollis of Queensferry with a view to its preservation. Parts of this vehicle eventually went into the preserved Ribble Lion No. 295 which was put into the Manchester Bus Museum in 1994. Nos. 9-10 were broken up, probably in 1945.

In 1926-27 three demonstrators ran in Wallasey. The first was a Leyland Leveret 20-seater which was used on the Harrison Drive-Foreshore service and also for a short run along New Brighton Promenade between the pier and Marine Park which was as far as the roadway went at that time. It was a member of the same family of models as the Lion but was rejected, apparently because of its low capacity. The general manager, H.H. Lincoln, was attracted to the Karrier marque which was made in Huddersfield and two Karrier demonstrators were supplied for trials. One was a normal-control single-decker painted silver grey which ran on the Seacombe-Harrison Drive and the cross-docks services. The other, nicknamed HMS Rodney because it was painted grey, was originally a solid-tyred double-decker but, after a period of unsatisfactory service in Wallasey, went back to Huddersfield, returning soon after as a single-decker! The performance was improved but it was still inferior to the Leyland TD1s. The double-decker was in Wallasey on 30 June 1927 when it brought a crowd back from Bidston Hill where they had been watching an eclipse of the sun.

The Karriers

These events heralded the delivery of three Karrier single-decker buses. The first (No. 11) arrived on 2 July 1927 and was a two-axle JKL with a special Hall Lewis body designed by Mr Lincoln, the total cost being £1,137-12s.-0d. It could be used as a normal 31-seat single-decker bus or, by removing four of the nearside panels, as a toastrack. This was its normal summer role on the Harrison Drive-Foreshore service but it was used during the winters of 1927-28 and 1928-29 in ordinary service, often on the cross-docks services, and again in 1933-34 on route 9 between New Brighton and Moreton. The climb up Gorsey Lane proved to be a severe trial. No. 11 entered service on 2 July 1927; in general appearance it resembled the Lions. It had a Karrier 4-cylinder engine of 6.25 litres, theoretically much more powerful than the Lions but nevertheless very sluggish; the final drive was by underslung worm gearing.

After the outbreak of war it was adapted as a mobile canteen and converted to coal gas propulsion. However, the body was destroyed by fire at the gas works and apparently No. 8 took over its canteen role. However, enough was saved for it to be used as a Fire Service tender and it was last seen by the author in this role parked on the upper storey of Seacombe ferry car park in 1941.

On 1 August 1927 two three-axle Karrier WL6 40-seat single-decker buses (12-13) entered service. They had dual door Hall Lewis bodywork and were nicknamed 'snakes' because of their low, sleek lines; their overall height was 8ft 9¾in. compared with the Lions' 9ft 0¼in. They had a wheelbase of 17ft 6in. and were powered by Dorman 6JUL 6-cylinder engines with a capacity of 6.597 litres and a maximum output of 80bhp at 2,000rpm. On delivery, the rear wheels were partly obscured by black waterproof covers but these were removed after a time as they restricted access to the wheels and tyres. Following a collision between Nos. 12 and 16 (a double-decker), both chassis were sent back to the works at Huddersfield where new frames were fitted. While they were there some unknown modifications were made to try to improve their reliability in service. Both suffered cylinder head damage due to being frozen up in February 1929, probably through being parked out of service outside. There were frequent problems with the brakes and clutch, the latter requiring regular relining. The transmission was noisy and these buses were not much seen in service after 1929. They were withdrawn in August 1931 following an accident to one of the double-decker Karriers as described below but they stood outside the depot for a considerable time before disposal showing 'MARTINS LANE', which had been added to the blinds for a service which started over a month after their withdrawal.

A feature of all the Karriers was the unusual positioning of the fleet number compared with the other buses. On Nos 12-13 the fleet number appeared behind the rear bogie on the nearside, on the waist panel on the rear, and on the driver's cab door. It had originally been intended to order twelve Karrier and twelve Leyland Titan double-decker buses but the Council wisely changed the order to six Karriers and six Leylands. The Karriers were intended to be the first double-deckers to be operated by Wallasey Corporation but they were delivered late, entering service in May and June 1928. They were certainly impressive, with 27ft 6in.-long Hall Lewis bodies seating 66 passengers, the same as a Wallasey tram. The upper deck did not extend over the driver's cab and the rear platform was reached by two steps; there was a straight staircase. A large two-line destination box was mounted above the canopy and another in the nearside platform window. Single line indicators were also suspended in the rearmost lower saloon window on each side after a time. Much aluminium was used in the construction of the bodies and the semi-bucket-type seats were upholstered in brown antique hide.

The Karrier DD6 chassis also had a 17ft 6in. wheelbase but power came from a Karrier 6-cylinder sleeve valve engine of almost 9 litres' capacity. The engines had detachable heads, 10-bearing crankshaft and a central flywheel. There was an auxiliary engine oil cooler with a small radiator mounted below the main one. Like Nos. 12-13, they originally had covers over the rear wheels but these were removed to improve access. They were mechanically troublesome vehicles, most if not all going back to the works for attention. No. 15 in particular was nicknamed 'Bloody Jonah' because of its persistent unreliability. It was towed in on its first day in service and fitted with a new engine the next day. The whole batch suffered the same problems as the single-deckers with frequent clutch and transmission failures. Because of excessive engine oil consumption, supplies were kept at Seacombe terminus so that the sump could be topped up in service. It might be added that these problems were not peculiar to Wallasey as all Karrier owners suffered in the same way.

On 18 August 1931, there was a fatal accident to a passenger who had boarded No.16 at Trafalgar Road. The collar bolts fixed to the brake drum to connect the carden shaft through the flexible coupling sheared, causing the trap in the lower deck floor to give way causing the unfortunate woman to fall on to the open propeller shaft. All the three-axle Karriers were immediately withdrawn from service. A Ministry of Transport inspector carried out an investigation on 7 and 8 September with a trial trip on No. 19. He approved measures which the Corporation proposed to take to improve safety but, despite this, in December the Council decided to dispose of them. The two single-deckers and four of the double-deckers (Nos. 14, 17-19) were sold to a dealer, the Waterloo Motor Co. in London for £130 each with an option to purchase the other two 'when the Corporation can release them'. It is assumed that No.16 was retained pending the completion of legal formalities but the retention of 15 is a mystery; perhaps it was not a runner.

They finally left Wallasey in September 1932. The double-deckers saw further service with Canvey & District Transport Co. in Essex, for whom they ran until 1936-37; Canvey also bought all the spares for £65. The offer for the 'snakes' was withdrawn and they stood outside the depot for many months, being sold to a dealer in 1933-34 for £20 and £15 respectively.

The First Titans

In October 1927, Leyland Motors unveiled the T range – the Titan double-decker and the Tiger single-decker. The Titan was to do more than anything else to influence the spread of double-decker bus operation in Britain. The two sides of the Leyland organisation – chassis and body – had collaborated to produce a perfectly matched design of lightweight double-decker bus of low overall height on a much lower-built two-axle chassis. The chassis was cranked between the axles and tapered inward at the front end, allowing a platform height of only 1ft 2in., and an 8in. step to the lower saloon which was ramped over the rear axle to give a maximum floor height of 2ft 4in., 9in. lower than the PLSC Lion, itself considered a low-loader at the time. The upper deck was reached by an open but fully panelled staircase from the open rear platform, and access to the seats, arranged in rows of four, was given by a sunken offside gangway which protruded into the lower saloon. This was not an ideal arrangement but it reduced the overall height to almost exactly 13ft, two to three feet lower than a Leviathan. The composite body was panelled with aluminium sheeting, reducing the weight to 5½ tons of which 3½ tons was chassis. This was low enough to enable pneumatic tyres to be fitted all round without restriction.

The TD1, as it was designated, took the bus engine into the six-cylinder era. Its 6.8-litre overhead camshaft engine with 4in. bore and 5½in. stroke developed 90hp at 2000rpm; it was of monobloc construction with detachable head and had undergone 80,000 trial miles during an 18-month development period. The body design introduced the 'piano front' which took the upper deck over the driver's cab instead of stopping short over the lower deck bulkhead, as was usual on earlier models. The Titan was years ahead of its competitors and the range continued in production with various modifications for forty years.

One of the model's advantages was that it increased the mobility of double-decker buses, making them accessible to places where low bridges or overhanging trees were hazards. Wallasey suffered not at all from low bridges and it is surprising, therefore, that three batches of low-bridge TD1s, totalling thirty-six vehicles, all with open platforms and stairs, were placed in service in 1928-29.

The first batch of six (20-25) arrived just too late to inaugurate the Moreton services on 1 April 1928 but they were in service four days later. They seated 27 passengers upstairs on 6 x 4 and 1 x 3 benches and 24 in the lower saloon, a total of 51. They were equipped with destination and route indicators front and rear; side indicators, mounted in the rearmost lower saloon windows on both sides, were added later. A route number box was added to the nearside of the front destination and route indicators in 1931. Despite their awkward upper deck seating, these buses were an immediate success and it was decided to purchase a further twenty-four (26-49) for the first tramway conversion, the Seabank Road route, on 20 January 1929; Leyland was inundated with orders and the bodies of these are believed to have been built by Short Brothers under licence. A further six (50-55) entered service during May and June 1929.

In the late 1920s and early 1930s chalk was applied to both nearside wheels and if it was rubbed off due to striking a kerb, the driver was disciplined. These buses were the mainstay of the fleet until 1935 when the first twelve numerically (20-31) were withdrawn at the end of the year, all being sold for £240 each, through a dealer, to the large Scottish operator, W. Alexander & Sons Ltd of Falkirk who ran them for several years, Nos. 26, 29 and 31 running until 1949, twice as long as for Wallasey. Except for No. 33, the remainder followed a year later, several having their platforms and staircases enclosed and their petrol engines replaced by diesel power units. No. 33 was converted into an illuminated tableau for the coronation of the King and Queen in 1937; its units later found homes in other buses.

The Regent Demonstrator

In July 1929, an AEC Regent demonstrator, the ninth of twelve Regents originally built, was delivered in Wallasey colours and entered service as No. 56 on 19 July. Its body, built by Short Brothers, bore a superficial resemblance to the Titans but it had a raised hump to its roof, being nicknamed 'the camel'. There was normal seating for 26 on the upper deck, the hump giving the required headroom for the central gangway. The lower deck seated 24. The Regent was in fact AEC's answer to the Titan; it was powered by an AEC A131 6.1 litre six-cylinder engine and had a new accessory, a 'self-starter', which was somewhat troublesome, perhaps because the drivers did not know how to use it properly. Corporation records reveal that there were quite a few teething troubles, principally poor pulling power and weak brakes. On 18 September, by which time it had run 6,563 miles in Corporation service, it went back to AEC for modification, returning after only two days with a new steering wheel, induction manifold, exhaust valves and springs. The power output and brakes were still unsatisfactory and a new Dewandre servo motor was fitted. It went back to AEC on 23 September, returning on 26 when it was declared 'much better' after a test. However on 7 October the AEC Chief Engineer, G.J. Rackham (who, whilst with Leyland had designed the Titan) came to Wallasey and drove the bus himself. The bus went back to AEC once more on 19 October and this time did not return until 19 November, fitted with new brake drums and shoes and new clutch parts. Thereafter, the only complaint about the brakes was that they squealed.

There is no doubt that Wallasey's operations were being used as a test bed for the Regent and the model was much improved as a result. The vehicle was originally hired but, in 1930, the Corporation decided to buy it, the hire charges of 3½d per mile being deducted from the cost. Not having been built to Wallasey specifications, it had some peculiarities. notably the single line indicators back and front and white instead of brown handrails. A route number box was not fitted until November 1933, in the form of a separate box under the canopy, as on the single-decker fleet. The rear destination indicator was modified in about 1935 or 1936 to the normal two-aperture layout. No. 56 was withdrawn in March 1938 and sold for £50 to Hardings, the local coach operator who did not run it and sold it on almost immediately. It finished up as a horse box and finally as an annex to an Essex café.

Twin Doors and Twin Staircases

In 1930, the Corporation started a policy of dividing quite small orders between two chassis manufacturers but specifying similar bodywork. At the same time, in order to tackle the problem of rapid unloading at Seacombe ferry, the general manager designed a dual-entrance, dual-staircase layout calculated to empty a bus in half the normal time. The first dual-entrance bodies were built by Davidson of Trafford Park, probably after their acquisition by Eastwood and Kenning, and were mounted on three Leyland TD1 and three Daimler CH6 chassis placed in service in April and June 1930. The three Leylands (Nos. 57-59) were mechanically similar to the earlier Titans. The Daimlers were characterised by a very small radiator; they were powered by the Daimler 5.76-litre six-cylinder sleeve valve petrol engine with fluid flywheel transmission. They were said to have a higher compression ratio than poppet-valve engines thus giving greater fuel economy and no pinking. There was also no need to adjust tappets or grind valves. Nevertheless, they were soon regarded as underpowered.

The curvaceous five-bay bodies were fully enclosed and sat well on the Leyland chassis but the Daimlers seemed to be perched high up. Official records give the height of the Leylands as 12ft 11½in. though this seems unlikely as they had high-bridge seating on the upper deck and it is probably an error for 13ft 11½in. The Daimlers were recorded as 14ft 5in high. A new feature was the provision of a small rectangular route number box to the right of the destination indicators front and rear though these were not used until 1 January 1931. None of these buses ever had side destination indicators fitted.

The front staircase turned through 180 degrees and the casing incorporated a locker in which the batteries were placed, making them much more accessible than usual. The front jack-knife entrance was controlled by a horizontal lever mounted above the front bulkhead window. The driver leaned across the bonnet and pushed this lever to the nearside to open the door.

The drawback to this design was the reduction in the seating capacity to 48 – 27 upstairs and 21 in the lower saloon. Because of the sloping profile of the Davidson buses there was no room for seats in front of the stair casing upstairs and the other seats were therefore cramped. One of the TD1s (No. 59) was later reseated to 51 but it is not known how it was done. In 1936, No. 58 was converted to run on coal gas and this is described later in this chapter.

In general, the front entrances were used only when unloading at Seacombe ferry and occasionally when there were capacity loads to be set down at New Brighton, Harrison Drive or Moreton Shore. But the conductors used both staircases constantly, collecting the upper deck fares, descending the front stairs and working through the lower saloon back to the platform.

These buses were withdrawn on 24 March 1938 though two of the Daimlers had been delicensed for the 1937-38 winter. These underpowered buses had been used as little as possible for some time and their lifetime average mileage was only 154,801 miles compared with 242,971 for their Leyland contemporaries. No. 57 was bought by A. Harding, but was not operated by him. It became a holiday home at Talacre on the North Wales coast and was still there, albeit is a derelict state, in the 1950s. Nos. 58 and 59 went to Hicks Brothers of Braintree (58 via Blackwell of Earls Colne) and both were fitted with new Park Royal bodies seeing further service into the 1950s. The Daimlers went to a dealer, No. 61 being in use by a showman by 1948.

The First Diesel Buses

In 1931, diesel buses, or 'oil-engined buses' as they were termed at the time, were very rare and Wallasey's next two acquisitions were the first to run on Merseyside, entering service in June 1931, three months before Liverpool Corporation's experimental Crossley. Mounted on AEC Regent I chassis, they were powered by AEC A155 8.1-litre engines; these were replaced by A164 engines in February 1933. The five-bay bodies were by Park Royal, successors to Hall Lewis. They seated 26 on the upper deck and 24 below and did not have the front exit and stairs. When public service vehicle licensing was introduced, these vehicles failed the test as they were slightly overweight. It is not known how this was overcome. The fleet numbers were applied at the rear of the lower deck side panels instead of at the front and on the cream waistband on the rear. This was the style used on the Karrier double-deckers and it seems likely that the earlier paint specification was used in error. The more usual paint scheme was applied in about 1934-35. These buses were numbered 63-64 and were preceded in May 1931 by four further Leyland Titan TD1 petrol-engined vehicles with 48-seat bodies by Eastwood and Kenning (Nos. 65-68). The later Kenning motor group was descended from this firm. The five-bay dual-entrance, twin-stair bodies resembled the earlier ones but were less pleasing. The front 'tween-deck' panels housing the destination equipment had the appearance of being added on as an afterthought and there was an exaggerated 'piano-front' effect. They were among the last TD1s built as the longer TD2 was already on the market, a demonstrator being placed in service in Wallasey briefly in 1932.

Like all early diesel buses, 63-64 were comparatively noisy and emitted a characteristic oily smell. They were unpopular in Wallasey and there was much comment in the press. As a result, no more diesels were bought until 1937. When they were withdrawn in 1939, their lifetime average mileage was 201,652 compared with 240,533 for the four Leylands, However, they saw many more years' service in Essex, first with Benfleet & District Motor Services, then with Westcliff-on-Sea Motor Services and 63 finally with the Eastern National Omnibus Co. Both received new utility bodies by Northern Counties in 1944. No. 63 was scrapped in 1956 and No. 64 in 1951.

Nos. 65-68 were withdrawn in March 1939 and sold to a dealer. No. 67 was converted into a lorry and 68 received a coach body, often visiting New Brighton in the post-war period in the ownership of A.E. Lingley of Sale.

The English Electric Era

The new buses for 1932 were again divided between Leyland and Daimler, all with twin-door dual-staircase bodies, by the English Electric Co. Ltd of Preston. The capacity was still 48 (27/21) but, as the front rake of the body was less and the rear was less upright, it was possible to fit four seats in front of the staircase on the upper deck in the form of a seat for three on the offside and a single seat on the nearside. Behind the latter were two more singles and the rest were in pairs. The front upper deck windows were arranged in a slight V-formation and there was a small 'piano-front'. The nearside destination indicator was fitted over the platform instead of in the rearmost saloon window.

The Leyland chassis were the new TD2 model which, following revised legislation, were 26ft long, one foot longer than the TD1 and the AEC Regent. There were other improvements, too. The Leyland petrol engines were of 7.6-litre capacity and there was a fully floating rear axle, triple- instead of single-servo brakes, and front springs anchored at the front end and shackled at the rear instead of the reversed way as had been Leyland practice. The Daimlers were of model CP6 with 6.6-litre petrol engines and pre-selector gearboxes. The Works Superintendent went to Coventry for instruction on these features and a chassis was lent to the Corporation for staff familiarisation. The Daimlers were noticeably sluggish compared with the Leylands. Three Leylands (69-71) and three Daimlers (72-74) entered service in March 1932 and a further three Leylands (75-77) in August.

All nine of these buses were formally replaced by similarly-numbered Leyland TD7c vehicles in July 1940 but, because of the wartime conditions, they were retained, unrenumbered for the time being. The Daimlers were sold to Kingston-upon-Hull Corporation in August 1941 to replace similar vehicles damaged in air raids; they were partially rebuilt by Halifax Corporation, losing their front doors and staircases, before entering service at Hull, and ran in service until January 1945. The others had a second more eventful life which is described below in the section headed Wartime Hirings.

The first part of the 1933 programme, which included tram replacements for the Rake Lane service, was very similar to that of the previous year though it comprised three Leyland TD2s (78-80) and five Daimler CP6s (81-85) which, except in matters of detail, were identical to their predecessors and eventually went to Hull with them. An unusual detail was that the three batches of TD2s, 69-71, 75-77 and 78-80 all had different styles of lettering on their destination and route blinds and could be instantly recognised from a distance.

For the final tram replacement programme on 1 December 1933, the Corporation ordered six Leyland Titan TD3s which differed from the TD2 only in the front-end treatment and the gearbox design. The bulkhead was brought forward by 3in., making for a roomier saloon, and a longer, more modern radiator was fitted. The bodywork was of similar design but much larger destination and route indicators were fitted at the front, rear and nearside. These became standard for the remainder of the undertaking's existence. Three (86-88) arrived in December and three (89-91) in January 1934. The transmission of the TD3 emitted a much more melodic note, lacking the scream of the TD1 and TD2. The later adventures of these buses are also described in Wartime Hirings.

The Roe Bodies

The intake of six TD3s was sufficient to cater for tramway replacement during the winter months when many buses would be delicensed in normal circumstances but several more vehicles were needed to cater for summer traffic. The now familiar English Electric bodywork was specified for six AEC Regents (93-98) which entered service in March. They had AEC A162 7.4-litre petrol engines and Wilson pre-selector gearboxes. However, following a visit by a Roe demonstration bus, centre-entrance five-bay Roe bodywork was ordered for a further two Regents (99-100), a Leyland TD3c (92) and two of the revolutionary AEC 'Q' side-engined chassis (101-2). Blackpool Corporation had adopted this style of bodywork, incorporating sliding doors and a split staircase rising towards both the front and rear. However, the design produced an untidy lower deck layout with several inward-facing seats. The centre-entrance Regents appeared in April followed by the Qs in July and, finally, the Leyland TD3c in August. The C suffix denoted the fitting of a hydraulic torque-converter, a fluid drive claimed as helpful to ex-tram drivers who often had difficulty mastering gear changing. By this time, however, Wallasey had already trained its tram drivers. The drive was controlled by a lever with four positions – neutral, converter mode, direct drive and reverse. It was simple to operate but harder to maintain and less fuel-efficient, consumption increasing by about one mile per gallon because of the inherent slip in the device. Refinement of the design accounted for the late arrival of No. 92.

The centre-entrance Regents and the TD3c seated 29 upstairs and 23 in the lower saloon, a total of 52, while the Qs seated 28 on each deck. One lower deck double seat on the latter was alongside the driver and was much sought after. The Qs, with the front axle set back, the engine mounted behind the front axle on the offside and single rear wheels because of the good weight distribution, was years ahead of its time and only twenty-three two-axle double-deckers were built. Four of these ran in Wirral as Birkenhead had one, as did Crosville. They were powered by the same 7.4-litre engine fitted to the Regents but the transmission incorporated a fluid coupling and Wilson pre-selective epicyclic gearbox. They were sold in 1943, probably after a period of storage, to Yeomans Motors of Hereford and both eventually became caravans. The other 1934 vehicles had an adventurous wartime and their subsequent disposal is dealt with later.

The Last English Electrics

The only two buses added to the fleet in 1935 were two small Leyland Cub 20-seaters with English Electric bodywork incorporating opening canvas roofs. They had Leyland six-cylinder 4.4-litre petrol engines and were finished in reversed livery. Their capacity was limited to 20 to meet current legislation for one-man operation and they were equipped with stand model TIM ticket issue machines. An unusual feature was the fitting of the rear destination and route number indicators at waist level. They were numbered 12-13 and whilst they were ordered with Promenade service in mind, their arrival in September ruled that out in 1935 and one was placed in service on route 9, New Brighton-Moreton via Warren Drive and Grove Road which involved some short trips on route 8 in the early morning. The other could turn up almost anywhere and was once encountered working a peak hour turn on route 14 with a conductor. One was often used on route 7, Egremont Ferry-Albion Street, in its last days but their usual summer duties were on routes 18 and 19.

The need to pay the driver led to people queuing outside the bus, sometimes in the rain, and there were many complaints and letters to the press about this. Little did the complainants know what was in store in the distant future.

Being of such small capacity, these buses were used mainly on special duties during the war and, early in 1947, they were refurbished with fixed roofs, reseated to 25 and renumbered 5-6. They ran like this until withdrawal in 1949, seeing further service with independent operators in South Wales.

In accordance with current policy, the first Titans were due to be replaced at the end of 1935 and the Corporation ordered eighteen TD4c chassis, to replace twelve TD1s (20-31) and six Lions (1-6). The bodywork was the familiar 48-seat twin-stair, dual exit English Electric six-bay, identical in all but minor detail with that fitted to the TD3s and the Regents. They were, however, fitted with torque-converters similar to that in No. 92 and the radiator was emblazoned with the words 'Gearless Bus'. The TD4 was broadly similar to the TD3 but had Lockheed vacuum-hydraulic brakes and an improved rear axle. These buses entered service on 1 January 1936 carrying fleet numbers 14-31. Once war came they had eventful careers which are described later.

The Metropolitan-Cammell Era

The year 1937 saw the beginning of a remarkably long period of bodywork standardisation because the basic shape first seen on the streets of Wallasey on 1 January 1937 could still be seen in the district until 1972. The remaining twenty-four open-staircase TD1s (32-55) were replaced by twenty-four similarly-numbered TD4cs with Metropolitan-Cammell five-bay all metal bodies seating 54 (28/26). The rear route number indicator was moved to the nearside, a feature which became standard. The dual-staircase front exit concept was abandoned because it had been found to have little practical benefit and the loss of so many seats was a serious matter. There were fifty-seven dual-entrance buses and the seat loss was equivalent to more than seven double-decker buses.

Nos. 32-53 entered service on 1 January 1937 and were mechanically similar to 14-31. Nos. 54-55 appeared one month later; they were fitted with Leyland 8.6-litre diesel engines as the manager had persuaded the committee that the economies given by the diesel engine were worthwhile and consideration should be given to abandoning the all-petrol policy as Birkenhead and many others had already done. The advantages of the diesel compared with the petrol engine were stated to be as follows:

1   Increased miles per gallon, so reduced costs (petrol 2.57d per mile; diesel 1.39d). Saving 1.18d per mile.
2   More power at lower engine revs.; will pull longer in direct drive and may be run into service from cold, thus there is less cylinder wear.
3   Less carbon formation on valve heads, therefore longer interval between overhauls.
4   Fewer auxiliary parts to give trouble.
5   Less pollution, as exhaust contains less carbon monoxide.

The points against were:
1   Slower acceleration.
2   Uneven torque when idling increases wear on torque converter clutch and slight vibration which, however, is not detrimental.

There was a strong pro-petrol lobby on the Council and the comparison of the two types was not considered conclusive when the time came to order replacements for 1938 delivery so another seven identical petrol-engined Titans of model TD5c, which was identical to the TD4c except in chassis detail, were ordered. These replaced the 'Camel' (No. 56) and the three TD1s and three Daimlers with Davidson bodies (57-62). These identically numbered buses entered service on 25 March 1938.

However, by 1938 costs were rising and the petrol lobby capitulated, finally accepting that the economies of the diesel engine could not be ignored. The order for six replacement chassis for 1939 delivery went to AEC and they were powered by AEC A173 7.7-litre diesel engines. Their Metropolitan-Cammell bodies were identical except that, because of their slightly heavier chassis, they were restricted to 52 seats, there being only 24 on the lower deck. Nos. 63-68 entered service in March 1939. Their bodies resembled those of their predecessors except for the design of the cab dash. The first two were, of course, diesels replacing diesels.

Four more Leyland Cubs, model KPZ4, Nos. 1-4, were placed in service in May 1939, their first duty was to take councillors to the opening of the Kings Parade extension. They had Burlingham 25-seat coach bodies with curved glass cove panels. They had 4.7-litre petrol engines and were used initially on promenade services. They saw limited use during the war, resuming service in 1946. They were used on tours and some town services before withdrawal in 1952, after which 1 and 2 eventually became mobile shops.

The Corporation ordered nine more replacement buses (69-77) and were fortunate enough to secure delivery in July 1940, ten months after the outbreak of war but before the government stopped normal bus production. Subsequent orders were not fulfilled until after the war. These were Leyland Titan TD7c chassis which were little different from their predecessors and fitted with the now familiar Metropolitan-Cammell bodywork seating 54. Torque converter maintenance was difficult during the war and No. 73 was fitted with a crash gearbox in July 1944.

Taking advantage of wartime relaxation of weight restrictions, thirty buses had their seating capacity increased in 1942-43; the increase was modest thus 51, 52 or 53 to 54 and 54 to 56. Nevertheless, in the exceptional conditions of the time, any increase was welcome.

There were now forty-six Metropolitan-Cammell all-metal bodied buses in the fleet (32-77) and they formed the backbone of the Wallasey Corporation fleet during the war years. They were not involved in any of the wartime hirings. The exceptional demands in the post-war era resulted in them having much longer lives than had earlier been considered normal. After the war, the Corporation continued the policy of numbering new buses with replacement numbers but quite frequently the earlier buses were still in service and there was an overlap between delivery of the new and withdrawal of the old. The old buses then had 100 added to their fleet numbers but strictly on an individual basis, not as a batch. Thus when new buses 11-34 arrived, the old 32-34 were renumbered 132-4 but none of the others. Eventually 36-7, 40, 48, 50 and 54-5 of this batch had 100+ numbers.

Withdrawal of 32-62 was spread over 1950-51 being based on vehicle condition, followed by 163-8 in 1952 and 169-70, 71-7 in 1951-2. The diesel engines of 154-55 were replaced by petrol engines after withdrawal. Sixteen vehicles were bought by Ribble Motor Services who removed the bodies and placed them on wartime chassis. In some cases the old bodies were mounted on the Wallasey chassis and sold to Bankfield Engineering of Southport; other chassis were dismantled for spares. Another sixteen buses, including all the Regents, were bought by Metropolitan-Cammell, for what purpose is unknown and some went back to Leyland who exported them to Yugoslavia. Several saw service with other operators. No. 74 became a mobile control point for Lancashire Police and was eventually preserved. Finally, No. 53 was retained and used as the coronation tableau in 1953; it was stripped down to chassis and cab and given a timber frame on which were displayed paintings by a local artist, Mr Alf Button. The nearside depicted galleons from the reign of Elizabeth I while the offside featured modern scenes. The large crown and town crest taken from the previous illuminated bus No. 8 surmounted the cab and radiator respectively. On 2 November 1956 it was used by a Liverpool multiple store's Father Christmas on a drive through the city but by 1957 it was stored in the running shed under dust sheets fabricated from old destination blinds; the superstructure was dismantled in 1959 and the remains were finally scrapped on site in May 1961.

Wartime Hirings

The reduction of services at the outbreak of war left Wallasey with a surplus of buses and this was increased in July 1940 when the nine new TD7cs arrived and their predecessors were retained in stock. Soon after the TD7cs arrived, the so-called 'phoney war' came to an end and enemy aircraft began to attack targets on Merseyside. The establishment of new munition factories created a demand for vehicles in certain places and the North Wales territory of Crosville Motor Services Ltd. was a case in point. Designated as a 'safe area', many businesses and government offices were evacuated to the coastal region, increasing the demand for transport far beyond the company's means. In addition, the giant Royal Ordnance Factory at Marchwiel, near Wrexham required two hundred buses to convey its workers.

The Regional Transport Commissioner set up an organisation for tracking down spare vehicles and arranging for them to be hired to operators in need. Drivers were usually recruited locally though some coach firms such as Yelloway Motor Services Ltd. of Rochdale, whose proprietors co-ordinated coach hirings in the North West, hired vehicles with drivers.

However, emergency services occasioned by air-raid damage intervened before more or less permanent arrangements were made. Following damage to Birkenhead Corporation's Laird Street depot in March 1941, three of the redundant TD2s (75-77) operated on the cross-docks services at peak hours with Birkenhead crews. Their destination and route blinds had already been removed but they were able to display route numbers. This lasted only for a few days. In earlier attacks, the electrified railway lines from Southport and Ormskirk to Liverpool Exchange sustained severe damage necessitating an intensive shuttle service between Bankhall or Kirkdale and Exchange. This was organised by Liverpool Corporation, as were the many bus services laid on to cover interruptions to the Liverpool Overhead Railway service. Six Wallasey TD2s (69-71, 75-77, 80) and three Daimlers (72-74) participated in these with Wallasey drivers and railway staff acting as conductors. They were joined for a time in 1941 by TD4cs 14-21. This operation continued from October 1940 to June 1941 during which period the worst of the air raids occurred, resulting in tremendous damage to the North Docks and its hinterland. The position was fluid and it is possible that these buses participated in other emergency services of which there is no record.

On 13th March 1941 many buses were damaged when a high-explosive bomb hit the waterworks alongside the former tram depot and in the case of ten of them the damage was so severe that they were sent to the body-builders for repairs, most of which was finished by the end of May. These buses were as follows:

Metropolitan-Cammell-Weymann	37, 52, 68
C.H. Roe	92, 101, 102
East Lancashire Coach Builders	17, 31, 83, 87
(on behalf of English Electric Co.)	

In about July 1941 the Marchwiel ROF came into full production and the Regional Transport Commissioner arranged for no fewer than thirty Wallasey vehicles to be hired to Crosville. These were TD2s 69-71, 75-80, TD3s 88-91, TD3c 92, AEC Regents 93-98 and TD4c's 22-31. They were all given new fleet numbers by adding L400 to their existing numbers. The Regents ran in Liverpool, being returned in August; 69, 70 and 79 went to Crewe but the others were sent to Wrexham depot where they were soon joined by 70 and 79. For an unknown reason, in November 1941 28 and 77 were returned to Wallasey where 77 re-entered service numbered 77A. In late 1945 it was again renumbered 11 and, in 1946, when the 100+ policy was adopted, it became 177. In October 1944, a visitor to Wrexham told the Wallasey rolling stock superintendent that the paintwork of 76 was in a deplorable condition and it was immediately recalled and repainted grey with red oxide wheels and mudguards at a cost of £9.14.0d (£9.70). Surprisingly it was given full transfers. Many of the others were fully or partially painted grey in parts by Crosville.

Whilst primarily intended for use on the ROF services, the Wallasey buses were seen on other services such as the long Chester-Wrexham-Llangollen route. As the war turned in favour of the Allies and new utility buses were made available to operators such as Crosville, the Wallasey buses were returned piecemeal as shown below. However, the repainted 76 remained until well after the end of the war.

October 1943	91
February 1944	90
February 1946	22, 23
May 1945	89
March 1946	27, 30
September 1945	88
October 1945	25
November 1945	26
January 1946	24, 29
September 1946	71
October 1946	78-80, 92
November 1946	69, 70, 75
December 1945	31
December 1946	76

It is interesting to note that the oldest vehicles, the TD2s, were among the last to be returned, possibly because they had a normal transmission and were preferred by Crosville to those with torque converters which used more fuel.

Daimlers 81-2 were briefly on hire to Lancaster Corporation in early July 1941 and on return went to Hull. In November 1941 they were sold to Kingston-upon-Hull Corporation as were all the other Daimlers. They replaced similar buses destroyed in an air raid. The only two TD3s not to be hired out, 86-7, were used in gas propulsion experiments, as was TD4c No. 20 (see later in this chapter). No. 86 was at Chester for a month in June 1941 in connection with the gas experiments there.

Refurbishments and Sales

Following their return from Crosville, TD3s 90-91 needed some body attention and the front staircases and entrances were removed, increasing the seating capacity to 56 (31/25); 86-88 were then done, all between January and April 1944. No. 89, still at

Crosville until May 1945, was the only bus in this batch not to be so treated. The process continued with TD4cs 14-17, 28 between June and November 1944 and 18, 19 and 21 in the first half of 1945.

The Corporation then decided that ten of the best pre-war chassis should be rebodied, six as double-deckers and four as luxury coaches, which could be used for promenade service or for private hire. The Regents (93-98) were considered for the latter role and a drawing exists, but it was decided to use TD4cs for all ten and 14, 22, 23, 25, 26 and 30 were chosen for new double-deck bodywork and 24, 27-29 for coach bodywork. The coaches went first and escaped renumbering but the others were all renumbered under the 100+ scheme as new buses arrived.

Salford Corporation was in desperate straits with its near-derelict tramway system and collected together a number of second-hand buses so that conversion could proceed while new buses on order were awaited. Wallasey agreed to sell twelve vehicles for £250 each and they were sent to Salford in November 1946. They were TD2s 69, 71, 78-80, TD3 87, TD3c 92, Regents 93-4, 97, 99, 100, some of which already had 100+ numbers before sale. They were numbered 1009-20 at Salford.

Several old buses were kept in service, viz. 170, 175-7, 186, 188-91, 195-6, 198, all except 196 (withdrawn 1946) remaining in service until 1948. Several of the 1936 TD4cs also lasted until 1948 and three (115-6, 118) until 1949. No. 120 which, it will be recalled, had a 1929 engine and gearbox, was painted green and used as a driver instruction and towing vehicle. Its chassis was used in 1951 in an exhibition commemorating the fiftieth anniversary of the undertaking, demonstrating how the various component parts of a bus worked. It remained in the garage unused for ten years until put into the yard in July 1961 and scrapped on site in September.

It is interesting to note that 119, 191 and 196 received coach bodies after sale, the second being operated by Sykes Motor Tours of Sale for whom it no doubt visited New Brighton frequently. TD2 No. 177 was eventually bought by Davies Brothers of Summerhill, thus taking it back to Wrexham.

The four chosen chassis received their 29-seat Burlingham coach bodies in 1947 and were licensed from 26 March 1948 numbered 7-10 in the correct order. They were luxuriously appointed and it was normal to have 33 seats on this chassis. They re-entered service with their original petrol engines and torque converters but 9 and 10 subsequently received the gearboxes from TD3s 188-9 when the latter were withdrawn in August 1948. The six double-deckers took rather longer, not entering service until December 1949 as 102-7, again in the correct order. Their bodies were also by Burlingham being well appointed and with seats for 56 (30/26). They retained their petrol engines but the torque converters had been replaced by gearboxes. In 1951, 103-4 received the diesel engines from TD4cs 154-5. Between March 1955 and January 1956, the TD4 chassis were replaced by new PD2 chassis and the diesel engines from 103-4 went into coaches 9-10. In June 1957 the TD4c chassis of coaches 7-8 were replaced by new PD2 chassis but the last two TD4 chassis (9-10, by then renumbered 83-4) were withdrawn in July 1961 when they were 25 years old; they were not disposed of until 1965.

The Post-War Titans

Soon after the delivery of the TD7s in 1940, an order was placed with Leyland Motors and MCW for a further twelve similar vehicles but it soon became clear that there was no prospect of delivery in the foreseeable future. In August 1942 the manager, probably due to a tip-off, placed an order for a further twelve vehicles, apparently on his own initiative, but this was endorsed by the Committee at their meeting on 18 August. It was a wise move as, with so many fleets running time-expired buses, the demand for new vehicles when the war ended was virtually insatiable but Wallasey, having had the foresight to place firm orders during the war, fared better than some other operators. Leyland, having been engaged on the manufacture of tanks, was a little slower off the mark than some other manufacturers and its first post-war product was not up to the standard of some of its pre-war models. A new series of model numbers was started and the designation of Wallasey's first deliveries of new buses for six years was PD1 (post-war double-decker 1). The order was for twenty-four chassis on Metropolitan-Cammell bodies of the same design used since 1937. They were numbered 78-101 and entered service between July and November 1946. They were powered by the Leyland E181 7.4-litre diesel engine and the transmission included a four speed constant mesh gear box. They had half-drop windows and seated 56 (30/26).

The Corporation had to wait almost two years for more new buses, a further delivery of twenty-four outwardly identical buses, numbered 11-34, being made in August and September 1948. Unfortunately, although built as 56-seaters, they were unable to pass the tilt test in that form and were altered to seat 54 (28/26). After suitable modifications, they eventually passed as 56-seaters in June 1951 and were reseated over the next nine months.

The last buses carrying the now traditional Metropolitan-Cammell metal bodywork took to the road between January and March 1951. They were mounted on the improved Leyland PD2/1 chassis powered by the new Leyland O.600 9.8-litre engine. There were synchromesh gears except on first and the handling qualities were much improved. There were some modifications to the body such as the replacement of half-drop windows with sliders and the consequent elimination of the louvres. There were no offside route indicators either. The seating was for 56 as before (30/26) and fleet numbers 35-58 were allocated.

Wallasey had bought 118 of these Metropolitan-Cammell bodies spread over fourteen years and all but seventeen were still in service when this final batch arrived.

Wider Buses

Buses which were 8ft wide, six inches more than the earlier maximum, had first appeared in Britain during the war when frustrated export orders had been diverted to home operators and run under special dispensation. From 1948 such vehicles had been permissible on approved routes but from 1950 they had been approved for general use. Wallasey's first twelve wide buses were on Leyland PD2/12 chassis with Weymann bodies and were delivered in October and November 1951, numbered 59-70. They were followed by a further ten identical vehicles (71-80) in December 1952. Using the extra width, two-column route number indicators were fitted and other refinements were saloon and cab heaters. No. 80 was fitted experimentally with fluorescent lighting for a time.

Many of the old buses were renumbered on the 100+ principle but remained in service for a time. Exceptions, however, were PD1s 78-80 which became 108-110. The post-war replacement programme was now complete except for the rebodied vehicles. New PD2/10 chassis for 102-7 were acquired between March 1955 and January 1956 on which the 1949 Burlingham double-deck bodies were mounted. Two similar chassis were purchased in May 1957 to take the bodies of coaches 7-8. The body of 8 was transferred almost immediately, the new combination being first licensed on 6 June 1957, but No. 7 did not take to the road with its new chassis until 7 April 1958. Double-deck chassis were necessary as the bodies had originally been mounted on such chassis. In June 1959, the body of 8 was taken off this chassis and placed instead on the chassis of PD1 89 which was then renumbered 8. The chassis received the body (and fleet number) of PD2 43, the original chassis of which was dismantled after a serious accident with similar bus 39. All four coaches 7-10 were renumbered 81-4 in January 1960 to make way for new buses.

Atlanteans

Wallasey was at the forefront of the changeover from half-cab front-engined buses to front-loading rear-engined vehicles which paved the way for one-man operation of double-decker vehicles. Wallasey's No. 1 was the first production Leyland Atlantean PDR1/1 and was displayed at the Commercial Motor Show as a 78-seater (44/34) in September 1958. It was the first to enter municipal service when it made its debut on route 1 as a 77-seater (44/33) on 8 December 1958, the front nearside inward facing seat over the front nearside wheel arch having been reduced from three to two. It ran for two days and on the 10th there was an official handing-over ceremony. It was powered by the same O.600 engine as the PD2s but its rear engine cover differed slightly from those fitted to later production vehicles. The transmission incorporated the Leyland pneumo-cyclic gearbox; there was no clutch pedal, gears being selected by a finger-tip lever on the steering column. Its rear route number equipment was on the offside, the first to occupy this position since the 1936 TD4cs, but all subsequent Atlanteans had it on the nearside. There was no side destination equipment on either side. No. 1 went back to Metropolitan-Cammell for adjustments and, on its return, was used for driver familiari-sation. Five further Atlanteans (2-6) arrived in September 1959 followed by fourteen (7-20) in March 1960 and another ten (21-30) between July and September 1961.

Between 1957 and 1961 46 of the 48 PD1s were withdrawn though not before 11-30 (except 24) had been renumbered 111-130. This was the last application of the 100+ scheme; 11-20 became 111-120 in January 1960 and 21-3, 25-30 received their new numbers in March 1961. Several had been stored for lengthy periods. Five were exported to Yugoslavia and many others saw service with other operators including Phillips of Holywell who bought many Wallasey buses over the years. PD2 No. 37 was retained as a driver instruction vehicle until 1970, succeeding PD2 102 which had been used between about April 1965 and August 1966. This in turn had replaced coach 82 which had been used from October 1964. Dedicated buses for driver training followed the passing of the Industrial Training Act, 1964.

No. 127 was withdrawn from service on 31 January 1962 but reinstated during August of that year making it the last PD1 double-decker in service. In May 1963, the upper deck and staircase were removed and the panels removed from the lower deck. It was then transformed in the bodyshop into a likeness of the Ferries Department cruise vessel Royal Iris, work being completed in December 1963. The interior was equipped as an information office and a power-operated sliding door was fitted on the nearside. It was 14ft 1in. high. It was allocated fleet number 84 but this was not carried and commenced its new role on 20 January 1964 after being 'launched' by Ken Dodd, the comedian. Its original regular driver was Eddie Taubman, nicknamed 'Captain' for obvious reasons. It toured towns in the North and Midlands publicising New Brighton and the River Mersey cruises. It was later decided to license the vehicle as a PSV and 22 seats were fitted. It was used in summer on Promenade route 19, commencing on 26 July 1964. Visibility was very restricted through the small side windows. Thereafter it was used on promotional work from February to May, on service June-September and delicensed October-January. It was duly transferred to Merseyside PTE but it is not clear whether it was used. In 1971 Wallasey Corporation refused to support it as New Brighton ferry had ceased to operate. It was sold for preservation to T. Hollis in January 1973 but subsequently went to the Isle of Man where it was given a new bow section and detachable funnel and painted to resemble Lady of Mann. It was still in existence in July 1986 but its ultimate fate is unknown.

In 1964, two Daimler Fleetline demonstrators and a Halifax forward-entrance Leyland PD3 were tried out in service, the latter being exchanged for Wallasey Atlantean 22 during September and October.

Small Buses

Attention now turned to the acquisition of small buses suitable for the new services which were being planned to penetrate into residential areas. The first of these arrived in November and December 1962 in the form of four Albion NS3N Nimbus front-entrance saloons fitted with 31-seat front-entrance bodies by Strachan and equipped for one-man operation. They were powered by 4-cylinder Albion 4.1-litre diesel engines. The Nimbus was regarded as a troublesome vehicle in some fleets but these do not seem to have given much trouble at Wallasey. Although regarded as 'small vehicles', their capacity was the same as the Leyland Lions which had been the standard vehicles in the late 1920s.

However, the next acquisition was certainly a small vehicle as it was a Trojan 13-seater powered by a Perkins diesel engine. New in October 1960 and numbered 100, it was purchased from Banstead Coaches Ltd, Banstead, Surrey in March 1963 and was the first second-hand purchase since 1922. The Trojan body had a mechanically operated folding door and was, of course, equipped for one-man operation. It ran in service in Wallasey until August 1966 when it was temporarily replaced by an Albion Nimbus pending the delivery, in February 1967, of a Bedford J2SZ10 with a 19-seat Duple Midland body with mechanically operated door. It was numbered 99 but the remarkable feature was that it had a Bedford 214 six-cylinder petrol engine as there had been many complaints about the interior noise made by the 4-cylinder Perkins diesel. It was strange that, after being a late convert to diesel engines in the 1930s, the very last bus to be purchased by Wallasey Corporation should have been petrol-powered.

There had been several trials of full-size single-decker vehicles during the 1960s, the main object being to ascertain whether such vehicles could be used as one-man buses on services currently using double-decker buses without inconvenience to passengers. There had been experiments of this kind in the early days of underfloor engined buses when a Daimler G6H/S36-seat dual-entrance bus, an AEC Regal Mk IV and a Leyland Olympic/Weymann HR44 integral 44-seater had been operated in 1952-53. However, the capacity was just insufficient at that time. January 1967 saw trials using Leyland Panther and AEC Swift full-size single-deckers as one-man buses on routes 1, 2 and 14 and with a conductor on route 16. In July of the same year a Daimler Roadliner and a Bristol RE standee bus were demonstrated, seeing service on routes 1, 3, 14, 16 and 26.

However, there were no more orders as Wallasey already had too many buses and, with the Transport Act 1967 on the statute book, the future seemed uncertain. Several PD2s including three eight-footers were withdrawn in the late 1960s. Burlingham 103 ran as a works bus for Castrol Ltd. at Ellesmere Port and No. 106 has been saved for preservation.

When the undertaking was handed over to Merseyside Passenger Transport Executive on 1 December 1969, there were 74 vehicles in the fleet comprising:

Leyland PD2/1	18	Nos. 40-42, 44-58
Leyland PD2/10	1	No. 43
Leyland PD2/12	20	Nos 59-62, 64-68, 70-80, (including 1 withdrawn [68])
Leyland PDR1/1	30	Nos. 1-30
Albion NS3AN	4	Nos. 31-34
Bedford J2SZ10	1	No. 99

TOTAL   74
plus 1 Training Bus (37) and Royal Iris replica bus (84).

Coal Gas Propelled Buses

Wallasey Corporation was anxious to promote the sale of compressed gas as a fuel for road vehicles. The technology had been developed early in the century and three tramway systems, Trafford Park, Neath and Lytham St Annes (the latter until 30 July 1920) had been successfully operated with this fuel. During the 1914-18 war, the London General Omnibus Co. had developed a sophisticated high-pressure system (2,000 or 3,000 psig) with substantial compressor and storage installations in depots at Hendon and elsewhere; large numbers of buses were converted. However, many thousands of vehicles converted in London and elsewhere were suddenly restricted about the end of 1917 by a government regulation restricting the sale of gas for traction because of a serious shortage of carbonising coal. Despite the serious shortage of motor spirit, the gas was more urgently required for other war work. From the early 1930s several munici-palities became interested in selling gas for traction, among them Birmingham, Chesterfield, Lincoln and Rotherham. The Chesterfield Tube Co. made considerable progress in the design of high-pressure tubular bottles and a neighbouring company, the Bryan Donkin Company, sold a large number of compression plants, essential equipment for high pressure gas filling stations.

Limited range and weight were discouraging factors and most operators lost interest after a time. In France and Germany there were national policies to maximise coal as an all-purpose fuel and there were scores of filling stations in industrial Germany for buses and commercial vehicles until the mid-1940s.

Enthusiasm in Wallasey for town gas as a fuel for motor vehicles originated in 1934 and, over a period of about 18 months, the Corporation Gas department converted five lorries. The driving force was H.B. Holliday, the Gas and Water Engineer and F.N. Booth, Chief Assistant Engineer. The gas was carried in two 6ft sealed cylinders carrying 350cu.ft, sufficient for 12 miles. A demonstration for councillors, using a 1930 Leyland TD1, No. 58, was held on 29 May 1936 and further experimental work was authorised. In February 1937 Wallasey Corporation was authorised to borrow £1,000 for gas compression equipment and recharging facilities were installed at the Gas Works in Gorsey Lane which was passed by routes 10 and 11. Bus 58 had only two gas storage cylinders necessitating 24 calls at the Gas Works daily to recharge, occupying a total of 40-50 minutes in the day. It was also very slow. On 4 August the same year, Gas Journal reported that the Motor Bus Committee had decided to discontinue experiments with a gas propelled vehicle until new and improved equipment became available. The problem was that the cylinders were so heavy that the vehicle exceeded the legal unladen weight and the Ministry of Transport was disinclined to make any concessions. Bus 58 was converted back to petrol operation and withdrawn from service in March 1938 together with five others of the same age.

Under war conditions, relaxation of weight restrictions was possible. Normal high-pressure cylinders were now virtually unobtainable and eventually some marine cylinders were found that could be adapted. However, they were unsuitable for the normal 3,000 lb. high pressure but could be approved for a working pressure of 1,800 lb. They were 7ft 10in. long and about 1ft 9in. in diameter, weighing 8¾cwt. The capacity was 2,100cu.ft, the equivalent to eight gallons of petrol, with a range of 30-35 miles. A drawing of the General Layout of Equipment for Conversion to Gas Propulsion of bus 86, a 1933 TD3, is dated 28 December 1939. It was proposed to remove the front staircase and place the cylinder upright in the stairwell, encased in a three-ply cover. Unfortunately the bus could not pass the tilt test so, on 11 January 1940, the battery blocks, weighing 3cwt 1 qr, were moved to the nearside front entrance step and cased in, and a 50lb auxiliary gas cylinder fitted to the nearside. On 17 January this was replaced with a 110 lb cylinder with a capacity of 100cu.ft. (another report says 350cu.ft.) to counterbalance the weight. The extra weight was now almost half a ton. It was passed by the Ministry of Transport certifying officer at Edge Lane, Liverpool on 19 January 1940 and put to work on route 10 which passed the Gas Works in Gorsey Lane where the gas was topped up every second trip, about every two hours. The recharging occupied 2½ minutes. The bus could be changed over to petrol at will and it operated thus at night as it was considered undesirable to refuel during the blackout. This bus does not seem to have been particularly successful at first, probably because of the tremendous extra weight, but information is scanty. It was on loan to Chester Corporation for a month in June 1941.

In July 1940, it was announced that three more Wallasey buses were to be converted to gas propulsion and a charging point would be installed at Seaview Road depot.

Manchester Corporation Leyland TD5 No. 942 had been converted and came to Wallasey during a gas conference, running on route 16 during July. However, Manchester was not impressed and 942 was converted back to diesel soon after. It is perhaps significant that only petrol-engined buses were converted in Wallasey.

There was then a hiatus as air raid damage to the Gas Works interrupted experimental work. A report in a North Western Gas Board staff magazine many years later recalled the conversion of Karrier semi-toastrack No.11 to a mobile kitchen fuelled by gas for both propulsion and cooking but it is not mentioned as gas-propelled in any departmental documents. However, it was no longer a PSV by this time. It was severely damaged by fire and, by early 1941, had been rebuilt as an Auxiliary Fire Service tender. It was parked on the upper floor of Seacombe ferry car park and it was certainly not gas propelled at that time.

The order of events is now unclear. The Gas department had been experimenting with crude naphtha as a fuel, one lorry having been successfully converted. The Engineer reported to the Gas Committee on 20 August 1942 that a special licence had been received from the Ministry of Fuel and Power for use of the total output of crude naphtha for the propulsion of motor vehicles. The special equipment for vaporising purposes and mixing liquid and vapour was developed by Mr W. Baxendale, deputy general manager, and the Corporation had applied for a patent. In April 1942, the Council was told that fifty vehicles (cars, lorries and four buses) were running on gas. In June 1942, it was agreed to make a bus available for naphtha experiments. It seems that the next two gas buses were Leyland TD4c Nos. 35 and 47 but they did not have a front staircase so their equipment must have been stowed beneath the floor. Some records indicate that this pair ran only on naphtha but they did not operate in this form for long as they needed a high fuel intake when starting from rest in order to overcome the inertia inherent in the torque converter transmission. However, their heavy gas consumption called for more frequent refuelling than had been forecast as their equipment comprised 12 cylinders, which weighed no more than the original two fitted to No. 58 and which potentially reduced the number of refuelling calls to eight of two minutes each. There were only three double-decker buses in the operational fleet with crash gearboxes (TD2 77A and TD3s 86 and 87). In addition, TD4c No.20 was given the 6.8-litre engine and the gearbox from TD1 No.33 which had been retained on withdrawal as the Coronation tableau. All four were converted in 1942 though the position with 86 is not certain. Some records state that 20 and 77A ran on naphtha and that 87 had periods on gas only and a gas-naphtha mixture.

In 1942 *Transport World* reported that the three buses being run on liquid fuel made from coal gas gave more miles per gallon than petrol. Gas was charged to the bus department at 3s. (15p) per 1,000 cu. ft which was equivalent to 1s.3d per gallon (about 6½p); the actual production cost had previously been quoted at 6½d, (just over 2½p). Unofficial Corporation records quote fuel costs as:

Diesel	2.42d
Petrol	3.98d
Naphtha	2.63d
Gas only	3.99d
Naphtha & gas	2.94d
Petrol & Gas	4.54d

On 30 July 1942, a joint meeting of the Motor Bus and Gas Committees agreed to convert the whole bus fleet. There were plans to install recharging equipment at the depot and at Seacombe ferry, the strategy being to run the gas buses at peak hours only so that they would only need recharging on the road in an emergency. But there were no further conversions, probably due to the unsuitability of the torque converter and the non-availability of high pressure cylinders. Furthermore, despite the desperate petroleum situation, the government was unhelpful and insisted that gas should be used instead of petrol, not as an addition. It is not known when gas and naphtha propulsion was abandoned; the minutes of the Motor Bus Committee are strangely silent on the whole topic; perhaps they regarded it as Top Secret though there several reports in the newspapers in the early stages. In October 1942, it was decided to supply surplus naphtha to private motor owners who had obtained the necessary licences but, in January 1943, the Gas Committee asked the Town Clerk to press the appropriate government departments for the renewal of licences for the use of naptha as a motor fuel. However, with the tide turning in favour of the Allies, the government seemed to lose interest in gas propulsion. The requirement to convert 10% of the fleet to producer gas propulsion, which was applied to many operators including Birkenhead Corporation and Crosville, did not affect Wallasey and the whole government scheme was cancelled from 30 September 1944.

Wallasey's PD2/10 Titans with Weymann bodies, purchased in 1951-2, were the first and only half-cab 8-foot wide buses in the fleet. No.70, is seen here on jointly-operated route 10 at Bromborough Cross in March 1968, the most southerly terminus reached, some six miles beyond the borough boundary. (© Ted Jones)

WCMB No.102, an example of the new PD2/10 chassis on to which the 1949 Burlingham bodies from the prewar TD4Cs were transferred in 1955. (© T.G. Turner)

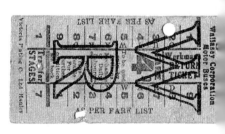

CHAPTER 7
FINANCE AND FARES

Unlike companies, municipal transport undertakings had no permanent capital and finance was raised by loans from the Public Works Loan Board. These loans had to be authorised by, originally, the Ministry of Health, which oversaw municipal affairs but, after 1921, by the Ministry of Transport. Loans were made at interest rates at the lower end of the prevailing scale and Sinking Funds were established for repayment. 'Debt Charges' was a major element in the accounts as, in effect, both capital and interest had to be repaid simultaneously. The government laid down specific repayment payments for different kinds of assets. Motor buses were paid for over seven or eight years in the pre-war era when this represented the usual life of vehicles. The war period demonstrated that buses could be made to last much longer so that 10 years became the repayment period in later years. The expected life of other assets determined the loan repayment period though 30 years was the normal maximum. Unlike a joint stock company, the general manager had no authority over financial matters which were handled by the Borough Treasurer though the appropriations would be decided by the elected representatives on the Motor Bus Committee and confirmed by the full Council.

Municipal enterprises were not in business to make profits but if they did so the surplus could be used in different ways and the table below shows the way in which the Wallasey Corporation Motor Bus department used its revenue over the life of the undertaking. If there was a surplus after everything else had been paid, it could be transferred to the General Rate Fund to reduce the rates and this, of course, was the equivalent of paying a dividend to the shareholders. However, there were always demands for fares to be reduced so that the benefits of successful trading could be passed on to the users, not all of whom were necessarily direct ratepayers and this was done on several occasions.

Some undertakings adopted a policy of accumulating provisions out of which new buses were bought thereby eliminating or reducing interest charges. In Wallasey, the tramways and motor bus accounts were kept separate although both modes were operated by the same undertaking. In their first year, the buses were subsidised by the trams to the extent of £2,368 but £1,228 of that was repaid the following year and the balance in 1928. The trams were abandoned progressively during the financial years 1928-29 and 1933-34 and the outstanding debt on the tramways undertaking, amounting to £44,686, was redeemed by the buses over this period. In addition, in each of the years ended 1934 to 1939, the General Rate Fund received £5,000 and £8,500 in 1940. During the war period, when money could not be spent on new buses, loans were paid off prematurely and £20,000 was set aside to meet possible taxation but was not needed and was transferred back to the Reserve. Payments to the rates were resumed in 1945 at £5,000 per year but, in view of the threat of nationalisation, £70,000 was paid into the rate fund in 1948-50, a practice which was criticised by the Ministry of Transport. A fares increase having been refused because of this, the undertaking then ran into debt. There were no further contributions to the rate fund and, as traffic contracted under the impetus of social changes and the growth of motor traffic, there were only four years during the remaining life of the undertaking as a separate entity when small surpluses were generated. Total contributions to the General Rate Fund amounted to £123,500 but in the final years, 1966-69, the undertaking made losses of £340,074 which were borne by the Rate Fund. The differences in these sums should be seen in the context of inflation and the purchasing power of the contributions in the years 1930-50 was much greater than the calls made in 1966-69.

APPROPRIATION OF MOTOR BUS REVENUE
1920-69

Year Ended 31 Mar	Revenue	Working Expend- iture	Income Tax	Debt Charges etc.	Surplus	Depreci- ation & Reserve	Capital Expend- iture	To Rate Fund	Deficit Met by Rates	Carried Fwd
	£	£	£	£	£	£	£	£	£	£
1921	9,174	9,002	-	640	(468)	1,000		*(2,368)		
1922	12,212	9,464	-	520	2,228	1,000		* 1,228		
1923	12,882	9,323	-	540	3,019	3,019				
1924	12,821	9,018	-	387	3,416	3,416				
1925	11,228	8,440	-	217	2,571	2,571				
1926	12,163	7,905	458	88	3,712	1,738	1,900			74
1927	19,611	8,884	265	1,014	9,448	9,322				200
1928	27,225	12,214	1,236	3,662	10,113	8,800		* 1,140		283
1929	53,540	33,376	2,240	10,122	7,802	4,890	295			2,900
1930	100,284	67,940	202	17,095	15,047	7,890	4,044	* 9,534		5,479
1931	116,933	75,588	5,028	20,800	15,517	6,322	916	*12,000		1,758
1932	131,092	83,633	5,908	23,338	18,213	6,854	80	* 6,040		6,997
1933	136,137	90,273	3,649	23,379	18,836	10,915	485	* 7,079		7,353
1934	159,750	110,667	4,362	24,371	20,350	10,000	804	#15,033		1,866
1935	174,616	131,992	-	21,674	20,950	10,000	227	5,000		7,589
1936	173,532	136,624	2,925	18,608	15,375	10,000	3,034	5,000		5,359
1937	171,693	139,850	2,215	23,383	6,245	-	555	5,000		6,991
1938	177,025	141,828	648	28,063	6,486	-	415	5,000		9,064
1939	172,971	141,570	2,036	24,739	4,626	-	1,454	5,000		7,236
1940	166,982	135,204	1,723	25,766	4,289	-	1,506	8,500		1,519
1941	151,492	126,363	3,184	24,117	(2,172)	-	1,260	-		(2,003)

Year Ended 31 Mar	Revenue	Working Expenditure	Income Tax	Debt Charges etc.	Surplus	Appropriation of Surplus				
						Depreciation & Reserve	Capital Expenditure	To Rate Fund	Deficit Met by Rates	Carried Fwd
	£	£	£	£	£	£	£	£	£	£
1942	153,424	122,952	1,903	19,346	9,223	6,750	348	-		122
1943	175,123	126,488	8,977	12,368	27,290	Ÿ20,000	363	-		7,049
1944	182,044	130,672	34,726	9,309	7,337	13,694	693	-		-
1945	196,700	146,756	21,711	1,325	26,908	14,265	5,576	5,000		2,067
1946	209,024	163,223	26,931	-	18,870	-	4,956	5,000		10,981
1947	243,244	203,469	1,296	-	38,479	5,270	2,623	5,000		36,567
1948	279,455	235,802	1,980	1,520	40,153	^29,155	6,374	40,000		41,191
1949	286,147	253,772	3,947	9,988	18,440	9,155	12,418	15,000		23,058
1950	283,036	264,283	82	13,671	5,000	-	3,820	15,000		9,238
1951	267,233	274,623	-	21,415	(28,805)	(21043)	1,476	-		-
1952	314,963	290,166	-	31,231	(6,434)	(7,235)	801	-		-
1953	355,294	310,399	-	37,914	6,981	-	2,673	-		4,308
1954	352,358	314,000	-	41,852	(3,494)	-	2,527	-		(1.713)
1955	353,164	317,625	-	42,522	(6,983)	+11,219	2,523	-		-
1956	374,439	335,373	-	41,840	(2,774)	-	1,570	-		(4,344)
1957	394,952	348,836	-	33,415	12,701	-	338	-		8,019
1958	381,308	369,886	-	30,542	(19,120)	-	1,232	-		(12333)
1959	415,865	381,508	-	23,807	10,550	-	34	-		(1,749)
1960	419,881	390,779	-	14,962	14,140	-	432	-		11,959
1961	423,392	413,352	-	21,369	(11,329)	-	484	-		146
1962	446,328	428,675	-	23,821	(6,168)	-	566	-		(6,588)
1963	437,925	437,636	-	27,873	(27,584)	-	3,060	-		(37232)
1964	464,046	447,262	-	26,547	(9,763)	-	5,188	-		(52183)
1965	467,232	451,960	-	27,596	(12,324)	-	9,579	-		(74086)
1966	462,646	457,915	-	29,268	(24,537)	-	1,716	-	70,000	(30339)
1967	443,707	481,718	-	25,993	(64,004)	-	2,147	-	50,000	(46490)
1968	401,810	470,049	-	27,713	(95,952)	-	-		142442	-
1969	417,555	512,709	-	26,441	(121595)	(=44381)	418	-	77,632	-

NOTES:
* Payment in redemption of Tramways debt.
# £10,033 to clear Tramways debt and £5,000 to rates.
^ £20,000 to Taxation Suspense 1943 then transferred to Reserve Fund 1948.
 Additional redemption of debt.
+ £7,284 superannuation equal annual contribution overcharged.
= Credit on appropriation of land & buildings to General Rate Fund.

The basic principles of fare fixing on Wallasey buses originated in tramway days. When the electric tramways commenced running in 1902, fares were 1d and 2d, children up to 12 being charged half fare. In order to discharge a statutory duty to provide cheap facilities for workmen, a 2d workmen's return was issued for any distance on early cars from Molyneux Drive or Liscard Village to Seacombe ferry. A 1d workmen's single was later introduced and these facilities were extended to Victoria Road (Rowson Street) and Earlston Road from 5 April 1907 when several 1d stages were lengthened. There was no scientific basis for fare fixing at the time; they were based on what the Committee thought to be equitable and it was quite common for councillors to campaign for the lengthening of stages, sometimes successfully. When the Poulton route was completed in 1911, there was a 3d through fare (1½d child) to New Brighton and 1d and 2d transfer tickets to enable passengers from Poulton cars terminating at Grove Road to continue their journeys on Warren Drive cars running to New Brighton. The management did not like transfer tickets but this was seen as preferable to running an unnecessary through service.

Fares remained stable until inflation towards the end of the 1914-18 war increased costs. From 16 December 1918, the 1d and 2d stages were shortened and a 1½d fare introduced. Through fares went up from 2d to 3d (4d on the Poulton route) and workmen's returns from 2d to 3d, though the 1d single was unchanged, but the last time for issue was changed from 7.45am to 7.00am. In about December 1920 or January 1921, the minimum fare became 1½d and the through fare to New Brighton on the Poulton route became 5d.

Penny fares for distances of about ¾-mile were reintroduced on 8 January 1922. Workmen's tickets remained at 1d single and 3d return but were issued up to 7.30am. The age for children's fares was raised from 12 to 14. Prepaid tickets were sold at 2d in the shilling discount. From 28 July 1922, the 1d stages were lengthened and the fares in operation between 1918 and 1920 were restored. The through fares remained at 3d and 4d and the 2d maximum on the direct routes between Seacombe and New Brighton was never restored.

When buses were first introduced on 3 April 1920, fares were relatively high and some were fixed to give protection to the trams over common sections. The through fare between Seacombe and Harrison Drive was 6d, double the tram fare, and there were originally short 1d stages though, from 10th May, the scale was revised, all the 1d fares being abolished in favour of slightly different 1½d fares. Some fares were reduced from 1 April 1925, the 6d fare coming down to 5d. Fares on the cross-docks services were also expensive, 5d being charged from Seacombe to Charing Cross and 6d from Harrison Drive or Liscard to Charing Cross. Birkenhead Corporation, having quickly learned the economics of bus operation, proposed lower fares which came into effect on 8 March 1926 when the 2d and 3d fares became 1½d and 2½d and the higher fares were reduced by 1d, the through fares becoming 4d to Liscard and 3½d to Seacombe. Cross-docks fares were again reduced from 2 April 1929. There was a general trend towards lower fares throughout the late 1920s but, except at the outer end of the Moreton routes, the minimum bus fare remained at 1½d until 16 April 1928 when a few short 1d stages were fixed. At the same time the through express fare between Harrison Drive reverted to 5d from 4d but passenger resistance soon brought it down again.

Workmen's Fares on Buses

The first tramway conversion on 20 January 1929 raised some problems over fares. It was desired to retain the tram fares as far as possible but there was no statutory duty to provide workmen's fares on buses. In the event, the facility was retained but at 2d single 4d return up to 7.00am, an increase which caused some public dissatisfaction and raised the whole question of cheap workmen's fares on buses. At the same time, 1d ordinary fares were introduced on all bus routes.

The debate on workmen's fares culminated in the introduction of workmen's day return fares at single fare for the return journey (minimum 2d) on all except the cross docks services with effect from 1 December 1930. On the New Brighton-Moreton service on which the through fare was 7d, the workmen's fare at 6d was less than the single fare. Tickets were issued on all buses leaving a terminus up to 7.40am on weekdays, officially to 'artisans, mechanics and daily labourers' though they tended to be issued indiscriminately. In the immediate post-war years, they were issued to all passengers tendering 2d or more whether requested or not but it is not known if this applied in the 1930s.

The Traffic Commissioners had circulated standard conditions on workmen's fares which were applied as conditions to all road service licences but Birkenhead Corporation did not agree with them. Their conditions were slightly different as the fare for a 2½d stage (of which there were very few) was 3d and tickets were issued up to 8.00am. Furthermore, they were made available for return over any correspondingly priced stage in any direction and not just on the day of issue. Their argument was to the effect that great hardship would be caused by adopting the Traffic Commissioners' rules which provided for day returns to be valid for return only over the same stage, the conditions which applied on most systems everywhere. Birkenhead said that many tickets were issued to casual dock workers who, if they did not get work, walked home and used the return half for the same journey the next day. Birkenhead won the day but the Commissioners initiated a campaign for equalisation of workmen's and children's fares and conditions of issue on all buses, including Crosville, in the areas served by Birkenhead and Wallasey Corporation buses.

More or less common conditions for workmen's return tickets were introduced on

1 August 1935 and on the same day these tickets were made available on the cross docks services. However, Wallasey retained their 'up to 7.40am from a terminus' time and Birkenhead the 'up to 8.00am' time which, in practice, was just about the same thing; Birkenhead still did not issue a 2½d workmen's return ticket, the return fare over their few 2½d single fares remaining at 3d. Crosville fell into line on the appropriate routes and, in some cases, extended the facilities beyond the Corporations' operating areas to avoid anomalies. There were no 2½d fares on any of the cross-docks services even though, if Wallasey practice had been applied, one could have expected to travel between New Brighton and Poulton Road for 2½d.

Meanwhile, there had been some bus fare reductions from 10 April 1932 and more from 1 December 1933 following the final abandonment of tramways in Wallasey. Fares were not entirely reduced to tramway levels; however through fares of 3½d fell to 3d on some routes, the maximum fare became 6d and there were various stage length concessions.

Average Distance of Fares – 1935

1d	.759 miles
1½d	1.359
2d	2.097
2½d	2.702
3d	3.414
3½d	4.029
4d	4.911
5d	6.015
6d	7.132

Average fare .98d per mile

Children's Fares

A ½d child's fare for 1d stages was introduced on buses in Birkenhead and Wallasey at the same time but conditions could not be synchronised as the LMS Railway objected to the change of the age for free travel from 3 to 5 years and a lengthy public hearing before the Commissioners was necessary. The changes were implemented on 1 August 1935 when free travel was granted up to 5 years and half fare up to 14 (and 16 when travelling to and from school). Children were given the benefit of fractions, the 1d fare applying to 2½d stages, 1½d to 3½d stages. 2d to 5d stages and 3d to 7d stages (of which Wallasey no longer had any).

Bus and Ferry Tickets

The first example of a ticket available by ferry and tram was issued from 14 May 1923.

It permitted a circular tour by ferry from Liverpool to New Brighton then by the Poulton tram to Seacombe and by ferry back to Liverpool at a fare of one shilling. Tickets could also be bought on the trams. As the Poulton tram ran through to New Brighton only on Sundays, it is assumed that it was available by the Warren Drive car to Grove Road. The attraction of the Poulton tram route was the extensive view across to North Wales which could be obtained (briefly) from the higher parts of the route. The facility was withdrawn for the winter by which time 885 had been sold at the ferry and 1,207 on the trams. It was resumed on Good Friday, 18 April 1924 and lasted only for one or two seasons.

Through tickets to and from Liverpool by tram and ferry had been available in Birkenhead on a selective basis since early in the century and almost universally since 1 April 1928. Birkenhead's incentive was competition from the underground Mersey Railway. Wallasey did not have this problem and hence through tickets were unknown until buses started to run to the newly-incorporated districts of Leasowe and Moreton on 1 April 1928. As this was the very day that Birkenhead started to issue bus and ferry day returns on all routes, Wallasey introduced a 1s. return but was soon obliged to come down to Birkenhead's price with a 10d return to or from Bermuda Road and an 8d to or from Leasowe Castle, the equivalent of a free trip on the ferry. Tickets were valid for return on the day of issue or following day; later Saturday's tickets were accepted on Mondays. Receipts were divided 75% to the buses and 25% to the ferries. When the summer service to Moreton Shore started in 1931, the 10d fare was applied to this also. Through tickets were not issued or accepted to or from points between St. Nicholas Road and Seacombe. Whilst Birkenhead's tickets were based on a single fare formula, Wallasey's were based purely on Birkenhead's bus and ferry ticket prices. When the Egremont Ferry-Albion Street route started on 10 June 1928, the 10d return was made available; it was reduced to 9d (children 4d) from 20 January 1929 when some fares were reduced. The original revenue split was buses 7d, ferries 3d. At first it was available only as a day return but it was brought into line with the Moreton tickets making it available also on the following day, probably when the ferry reopened after its suspension in 1932. With the bus service reduced to peak hours from 1 January 1930, this facility, designed to boost revenue on the ferry, was little used.

For the year ending 31 March 1935, only 10 tickets were issued and the through tickets were discontinued from 1 April. It is believed that the through returns were issued and accepted on route 5 between Albion Street and the top of Tobin Street but they were not valid via Seacombe ferry.

Following the opening of the Derby Bathing Pool in 1932, combined travel and admission tickets were issued in 1932-33. The 1s.4d ticket was valid for travel from Liverpool to Seacombe, then by tram or bus to Harrison Drive, and presumably by the shuttle bus to the Derby Pool (if it was running) and return. For 1s.6d, one could extend the trip to New Brighton and admission to the Promenade Pier was included as well as to the Derby Pool. The return trip was by the New Brighton ferry. No records of the number of tickets issued have been found.

In June 1935, Wallasey proposed that the 8d Leasowe Castle ticket be extended back to Fender Lane to which point Birkenhead Corporation's fare was 8d. Birkenhead objected as the distance from Woodside was 4.2 miles compared with 5.0 miles from Seacombe. Leasowe station (4.8 miles from Seacombe, and not served by Birkenhead buses) was agreed as a compromise and introduced on 1 August. The anomaly caused by charging 8d to Leasowe station (4.8 miles) and 10d to Moreton Shore (4.65 miles) was ignored as it was considered commercially justifiable to charge the same fare to Moreton Shore via Seacombe ferry as via Woodside (5.8 miles). Birkenhead would have vigorously opposed any reduction to 8d as, having been first in the field, they carried the bulk of the substantial Liverpool-Moreton Shore traffic. It is doubtful if Wallasey would have had the resources to handle any major switch from Woodside to Seacombe.

As the Moreton services were loss-making, the additional fare was welcome. In October 1935, a Transport Co-ordination Sub-Committee called for a joint report by the Ferries and Buses managers on bus and ferry contracts, bus and ferry tickets and combined tickets of the Derby Pool type but no changes were made and it seems that there was no enthusiasm in either department. The Motor Bus Department considered through tickets a necessary evil and the following figures were produced in support of this view:

| | 1934-35 | 1935-36 | 1936-37 |
	d	d	d
Total receipts per bus mile - route 4	10.36	10.31	9.87
Working expenses per bus mile	10.75	10.54	10.70
Total expenses	12.65	12.32	12.73
Ord fares per bus mile	.92	.92	.92
Bus & ferry fares per bus mile	.59	.59	.59

Figures for total tickets issued in 1935-36 and 1936-37 are also recorded in official papers but without explanation for the enormous increase in 1937 and some reservations as to their accuracy must be entertained though the fall in the total receipts per bus mile could have been caused by such an increase. The summer of 1936 was cold and wet and traffic was poor all round.

	1934-35		1935-36		1936-37	
	By buses	By Ferries	By buses	By Ferries	By buses	By Ferries
4d child	1877	9138	1949	12019	2277	9708
5d child	1541	6986	1068	10244	982	8645
8d	39264	44024	39199	51565	41369	49431
10d	15017	31353	12984	39237	55520	102456
Total	57699	91500	55200	113065	100148	170240

Bus and Ferry Contracts

In January 1938, a councillor brought a motion proposing bus and ferry contracts and it was agreed that a scheme be prepared. The proposed scale of charges for 12 journeys was as follows:

Bus fare stage	Via Seacombe ferry	Via Egremont Ferry
1d	2s 3d	2s 11d
1½d	2s 8d	3s 4d
2d	3s 1d	3s 9d
2½d	3s 6d	4s 2d
3d	3s 11d	4s 7d

Again, there was no enthusiasm for the idea as it was estimated that the loss of revenue would be £90 per month and as with other matters, it was deferred pending firm proposals by the Merseyside Co-ordination Committee.

Unemployed Allotment Holders' Tickets

In a move to assist the long-term unemployed, Wallasey Corporation made a number of allotments available rent free to enable them to grow their own vegetables. The sites were in Beaufort Drive (near St Hilary Brow), Leasowe Road (near Twenty Row) and Leasoweside, all some way from the places where most of these people lived so cheap travel tickets were made available to them at 1d for 1½d and 2d stages, 1½d for 2½d and 3d stages and 2d for 3½d and 4d stages. The tickets were issued in bulk to the Secretary of the Unemployed Allotment Holders' Association who handed them out on the basis of 10 tickets per man per week. The passenger was supposed to show his membership card to the conductor when presenting his ticket for cancellation. Tickets were valid from 17 May 1934 and the scheme flourished until 1940 after which it gradually petered out, the last hundred tickets being issued in September 1941 by which time the total issues were 23,550 1d tickets, 12,118 1½d tickets, and 12 2d tickets.

Free travel was also given to unemployed persons resident in Moreton who were required to travel to and from the Unemployment Exchange in Ferry View Road, Seacombe to sign on and off. This facility was withdrawn after consultation with the Regional Transport Commissioner after 12 April 1940.

Long Term Stability

Despite wartime inflation, fares now remained stable for almost eighteen years. Faced with falling traffic in 1940, the Corporation examined the fare structure with a view to increasing revenue. Consideration was given to increasing the price of workpeople's returns to ordinary fare plus 1d or reducing the period of availability. It was revealed that about 51% of workpeople's returns were issued in the last available half-hour ie on buses due at a terminus between 7.10 and 7.40am and by increasing the fares, including the elimination of odd halfpennies, additional revenue of £5,040 was anticipated. If the period of issue was reduced by 30 minutes, the addition would have been £7,300.

The annual number of workpeople's return tickets issued was calculated as:

Fare	No	%
2d	805,400	74.6
2½d	57,000	5.3
3d	149,000	13.6
3½d	7,200	0.7
4d	43,500	4.0
5d	16,450	1.5
6d	850	0.3
Total	107,350	
Revenue	£10,361	

Raising ordinary fares or, alternatively, reducing the length of stages were also considered but rejected. The Corporation's application in February 1940 was to increase the cost of workmen's returns but leave the period of issue unchanged. Crosville agreed to come into line between Liscard and Moreton and agreement was reached with Birkenhead Corporation whereby workmen's fares would be increased for stages between New Brighton and Central station on route 10 and for the whole route on 11 and 12, excluding stages lying wholly in the Birkenhead area. Fares between New Brighton and points beyond Central station would have been unchanged. However, the application was refused by the Regional Transport Commissioner on 12 April and fares remained the same until 1950 except for the 'temporary' abolition of the ½d children's fare from 4 July 1943 in Wallasey (28 June in Birkenhead) to discourage short distance travel; it was never reintroduced.

There were so many extra passengers that transport undertakings could not make out a case before the Commissioner for an increase. After the war, the government's policy was to keep fares low even if reserves had to be depleted in doing so. At a time when the price of every other commodity was rising, there would have been little resistance to a commensurate rise in bus fares and this artificial capping had an unfortunate effect in the post-war period when bus fares had to rise at a much higher rate than inflation and were resisted that much more strongly.

Post-War Increases

In 1950 Wallasey Corporation applied to increase all single fares by ½d and workmen's and bus and ferry returns by 1d. The Commissioners, having noted the transfer of £15,000 to the Rate Fund in each of the previous two financial years, were not satisfied that this was totally justified and it was applied in two parts. In the first part on 27 November 1950 1d fares were increased to 1½d and the minimum workmen's return fare became 3d instead of 2d. The second part took effect from 1 April 1951 when the remaining fares from 1½d upwards were increased by ½d, workmen's returns by 1d and bus and ferry tickets by 1d to 9d and 11d.

The second increase came on 30 March 1952 when all fares except the 1½d and 4d were increased by ½d. This eased conductors' work as it eliminated the odd ½d from many popular fares. Workmen's returns were abolished and replaced by work singles at approximately half fare (minimum 2d); the children's scale was amended to give the Corporation the benefit of the fractions with a minimum fare of 1½d. Bus and ferry tickets went up by 3d.

Despite continuing rises in costs, two years elapsed before there was a further increase. Like many other operators, Wallasey put the fare scale on a more scientific basis, dividing the routes into stages of approximately half a mile in length and applying a scale as follows:

1 stage	1½d	6 stages	4d
2 stages	2d	8 stages	5d
3 stages	2½d	10 stages	6d
4 stages	3d	12 stages	7d
5 stages	3½d	14 stages	8d

Workmen's singles were increased to the level of those of Birkenhead ie 1d less than single fare up to 5d then 4d for 6d fares, 5d for 7d and 8d stages and so on. A 1d children's fare was reintroduced for the 1½d adult stage. These increases took effect from 5 April 1954.

From 28 November 1955 there was a further increase in which 1½d and 2d fares remained unaltered, the 2½d fare went up to 3d, the 3d and 3½d fares to 4d and 4d fares and over were increased by 1d. Workmen's fares were abolished altogether and the bus and ferry returns were increased by 2d. The next increase was a temporary one being prompted by the Suez emergency when fuel was rationed and increased in price. It consisted of increasing by 1d the second half of the 4d stages and the 5d and all higher fares. Bus and ferry tickets went up by a further 2d. This came into effect on 31 December 1956 but was cancelled from 10 April 1957 when the emergency ceased. Further increases up to 1967 are tabulated at the end of this chapter.

The pattern of bus and ferry ticket issue remained unchanged until the inflationary fare increases of the post-war years led to regular increases. From 1 April 1951, they were increased by 1d all of which went to the buses; there was a further increase of 3d from 30 March 1952 bringing the Leasowe fare up to 1s. and Moreton to 1s.2d. A third increase, from 28 November 1955 added 2d; there was a further 2d increase from 31 December 1956 to cover the additional tax arising from the Suez affair but this was removed in April 1957 and fares reverted to their previous level on 10th. There were further increases from 1 January 1961 when the fares became more mileage based and the Leasowe station and Moreton Shore fare became 1s.8d and the Bermuda Road fare 1s.10d. By this time, the Shore traffic had lost its importance, Birkenhead's fare having been higher than Wallasey's on occasions because of increases being introduced on different dates. By 1965 the Moreton and Leasowe tickets had been merged into one fare of 2s.4d which rose to 2s.6d in 1967. The Merseyside PTE continued to issue these tickets for a time but they disappeared with the introduction of Traveller tickets on 8th January 1972.

A Liverpool-Derby Bathing Pool through ticket at 1s. (7d child) was issued from 27 May 1950; no records of the numbers issued have been found. It was issued only at the ferry and remained unchanged until withdrawn at the time of the November 1955 increase.

In 1953, in an effort to reverse the loss of ferry traffic to the railway and private car, the Motor Bus and Ferries departments at last agreed to issue a comprehensive range of weekly through contracts at a discount. However, as ferry only contracts were reduced at the same time and the through rate offered no reduction on the sum of the parts, the scheme failed. In 1959, a further attempt was made to introduce through contracts. The scheme was adopted by the Council at a special meeting, the basis being Weekly Ferry Contract plus bus fares minus 10%. Following approval by the Traffic Commissioners, the scheme came into effect on 31 May 1959. Two types of tickets were sold at the ferry from 4.00pm on Thursdays; 10 journey available over five days and 12 journey available over seven days. Separate tickets were issued for men and women to avoid transference, this having been standard practice on the ferries for many years.

However, the finances of neither undertaking were in a position to be able to give 10% discounts. It was too little too late and the through contracts were discontinued from 2 October 1960.

Concessionary Fares

After the 1914-18 war, many operators granted free travel to leg-disabled and blind ex-servicemen and eventually there was interavailability of such tickets issued by the Liverpool, Birkenhead and Wallasey transport undertakings. Books of free tickets for old age pensioners of 70 years and over were issued for free travel on Mondays to Fridays in June, July and August from June 1934, and possibly earlier. The hours of availability were 10.00am to 12.00 noon and 1.45 to 4.00pm. In Birkenhead, the times were slightly different. They could not be used on Bank Holidays or at any time on the 'holiday' services along Harrison Drive or the Promenade neither could they be used on Route 10 and, in post-war years, on Routes 13 or 18. In post-war times, in response to pressure, availability was extended throughout the year except for the month of August. They could also be used in Birkenhead on services 9, 11 and 12.

The cost of these concessions was borne by the bus operators and, in the days when there were plenty of passengers, it was not a severe burden. However, by the late 1950s, the operators could see no reason why this social cost should be borne by them and eventually the Travel Concessions Act, 1964 transferred the cost to public funds at local authority level. This led to wider application of concessions under the auspices of Merseyside PTE.

Two of Wallasey's Leyland Atlanteans take time off in the layover area at Seacombe Ferry in July 1968. This pair were 1960-batch Nos.13 and 17. (© Ted Jones)

WALLASEY CORPORATION.

Motor Omnibus Service

HARRISON DRIVE & SEACOMBE FERRY
(via LISCARD VILLAGE and MANOR ROAD).

REVISION OF FARES.

ON and after MONDAY, 10th MAY, 1920, the following Scale of FARES will take effect:

HARRISON DRIVE to or from—	MARLOWE ROAD to or from—
Marlowe Road ....1½d.	Manor Rd (junc Sea Bk Rd) 1½d.
Liscard Village .... 2d.	
Manor Rd (junc. Sea Bk Rd) 3d.	LISCARD VILLAGE to or from—
Egremont Ferry .... 4d.	Egremont Ferry .... 2d.
Seacombe Fy. (through fare) 6d.	Seacombe Ferry .... 3d.
LEASOWE ROAD to or from—	MANOR RD. (junc. Sea Bk. Rd)
Liscard Village .... 1½d.	to or from Seacombe Ferry... 2d.
Egremont Ferry .... 3d.	EGREMONT FY. to or from—
Seacombe Ferry .... 4d.	Seacombe Ferry .... 1½d.

TIMES OF DEPARTURE:—

HARRISON DRIVE—	SEACOMBE FERRY—
A.M.	**A.M.**
8-6; 8-16; 8-36; 8-46; 9-6; 9-16; 9-36; 9-46; 10-6, and every thirty minutes till 12-36 p.m.; then 12-46 and every 6, 16, 36, and 46 minutes past the hour till 10-36 p.m.	8-30; 8-45; 9-0; 9-15; 9-30; 10 a.m., and every thirty minutes till 12-30 p.m., then 12-45 p.m. and every fifteen minutes till 10-30 p.m.

APPROXIMATE TIMES OF ARRIVAL:—

At LISCARD VILLAGE : 8 minutes after leaving HARRISON DRIVE or vice versa.

At SEACOMBE : 12 minutes after leaving LISCARD VILLAGE or vice versa.

THE BUSES WILL STOP to pick up or set down passengers at—Sandy Lane, Leasowe Road, School Lane, St. Hilary Brow (junction of Claremount Road), Marlowe Road, Belvidere Road, Coningsby Drive, Liscard Village, Liscard Concert Hall, Withens Lane, Penkett Road, Sea Bank Road (junction of Manor Road), Trafalgar Road, Rice Lane, Church Street, Bell Road, Brougham Road, Borough Road, and Railway Station.

Tramways Department,
Sea View Road, 7th, May, 1920.

APPENDIX 1

Copy of a Report appended to General Manager's Report for
Tramways Committee Meeting held on 14 January 1920

WALLASEY CORPORATION TRAMWAYS

To the Chairman and Members of the Tramways Committee.

Gentlemen,

Running of Motor Omnibuses

A glance at the Map of the District will show that the Borough is already fairly well provided with transit facilities by the existing Tramways system.

The lines run broadly from north to south somewhat in the form of an ellipse, the Northern and Southern ferries forming the two ends. There is no appreciable depth of territory intervening between the various routes which are within comparatively easy distance of each other. Hence the running of a service of Buses parallel and so close to the existing lines to pick up and set down short distance passengers would not be likely to be a remunerative proposition but a through running for the convenience of long distance passengers only might meet with more success.

What seems to be most required are facilities for crossing the Borough from east to west and the intersecting of the existing Tramway routes. To effect this the buses could be employed as follows:

In a service which would intersect the existing four routes of Tramways in or about the centre of the district, which would enable passengers to travel across the Borough or transfer at any of the points of intersection to the Tramcars going north or south.

The route which suggests itself as best adapted for this purpose would appear to be along Manor Road (from Sea Bank Road) through Liscard Village via Wallasey Road and along St Hilary's Brow and Wallasey Village to Harrison Drive.

It would probably be necessary to adopt Seacombe Ferry as the eastern terminus to ensure the necessary traffic to make the route remunerative as it is doubtful whether, at the outset at least, there would be a sufficient user of the vehicles for the purpose if the terminus were fixed at the junction of Manor Road and Sea Bank Road.

PHRG

1 Should the experiment be found to supply a substantial want it would of course become a regular and permanent service and the number of vehicles required for its operation would practically absorb the six buses now on order.

2 In the event of the experiment not meeting with success, the service might either be reduced or discontinued in which case the Buses so released would be available for other work and might be employed on a service between Wallasey and Birkenhead or in the carrying of long distance or through passengers in conjunction with the existing Tramway service as already referred to, though in my opinion this ought not to be necessary if and when the tramlines are doubled as has already been suggested together with a commensurate increase in the Tramway rolling stock which would then be capable of meeting for many years any demand that might be made on it. I would take this opportunity to urge the pressing necessity of doubling of the existing single tramway track which should be done with all possible speed.

3 The question of intercommunication with Birkenhead is of importance and worthy of consideration, though if the cross route foreshadowed proves to be successful, additional Buses would have to be obtained for any further work. Assuming the necessary vehicles were available, such inter communication could be effected either by the running of each Authority's Buses into the territory of the other on defined routes or by transferring passengers at the Boundary of the two boroughs, as for example the Birkenhead Buses might discharge passengers desirous of travelling in this Borough at the Duke Street bridge who would continue their journey in the Wallasey Buses and vice versa. I have reason to think that Birkenhead would be willing to consider favourably either proposition. The terms would of course be subject to arrangement by and between the two Corporations.
The making of Gorsey Lane would greatly facilitate the running of a Bus Service between the two communities while it would also act as a connecting link with other thoroughfares in a direct line to form a main artery North and South through the Borough to the Docks and would add much to the amenities of the Borough.

4 There would also I think be ample work for a considerable fleet of Buses in the summer if run as follows:

(a)   From St Luke's Church or Gorsey Lane to Harrison Drive via Breck Road and Wallasey Village. This would not only accommodate a great number of people who are wishful to travel to Harrison Drive in the summer from the immediate district but it would also provide additional accommodation for the large number of people who come from Birkenhead in the summer and make their way to Harrison Drive and whose number would be greatly increased if the latter authority ran to Duke Street bridge.

(b)   From New Brighton or Wallasey Village, according to circumstances, to Leasowe Common. In the latter case passengers would transfer from the Tramways to the Buses at Wallasey Village.

(c)   There would also be a demand in the summer for the Buses to go further afield, notably to West Kirby and Hoylake.

(d)   Special Buses for parties of various description would also be required if it was thought desirable to supply such requirements.

5   In communication with the subject of routes it will be necessary to consider that of fares and specially the minimum fare, having regard to the fact that from actual experience it has been demonstrated that the working expenses of a Motor Bus are practically double that of an Electric Car.
Birkenhead has a minimum fare of 2d. and Sheffield charges 1½d per bus mile. Whatever the charge decided upon for Wallasey, it should be such as not to involve a loss on the Undertaking if possible while not so high as to discourage reasonable use of the Buses.

6   The following is a scale of fares recommended by the Sub-Committee appointed to consider Motor Bus Routes &c. and adopted by the Tramways Committee.

Miles	Yds		
1	590	Harrison Drive to Liscard Village	2d
	1070	Harrison Drive to Cheshire Cheese, Wallasey Village	1½d
	1300	Cheshire Cheese to Liscard Village	1½d
	1050	Liscard Village to Manor Road (Sea Bank Road)	1½d
1	640	Manor Road to Seacombe Ferry	2d
1	1690	Seacombe Ferry to Liscard Village	3d
1	1500	Egremont Ferry to Cheshire Cheese	4d
3	400	Seacombe Ferry to Harrison Drive	6d
1	200	Egremont Ferry to Liscard Village	2d

7   The running of the proposed service will be an entirely new departure in Wallasey and the question of insurance against third party and other risks should, I think, be considered.

I am, Gentlemen,

Your obedient Servant R.R. Greene

General Manager

APPENDIX 2
LISTS OF SERVICES
1 January 1932

1	Seacombe-New Brighton via Seabank Road
2	Seacombe-Harrison Drive via Manor Road & Liscard
3*	Seacombe-Harrison Drive via Borough Road, Poulton Road & Breck Road
4	Seacombe-Moreton (Bermuda Rd) via Poulton, Leasowe Rd & Reeds Lane
4~	Seacombe-Moreton Shore via Poulton & Leasowe Road
5#	Seacombe-Albion St. (Hotel Victoria) via Penkett Rd, Mount Rd and Hamilton Road
6	Seacombe-New Brighton via Church St, Rullerton Rd, Belvidere Rd & Warren Drive
7*	Egremont Ferry-Albion St. (Hotel Victoria) via Penkett Rd & Mount Rd
8	New Brighton-Moreton (Bermuda Rd) via Rake Lane, Liscard, Leasowe Rd & Reeds Lane
9	New Brighton-Moreton (Bermuda Rd) via Warren Drive, Grove Rd, Leasowe Rd & Reeds Lane
10+	New Brighton-New Ferry via Rake Lane, Liscard, Gorsey Lane & Argyle St
11+	Liscard-Charing Cross via Gorsey Lane & Park station
12+	Seacombe-Charing Cross via Dock Road & Park station
13*	Seacombe-Martins Lane (Serpentine Rd) via Trafalgar Road
~	Grove Road (Harrison Drive)-Bathing station

1 December 1933

1	Seacombe-New Brighton via Seabank Road
2	Seacombe-Harrison Drive via Manor Road & Liscard
3*	Seacombe-Harrison Drive via Borough Road, Poulton Road & Breck Road
4	Seacombe-Moreton (Bermuda Rd) via Poulton, Leasowe Rd & Reeds Lane
4A	Seacombe-Moreton Shore via Poulton & Leasowe Road
5#	Seacombe-Albion St (Hotel Victoria) via Penkett Rd, Mount Rd and Hamilton Road
6	Seacombe-Grove Road (Warren Drive) via Brougham Rd, Poulton Rd, Oxton Rd & Belvidere Rd. (extended to New Brighton summer weekends)
7*	Egremont Ferry-Albion St. (Hotel Victoria) via Penkett Rd & Mount Rd
8	New Brighton-Moreton (Bermuda Rd) via Rake Lane, Liscard, Leasowe Rd & Reeds Lane
9	New Brighton-Moreton (Bermuda Rd) via Warren Drive, Grove Rd, Leasowe Rd & Reeds Lane
10+	New Brighton-New Ferry via Rake Lane, Liscard, Gorsey Lane & Argyle St
11+	Liscard-Charing Cross via Gorsey Lane & Park station
12+	Seacombe-Charing Cross via Dock Road & Park station
13#	Seacombe-Mill Lane Circular via Martins Lane, return via Poulton Rd
14	Seacombe-New Brighton via Wheatland Lane, Liscard & Rake Lane

15# Seacombe-Mill Lane Circular via Poulton Rd return via Martins Lane
16   Seacombe-New Brighton via Church St, Liscard & Warren Drive
16   Seacombe-Grove Rd (Warren Drive) via Wheatland Lane, Liscard, Seaview Road (early mornings, weekdays only)
17   Seacombe-Grove Rd (Warren Drive) or New Brighton via Wheatland Lane, Poulton Rd, Marlowe Rd, St. George's Road
~   Grove Road (Harrison Drive)-Bathing station

1 August 1939
1   Seacombe-New Brighton via Seabank Road
2   Seacombe-Harrison Drive via Manor Road & Liscard
4   Seacombe-Moreton (Bermuda Rd) via Poulton, Leasowe Rd & Reeds Lane
4A~ Seacombe-Moreton Shore via Poulton & Leasowe Road
5#   Seacombe-Albion St. (Hotel Vic.) via Penkett Rd, Mount Rd and Hamilton Road
6   Seacombe-Grove Road (Warren Drive) via Martins Lane, Rullerton Rd & Belvidere Rd (extended to New Brighton summer weekends)
8   New Brighton-Moreton (Hardie Ave) via Rake Lane, Liscard, Leasowe Rd & Reeds Lane
9   New Brighton-Moreton (Borrowdale Rd) via Warren Drive, Grove Rd, Leasowe Rd & Reeds Lane
10+ New Brighton-New Ferry via Rake Lane, Liscard, Gorsey Lane & Bridge St
11+ Liscard-Charing Cross via Gorsey Lane & Park station
12+ Seacombe-Charing Cross via Dock Road & Park station
14   Seacombe-New Brighton via Wheatland Lane, Liscard & Rake Lane
16   Seacombe-New Brighton via Church St, Liscard & Warren Drive
16   Seacombe-Grove Rd (Warren Drive) via Wheatland Lane, Liscard, Seaview Road (early mornings, weekdays only)
17   Seacombe-Grove Rd (Warren Drive) or New Brighton via Wheatland Lane, Poulton Rd, Marlowe Rd, St George's Road
18~ Grove Road (Harrison Drive)-Bathing station
19~ New Brighton-Wallasey Beach via Promenade
20~ Grove Road (Harrison Drive)-Wallasey Beach

1 August 1949
1   Seacombe-New Brighton via Seabank Road
2   Seacombe-Harrison Drive via Manor Road & Liscard (extended to Derby Bathing Pool as required summer weekends)
4   Seacombe-Moreton (Borrowdale Rd) via Brougham Rd, Poulton, Leasowe Rd, Castleway North & Birket Ave (peak hour short journeys via Borough Rd)
4A   Seacombe-Saughall Massie via Brougham Rd, Poulton, Leasowe Rd, Moreton Shore & Pasture Rd.
4B   Seacombe-Moreton (Hardie Avenue) via Brougham Rd, Poulton, Leasowe Rd & Reeds

Lane (peak hour short journeys via Borough Road)

4S~ Seacombe-Moreton Shore via Borough Road, Poulton & Leasowe Road

5# Seacombe-New Brighton Stn via Penkett Rd, Mount Rd and Hamilton Rd

6 Seacombe-Grove Road (Warren Drive) via Martins Lane, Rullerton Rd & Belvidere Rd. (diverted to New Brighton via Sandcliffe Rd summer weekends)

8 New Brighton-Moreton (Borrowdale Rd) via Mount Pleasant Rd, Liscard, Leasowe Rd & Reeds Lane

8A New Brighton-Saughall Massie via Mount Pleasant Rd, Liscard, Leasowe Rd, Moreton Shore & Pasture Rd (Saturdays & summer Sundays)

9 New Brighton-Moreton Cross via Promenade, Greenleas Rd, Castleway North & Birket Avenue (summer Sats & Suns)

10+ New Brighton-Bromborough Cross via Rake Lane, Liscard, Gorsey Lane, Bridge St, Old Chester Rd & New Ferry

11+ New Brighton-Gorsey Hey (Hr Bebington) via Earlston Rd, Liscard, Mill Lane, Poulton Rd, Gorsey Lane, Park station, Charing Cross & Prenton

11+# Liscard-Charing Cross via Oxton Rd, Gorsey Lane, Park station

12+ New Brighton-Bebington Stn. via Seabank Rd, Seacombe, Dock Rd, Park station, Charing Cross, St. Catherine's Hospital, Bebington Rd

14 Seacombe-New Brighton via Wheatland Lane, Liscard & Rake Lane

16 Seacombe-New Brighton via Church St, Liscard & Warren Drive

16 Seacombe-Grove Rd (Warren Drive) via Wheatland Lane, Liscard, Seaview Road (early mornings, weekdays only)

17 Seacombe-Grove Rd (Warren Drive) or New Brighton via Wheatland Lane, Poulton Rd, Marlowe Rd, Claremount Road, Sandy Lane

18+ New Brighton-Arrowe Park via Sandcliffe Rd, Belvidere Rd, Poulton Bridge, Bidston Hill & Upton (daily summer, weekends in winter)

19~ New Brighton-Wallasey Beach via Promenade

20~ Grove Road (Harrison Drive)-Derby Bathing Pool

1 August 1961

1 Seacombe-New Brighton via Seabank Road

2 Seacombe-Harrison Drive via Manor Road & Liscard (extended to Derby Bathing Pool as required summer weekends)

2A# Seacombe-Harrison Dr. via Manor Rd, Liscard, Green Lane & Bayswater Rd (off-peak only)

3 Seacombe-Moreton (Town Meadow Lane) via Brougham Rd, Poulton, Leasowe Rd, Gardenside, Birket Avenue & anti-clockwise loop

4 Seacombe-Saughall Massie via Brougham Rd, Poulton, Leasowe Rd, Moreton Shore & Pasture Rd.

4S~ Seacombe-Moreton Shore via Borough Road, Poulton & Leasowe Road

5 Seacombe-Moreton (Town Meadow Lane) via Brougham Rd, Poulton, Leasowe Rd,

Reeds Lane & clockwise loop

6#   Seacombe-Grove Road (Warren Drive) via Martins Lane, Mill Lane, Marlowe Road & Belvidere Rd

7   New Brighton-Moreton (Town Meadow Lane) via Mount Pleasant Rd, Liscard, Leasowe Rd, Gardenside, Birket Avenue & anti-clockwise loop

8   New Brighton-Moreton (Borrowdale Rd) via Mount Pleasant Rd, Liscard, Leasowe Rd & Reeds Lane

9+#   Liscard-Charing Cross via Poulton Bridge & Park station

10+   New Brighton-New Ferry or Bromborough Cross via Rake Lane, Liscard, Gorsey Lane, Bridge St, Old Chester Rd & New Ferry

11+   New Brighton-Gorsey Hey (Hr Bebington) via Earlston Rd, Liscard, Mill Lane, Poulton Rd, Gorsey Lane, Park station, Charing Cross & Prenton

12+   Seacombe-Charing Cross via Dock Road & Park station

12+   New Brighton-Bebington Stn. via Seabank Rd, Seacombe, Dock Rd, Park station, Charing Cross, St. Catherine's Hospital, Bebington Rd

13+*   Trafalgar Road-Birkenhead (Central station) via Brougham Rd, Wheatland Lane, Four Bridges, Bridge St.

14   Seacombe-New Brighton via Wheatland Lane, Liscard & Rake Lane

15#   Seacombe-New Brighton Stn via Penkett Rd, Mount Rd and Hamilton Rd

16   Seacombe-Grove Rd (Warren Drive) or New Brighton via Church St, Liscard & Warren Drive

16   Seacombe-Grove Rd (Warren Drive) via Wheatland Lane, Liscard, Seaview Road (early mornings, weekdays only)

17   Seacombe-Grove Rd (Warren Drive) or New Brighton via Wheatland Lane, Poulton Rd, Marlowe Rd, Claremount Road. Sandy Lane

18+~   New Brighton-Arrowe Park-Woodchurch via Sandcliffe Rd, Belvidere Rd, Poulton Bridge, Bidston Hill & Upton

19~   New Brighton-Derby Bathing Pool via Promenade

20~   Grove Road (Harrison Drive)-Derby Bathing Pool

21   Liscard-Frankby Cemetery via Leasowe Rd & Reeds Lane (Sundays)

22#   Holland Rd (Haydock Rd)-Moreton (Town Meadow Lane) via Trafalgar Rd, Martins Lane, Liscard, Gardenside, Birket Avenue & clockwise loop (off-peak)

23*   Seacombe-Woodstock Road via Line of Docks

13 February 1967

1   Seacombe-New Brighton via Seabank Road

1A*   Seacombe-Albion St. (Hotel Victoria) via Seabank Rd & Mount Rd

2   Seacombe-Harrison Drive via Manor Road & Liscard (Mon-Fri off-peak)

2A   Seacombe-Harrison Drive via Manor Rd, Liscard, Green Lane & Bayswater Rd (school times & Sats

2B   Seacombe-Bayswater Rd via Manor Rd & Groveland Rd (Mon-Fri off-peak)

3 Seacombe-Moreton (Town Meadow Lane) via Brougham Rd, Poulton, Leasowe Rd, Gardenside, Birket Avenue & anti-clockwise loop

4 Seacombe-Saughall Massie via Brougham Rd, Poulton, Leasowe Rd, Moreton Shore & Pasture Rd. (Mon-Fri peak hours & all day Saturday & Sunday)

5 Seacombe-Moreton (Town Meadow Lane) via Brougham Rd, Poulton, Leasowe Rd, Reeds Lane & clockwise loop (Mon-Fri off-peak, Sat & Sun)

7 New Brighton-Moreton (Town Meadow Lane) via Mount Pleasant Rd, Liscard, Leasowe Rd, Gardenside, Birket Avenue & anti-clockwise loop

8 New Brighton-Moreton (Borrowdale Rd) via Mount Pleasant Rd, Liscard, Leasowe Rd & Reeds Lane

9+# Liscard-Charing Cross via Poulton Bridge & Park station

10+ New Brighton-New Ferry or Bromborough Cross via Rake Lane, Liscard, Gorsey Lane, Bridge St, Old Chester Rd & New Ferry

10A+* Liscard-Birkenhead (Kings Square) via Gorsey Lane

11+ New Brighton-Hr. Tranmere (The Wiend) via Earlston Rd, Liscard, Mill Lane, Poulton Rd, Gorsey Lane, Park station, Charing Cross & Prenton

12+ Seacombe-Charing Cross via Dock Road & Park station

13+* Trafalgar Road-Birkenhead (Kings Square) via Brougham Rd, Wheatland Lane, Four Bridges, Bridge St

14 Seacombe-New Brighton via Wheatland Lane, Liscard & Rake Lane (Mon-Fri off-peak, Sat & Sun)

16 Seacombe-New Brighton via Church St, Liscard & Warren Drive

16 Seacombe-Grove Rd (Warren Drive) via Wheatland Lane, Liscard, Seaview Road (early mornings, weekdays only)

18+~ New Brighton-Arrowe Park-Woodchurch via Sandcliffe Rd, Belvidere Rd, Poulton Bridge, Bidston Hill & Upton

19~ New Brighton-Derby Bathing Pool via Promenade

20~ Grove Road (Harrison Drive)-Derby Bathing Pool

21 Liscard-Frankby Cemetery via Leasowe Rd & Reeds Lane (Sundays)

22# Wallasey (Grove Rd) Stn-Kirkland Rd via Liscard & Trafalgar Rd

23# Gorsedale Road-Leasowe Estate (Ross Ave) via Mill Lane, Mosslands Drive

24/25# Saughall Massie-Moreton-Leasowe circular service

26* Seacombe-Liscard via Wheatland Lane, Poulton Rd & Oxton Rd

28 Seacombe-Liscard Non-Stop

30/31 Liscard-Moreton (Borrowdale Rd) Circular via Grove Road or via St Hilary Brow, Gardenside, Birket Avenue

32/33* Seacombe-Poulton Rd-Belvidere Rd-Mount Pleasant Rd-Seabank Rd-Seacombe Circular

30 November 1969

1 Seacombe-New Brighton via Seabank Road

1A*	Seacombe-Albion St. (Hotel Victoria) via Seabank Rd, Mount Road Dudley Road
2	Seacombe-Grove Rd (Warren Drive) via Manor Rd, Liscard & Claremount Rd
2A	Seacombe-Harrison Drive via Manor Rd, Liscard, St. Hilary Brow, Green Lane & Bayswater Rd (school times only)
3	Seacombe-Moreton (Town Meadow Lane) via Brougham Rd, Poulton, Leasowe Rd, Gardenside, Birket Avenue & anti-clockwise loop
4	Seacombe-Saughall Massie via Brougham Rd, Poulton, Leasowe Rd, Moreton Shore & Pasture Rd. (Mon to Fri peak hours, all day Sat & Sun)
5	Seacombe-Moreton (Town Meadow Lane) via Brougham Rd, Poulton, Leasowe Rd, Reeds Lane & clockwise loop. (Mon-Fri off-peak, Sat & Sun)
7	New Brighton-Moreton (Town Meadow Lane) via Mount Pleasant Rd, Liscard, Leasowe Rd, Gardenside, Birket Avenue & anti-clockwise loop
8	New Brighton-Moreton (Borrowdale Rd) via Mount Pleasant Rd, Liscard, Leasowe Rd & Reeds Lane
9+#	Liscard-Charing Cross via Poulton Bridge & Park station
10+	New Brighton-New Ferry or Bromborough Cross via Rake Lane, Liscard, Gorsey Lane, Argyle St, Old Chester Rd & New Ferry
10A+*	Liscard-Birkenhead (Bridge Street) via Gorsey Lane
11+	New Brighton-Hr. Tranmere (The Wiend) via Earlston Rd, Liscard, Mill Lane, Poulton Rd, Gorsey Lane, Park station, Charing Cross & Prenton
12+	Seacombe-Charing Cross via Dock Road & Park station
13+*	Trafalgar Road-Birkenhead (Bridge Street) via Brougham Rd, Wheatland Lane and Four Bridges
14	Seacombe-New Brighton via Wheatland Lane, Liscard & Rake Lane
16	Seacombe-New Brighton via Church St, Liscard & Warren Drive
16	Seacombe-Grove Rd (Warren Drive) via Wheatland Lane, Liscard & Seaview Road (early mornings, weekdays only)
21	Liscard-Frankby Cemetery via Leasowe Rd & Reeds Lane (Sundays)
22#	Wallasey (Grove Rd) Stn-Kirkland Rd via Liscard & Trafalgar Rd
23#	Gorsedale Road-Leasowe Estate (Ross Ave) via Mill Lane, Mosslands Drive
24#	Saughall Massie-Moreton-Fender Lane via Town Meadow Lane
26*	Seacombe-Liscard via Wheatland Lane, Poulton Rd, Oxton Rd & Marlowe Rd
32/33*	Seacombe-Wheatland Lane-Poulton Rd-Belvidere Rd-Mount Pleasant Rd-Seabank Rd-Seacombe Circular.

NOTES

+	Joint service with Birkenhead Municipal Transport
*	Weekday peak hours only
~	Summer only
#	No Sunday service

PHRG

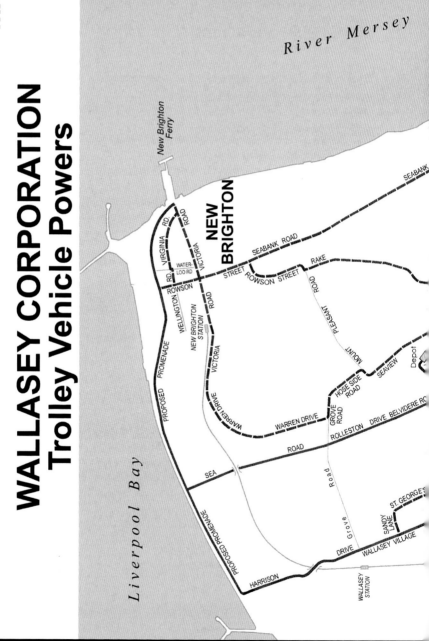

MAP 1

WALLASEY CORPORATION
Trolley Vehicle Powers

River Mersey

Liverpool Bay

New Brighton Ferry

NEW BRIGHTON

VIRGINIA RD.

VICTORIA ROAD

WATER-LOO RD

ROWSON RD.

WELLINGTON

SEABANK

SEABANK ROAD

STREET ROWSON STREET

RAKE ROAD

PLEASANT

MOUNT

Depot

SEAVIEW

HOSE SIDE ROAD

GROVE ROAD

ROLLESTON DRIVE

BELVIDERE RO

WARREN DRIVE

VICTORIA

WARREN DRIVE

NEW BRIGHTON STATION

ROAD

PROPOSED PROMENADE

SEA ROAD

Grove Road

DRIVE

HARRISON

PROPOSED PROMENADE

WALLASEY STATION

SANDY LANE

WALLASEY VILLAGE

ST. GEORGE'S

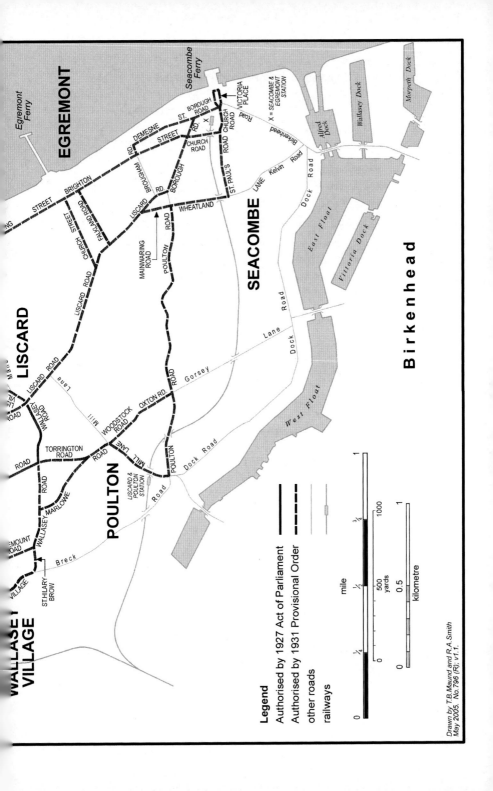

Legend

Authorised by 1927 Act of Parliament
Authorised by 1931 Provisional Order
other roads
railways

X = SEACOMBE & EGREMONT STATION

mile

yards

kilometre

Drawn by T.B.Maund and R.A.Smith
May 2005. No.796 (Ri): v1.1.

EGREMONT

LISCARD

WALLASEY VILLAGE

POULTON

SEACOMBE

Birkenhead

Egremont Ferry

Seacombe Ferry

VICTORIA PLACE

BOROUGH ROAD

DEMESNE STREET

ST. CHURCH ROAD

ST. PAULS ROAD

CHURCH ROAD

Birkenhead Road

BRIGHTON STREET

CHURCH STREET

FALKLAND ROAD

LISCARD ROAD

BROUGHAM RD

LISCARD RD

BOROUGH ROAD

WHEATLAND

MAINWARING ROAD

POULTON ROAD

Kelvin Road

Dock Road

Dock Road

Dock Road

Gorsey Lane

Lane

East Float

West Float

Victoria Dock

Alfred Dock

Wallasey Dock

Morpeth Dock

WALLASEY ROAD

TORRINGTON ROAD

WOODSTOCK ROAD

OXTON RD

MILL LANE

POULTON ROAD

LISCARD & POULTON STATION

ROAD

MARLOWE ROAD

ST.HILARY BROW

Breck

Mill Lane

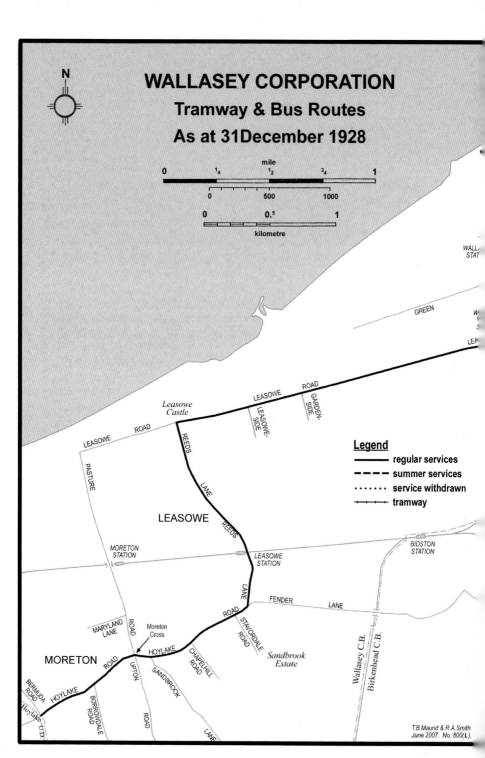

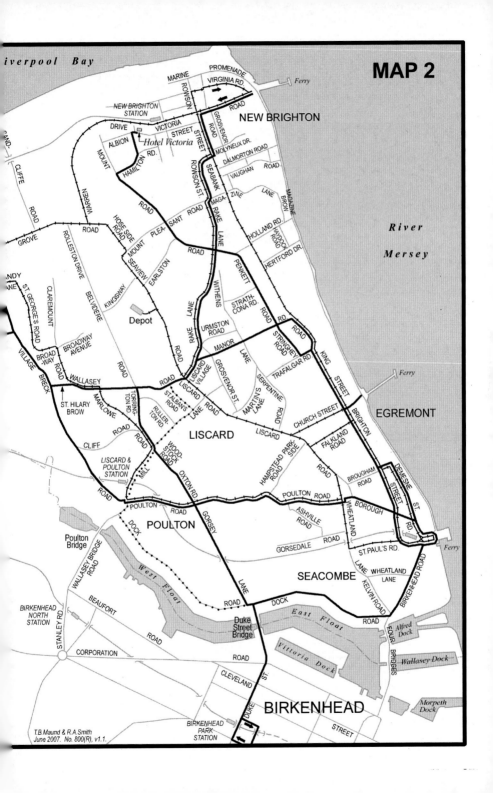

MAP 2

iverpool Bay

River

Mersey

NEW BRIGHTON

EGREMONT

LISCARD

POULTON

SEACOMBE

BIRKENHEAD

MARINE PROMENADE
VIRGINIA RD.
Ferry
ROWSON
ROAD
NEW BRIGHTON STATION
GROSVENOR STREET
VICTORIA
DRIVE STREET
ALBION RD.
Hotel Victoria
MOLYNEUX DR.
DALMORTON ROAD
SEABANK
VAUGHAN LANE
HAMILTON MOUNT
WARREN
ROAD
ZINE
MAGA-
RAKE
MAGAZINE BROW
HOLLAND RD.
HADLOCK ROAD
HOSE SIDE ROAD
PLEA- SANT ROAD
ROAD
MOUNT
SEAVIEW
EARLSTON
PENNETT
HERTFORD DR.
GROVE
ROAD
CLIFFE ROAD
ROAD
ROLLESTON DRIVE
BELVIDERE
KINGSWAY
ROAD
WITHENS LANE
STRATH- CONA RD.
ROAD
NDY
LANE
ST. GEORGE'S ROAD
CLAREMOUNT
BROADWAY AVENUE
Depot
URMSTON ROAD
MANOR LANE
STRINGHEY ROAD
RD.
ROAD
TRAFALGAR RD.
KING STREET
Ferry
VILLAGE
BROAD-WAY ROAD
BRECK
WALLASEY
ST. HILARY BROW
MARLOWE
ROAD
GORRING-TON RD.
RULER-TON RD.
ST. ALBAN'S ROAD
WOOD-STOCK ROAD
LISCARD VILLAGE
RAKE LANE
ROAD
LISCARD ROAD
GROSVENOR ST.
MARTIN'S LANE
SERPENTINE ROAD
CHURCH STREET
BRIGHTON
LISCARD
CLIFF
ROAD
MILL
LISCARD & POULTON STATION
OXTON RD.
ROAD
POULTON ROAD
GORSEY
LISCARD
HAMPSTEAD PARK SIDE
ROAD
FALKLAND ROAD
BROUGHAM ROAD
DEMESNE STREET
ASHVILLE ROAD
POULTON ROAD
WHEATLAND
BOROUGH ROAD
RD.
Ferry
Poulton Bridge
WALLASEY BRIDGE ROAD
DOCK
GORSEDALE ROAD
ST. PAUL'S RD.
West Float
LANE
WHEATLAND LANE
KELVIN ROAD
BIRKENHEAD ROAD
BIRKENHEAD NORTH STATION
STANLEY RD.
BEAUFORT
ROAD
CORPORATION
ROAD
LANE
ROAD
DOCK
East Float
ROAD
FOUR BRIDGES
Alfred Dock
Wallasey Dock
Duke Street Bridge
Vittoria Dock
DUKE ST.
CLEVELAND
BIRKENHEAD PARK STATION
STREET
Morpeth Dock

T.B.Maund & R.A.Smith
June 2007. No. 800(R), v1.1.

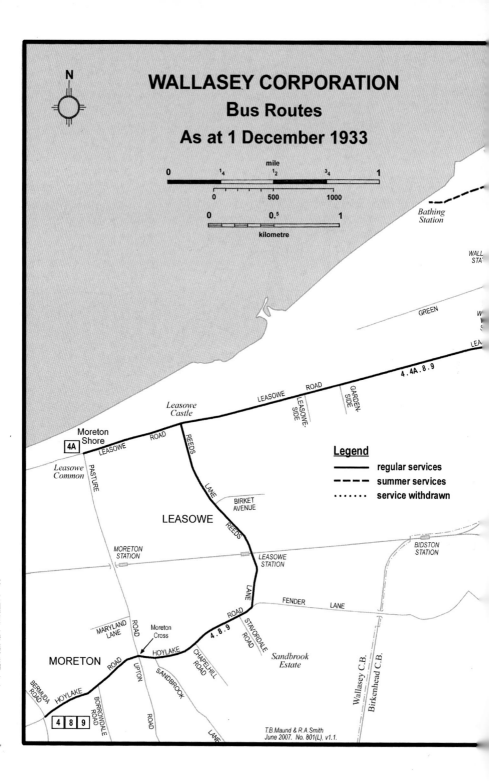

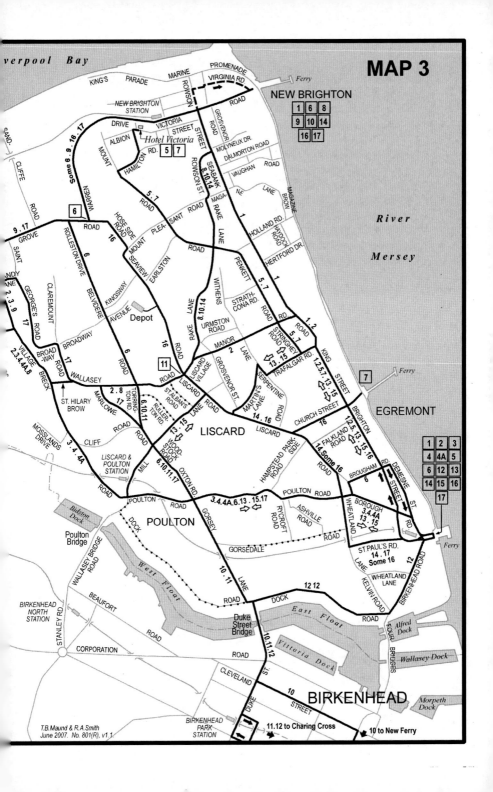

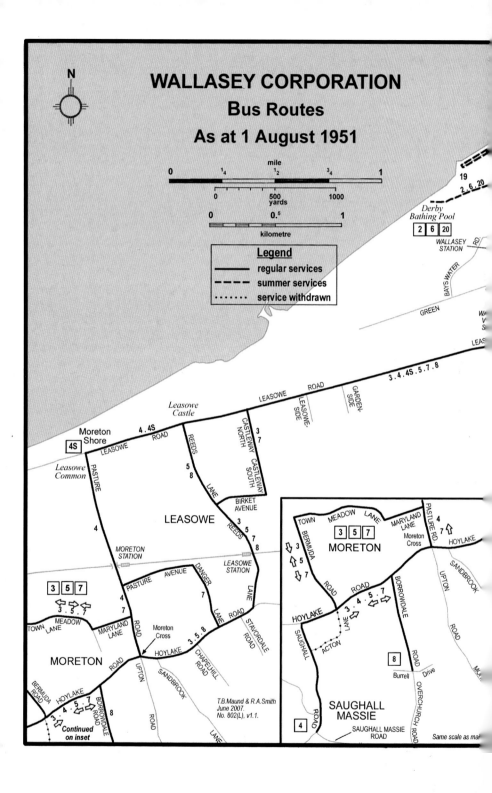

WALLASEY CORPORATION
Bus Routes
As at 1 August 1951

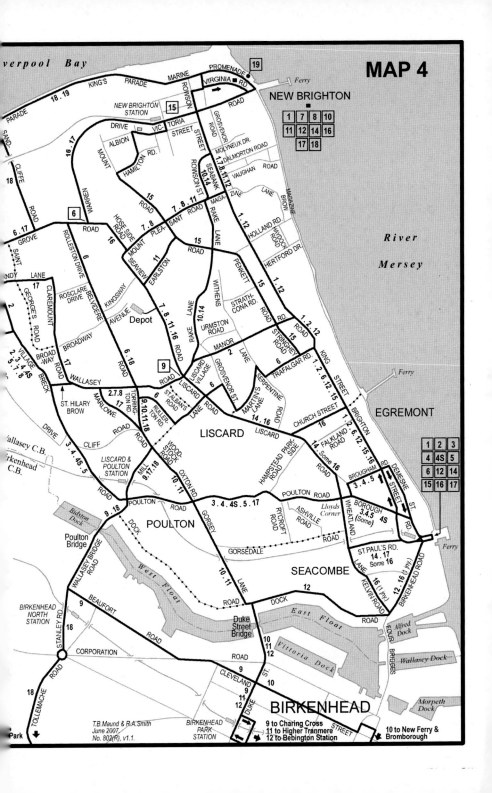

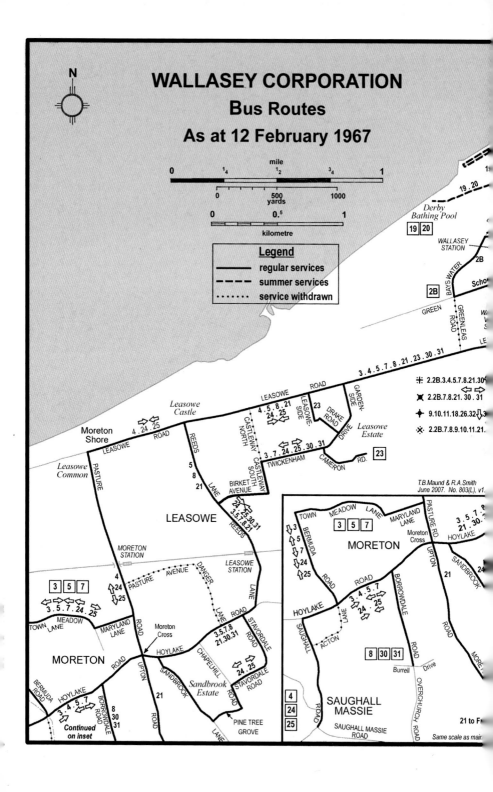

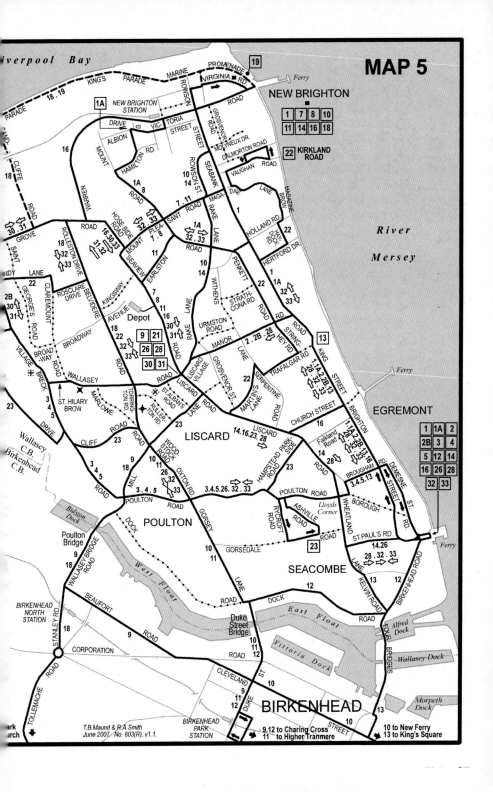

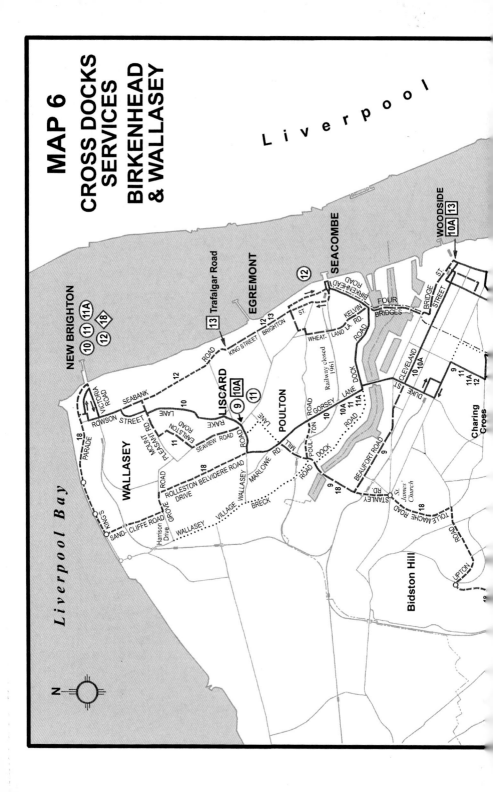

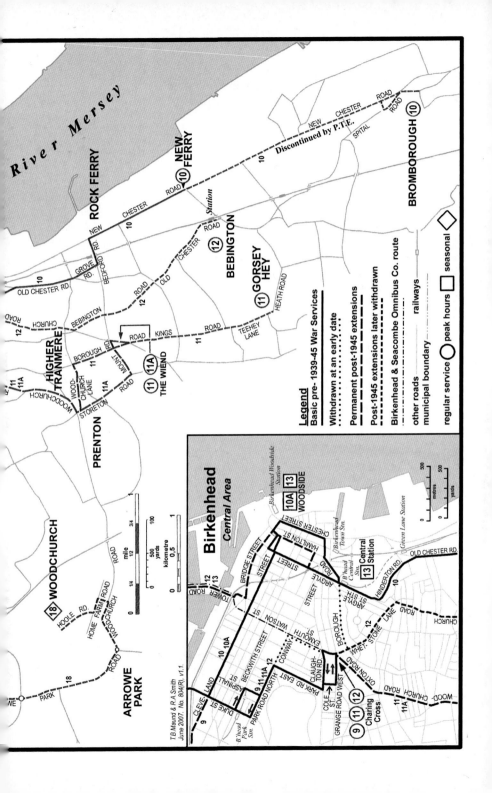

APPENDIX 4
LIVERY

The earliest buses adopted the tramway livery of primrose green and cream but there were many different shades, some probably caused by discolouration of the varnish. Some of the single-decker buses went through several paint schemes, some with the green relieved only by black beading lines. Gold lining out was employed, becoming more subdued in accordance with trends and disappearing on buses delivered after 1936. The undertaking's title on the original AECs was 'WALLASEY CORPORATION MOTOR BUSES', displayed along the side panels; from the Leyland Lions onwards it became 'WALLASEY CORPORATION MOTORS', and flanked the borough coat-of-arms. It was applied in lettering shaded with gold and blue. The three cream bands on double-decker buses were enclosed by black beading; window surrounds were also in cream. Roofs were off-white or cream until 1940 when dark grey or RAF-blue paint was applied to make the buses less visible to enemy aircraft. On the original AECs fleet numbers were applied below a coat of arms on the driving compartment doors on both sides of the vehicle and inside a circle at waist level on the rear panels. Thereafter the numbers appeared below the foremost saloon window on each side of the vehicle, low on the near and offside panels and on the rear, except on the Karriers and 1931 AECs where they were applied behind the rear wheels and on the waistband at the back. They were originally elaborately shaded up to 'Camel' No.56, less so on following buses up to Daimler 74 and thereafter in plain black numerals which were applied to earlier buses on repainting.

The livery was unaltered for very many years and the only variation was the use of reversed livery on Leyland Cubs and the Burlingham coaches. In 1952, fleet numbers on the rear were moved up to the cream band; the offside fleet number also moved up into the cream band on the cab door until 1954 after which it was applied lower down, also on the cab door. Even the early Atlanteans carried the, by then, archaic title and the large plain black fleet numbers. However, following the arrival of G.G. Harding, various livery changes were made. Fleet numbers on the cab dash began to appear in June 1961. On the rear, this was to enable the lower rear panel to be used for advertisements. Atlanteans 21-30 appeared with the existing livery modified to the extent of eliminating the fleet title and substituting neat 3in gold Gill Sans fleet numbers for the large 6in. black numerals formerly used which were really too large to fit between the black beading lines.

However a more radical change was introduced in September 1961 when No. 1 appeared with primrose green lower panels then cream up to the upper deck waistline and green upwards from there including the roof. This arrangement met with general approval and the whole fleet except 35-39, 102-7 and PD1s 127, 132 were gradually repainted, No. 63

being the first of the PD2s to be treated. However, several vehicles went through an intermediate stage with some old and some new features being carried simultaneously. The side fleet numbers now appeared above the municipal crest. The Albions were painted in reverse livery on delivery but this was changed at the first repaint.

An attempt to brighten up the interiors of buses was made in 1961-63 on the 8ft PD2s, various bright colours being used in the lower saloon and on the upper deck seat frames. It has been said that the designs originated with Mrs Harding. The original scheme consisting mainly of white ceilings and brown panels was restored during the 1966-68 repaints.

Some details of painting routines over the years have survived and it is of interest to note the changes, bearing in mind that modern paints are vastly superior to those of the 1920s. Leyland TD1 No. 23 was repainted between 15 July and 3 August 1929, the treatment comprising two days cleaning off, four coats of colour (4 days), three coats of varnish (three days) and three days lettering and lining. As it had been delivered only on 21 April 1928, it is surprising that it needed so much attention so soon.

A general painting schedule for 1935-36 comprised. Wash and rub down; clean all bad panels; two coats of green and cream, one coat of varnish paint; one coat of undercoating varnish; one coat of finishing varnish; transfers fixed. Interior: Wash down. Ceilings – two coats of white and one coat of white enamel; all iron work, two coats of paint; woodwork, one coat of paint then one coat of stain and, finally, one coat of varnish. Total cost £32-7-8d (£32.38), Man hours 388¾. The cost of repainting bus 40 in 1947 is given as £57-1-10d (£57.09) though there is no detail of the work done. An engine overhaul for the same bus cost £105. Bus 65, repainted in 1950, cost £78-9-0d (£78.45) so the trend of rising costs can be clearly discerned.

The standard Metro-Cammell body, which was available to operators from 1934 for over 18 years, graced this Leyland TD7c of 1939 at Seacombe Ferry terminus in the penultimate livery and full signwriting. (© Omnibus Society / R. Marshall collection)

APPENDIX 5
SUMMARY OF WALLASEY CORPORATION BUS FLEET
1920-69

KEY TO BODY TYPE CODE

B = Saloon Bus, H = Highbridge type double deck L = Lowbridge type double deck C = Single deck coach.

DP = Dual purpose vehicle (coach seats in bus body). Figures denote seating capacity, upper deck first.

Final letter denotes entrance position. F = Front, FD = Front with closing doors, R = Rear, RO = Rear with open staircase, C = Centre and D = Dual. TR = Toastrack.

Note: HF registration numbers. Only odd numbers were used for four-wheeled vehicles until October 1934 after which even numbers were filled up from HF 4402.

Fleet No.	Reg No.	Chassis Make and Type	Body Make	Type & Capacity	Year in Service	Year With-drawn	Notes
1-6	HF 589-99	AEC Y (Tylor)	E & A Hora	B32R	1920	1926	P
7-10	HF 1737-43	AEC Y (Tylor)	E & A Hora	B32R	1922	1926	Q
1-5	HF 4109-17	Leyland Lion LSC1	Leyland	B31R	1926	1935	
6-7	HF 4531-3	Leyland Lion PLSC1	Leyland	B31F	1926	1935-44	M
8-10	HF 4535-9	Leyland Lion PLSC1	Leyland	B31R	1927	1941	M
11	HF 4919	Karrier JKL	Hall Lewis	B31TR	1927	1939	S
12-3	HF 4923-21	Karrier WL6	Hall Lewis	B40D	1927	1931	R
14-9	HF 5337-47	Karrier DD6	Hall Lewis	H36/30R	928	1931	KR
20-5	HF 5349-59	Leyland Titan TD1	Leyland	L27/24RO	1928	1935	
26-49	HF 5851-97	Leyland Titan TD1	Leyland	L27/24RO	1929	1935-6	
50-5	HF 6033-43	Leyland Titan TD1	Leyland	L27/24RO	1929	1936	
56	HF 6069	AEC Regent 1	Short	H26/24RO	1929	1938	
57-9	HF 6701-5	Leyland Titan TD1	Davidson	H27/21D	1930	1938	
60-2	HF 6707-11	Daimler CF6	Davidson	H27/21D	1930	1938	
63-4	HF 7435-7	AEC Regent 1	Park Royal	H26/24R	1931	1939	L
65-8	HF 7439-45	Leyland Titan TD1	Eastwood & Kenning	H27/21D	1931	1939	
69-71	HF 7857-61	Leyland Titan TD2	English Electric	H27/21D	1932	1946-8	
72-4	HF 7863-7	Daimler CP6	English Electric	H27/21D	1932	1941	
75-77	HF 8253-7	Leyland Titan TD2	English Electric	H27/21D	1932	1948	NZ
78-80	HF 8259-63	Leyland Titan TD2	English Electric	H27/21D	1933	1946	
81-5	HF 8435-43	Daimler CP6	English Electric	H27/21D	1933	1941-2	

86-91	HF 9175-85	Leyland Titan TD3	English Electric	H27/21D	1933-4	1946-8	YZ
92	HF 9381	Leyland Titan TD3c	Roe	H29/23C	1934	1946	
93-8	HF 9383-93	AEC Regent 1	English Electric	H27/21D	1934	1946-8	
99-100	HF 9395-7	AEC Regent 1	Roe	H29/23C	1934	1946	
101-2	HF 9399-401	AEC Q	Roe	H28/28C	1934	1943	
12-3	HF 5008-10	Leyland Cub KP3	English Electric	B20F	1935	1949	T
14-31	HF 5224-58	Leyland Titan TD4c	English Electric	H27/21D	1936	1948-9	UYZ
32-55	HF 6208-54	Leyland Titan TD4c	Metro-Cammell	H28/26R	1937	1950-1	VZ
56-62	HF 7268-80	Leyland Titan TD5c	Metro-Cammell	H28/26R	1938	1950-1	
63-8	HF 8180-90	AEC Regent 1	Metro-Cammell	H28/26R	1939	1952	
1-4	HF 8656-62	Leyland Cub KP4	Burlingham	DP25F	1939	1952-3	
69-77	HF 9116-32	Leyland Titan TD7c	Metro-Cammell	H28/26R	1940	1951-2	
78-101	HF 9574-9620	Leyland Titan PD1	Metro-Cammell	H30/26R	1946	1957-60	W
11-22	AHF 189-200	Leyland Titan PD1	MetroCammell	H28/26R	1948	1961-2	
23-34	AHF 361-72	Leyland Titan PD1	Metro-Cammell	H28/26R	1948	1961-2	X
35-58	AHF 831-54	Leyland Titan PD2/1	Metro-Cammell	H30/26R	1951	1965-72	W
59-70	BHF 45-56	Leyland Titan PD2/12	Weymann 8ft	H30/26R	1951	1968-73	
71-80	BHF 490-9	Leyland Titan PD2/12	Weymann 8ft	H30/26R	1952	1971-4	
102-7	CHF 561-6	Leyland Titan PD2/10	Burlingham	H30/26R	1955-6	1965	U
7-8	EHF 391-2	Leyland Titan PD2/10	Burlingham	C29F	1957	1966	UW
1-6	FHF 451-6	Leyland Atlantean PDR1/1	Metro Cammell	H44/33FD	1958-9	1973-8	
7-20	HHF 7-20	Leyland Atlantean PDR1/1	Metro Cammell	H44/33FD	1960	1973-7	
21-30	JHF 821-30	Leyland Atlantean PDR1/1	Metro Cammell	H44/33FD	1961	1974-9	
31-4	LHF 31-4	Albion Nimbus NS3AN	Strachan	DP31F	1962	1972-4	
100	601 SPA	Trojan	Trojan	B13F	1963	1966	+
99	DHF 162E	Bedford J2SZ10	Duple Midland	B19F	1967	1975	

NOTES:

+ Ex-Banstead Coaches Ltd, Banstead, Surrey.

K Not consecutive; 18 was HF 5343 and 17 was HF 5345.

L First diesel engined buses.

M 7-10 converted to ambulances 9/39. 8,10 returned 12/40; 8 to mobile canteen, 10 to Public Assistance. Committee 12/40. 7,9 returned 6/41. 9/10 sold 7/41.

N 77 renumbered 77A 11/41, then 11 late 1945 and 177 late 1946.

P 2, 3 renumbered 8, 9 in March 1926, following delivery of new buses.

Q Purchased from Liverpool Corporation and re-registered from KB 1968-9/73/9

R Three-axle vehicles.

S Delicensed 9/39. CofF expired 28.3.40 and officially withdrawn. To AFS canteen and coal gas propulsion 12/40 and burnt out. Chassis sold to AFS for fire tender 1/41.

T Rebuilt as B25F 1947 and renumbered 5, 6

U 14, 22-3, 25-6 rebodied by Burlingham H30/26R 1949 and renumbered 102-7. Bodies transferred to new chassis 1955-6. 24, 27-9 rebodied by Burlingham C29F 1948 and renumbered 7-10. Bodies of 7-8 transferred to new chassis 1957. 9-10 renumbered 83-4 in 1959

V   32-53 had petrol engines. 54-55 had diesel engines.

W   Body of 89 scrapped after an accident in 1959. Coach body from 8 (EHF 392) mounted on chassis in 1959. EHF 392 received body from 43 the chassis of which was scrapped. 78-80 were renumbered 108-110 in December 1952.

X   27 received body in form of replica of Royal Iris cruise ship in 1963 and renumbered 84 (see back cover).

Y   TD3s 90-91 and TD4c 14-19, 21 & 28 rebuilt as H31/25R by removing front staircases and entrances in 1944-45.

Z   No. 58 (HF 6703) was the experimental coal-gas powered bus 1936-38 and at various times between   1940-44 buses 20, 35, 47, 77A, 86 & 87 operated on coal gas or naphtha fuel.

From time to time from 1940, buses were retained after their replacements had arrived and 100 was added to their fleet numbers from 1946 onwards.

Ex-Wallasey No.101, one of the 1934 Roe-bodied 56-seater AEC 'Q's, had a further lease of life from 1946 in the fleet of G.H.Yeomans of Canon Pyon, deep in rural Herefordshire. It is seen here in Hereford's country bus station. (The late C.F. Klapper)

APPENDIX 6
THE ANNALS OF WALLASEY TRANSPORT

c 09.1861	Seacombe-New Brighton via Liscard & Rake Lane Horse bus (James Hall)
by 1868	Several omnibus services in operation
28.06.1879	Wallasey Tramway Co.'s line opened from Church Road, Seacombe to Field Road
05.01.1880	New Seacombe ferry terminal opened and tramway extended to Ferry Approach
? 1880	Seacombe-Molyneux Drive by H. Gardner's Seacombe & Magazines Omnibus Co.
26.04.1884	Gardner's company reregistered as Magazines, New Brighton & District Omnibus & Carriage Co.
07.08.1885	Seacombe & New Brighton Omnibus Co. Ltd formed
Early 09.1885	S.& NB Co's Seacombe-New Brighton (Victoria Rd/Rowson St) service started in competition with Gardner
12.1887	Gardner sold Seacombe-Molyneux Drive service to Seacombe & New Brighton Omnibus Co.
02.01.1888	Wirral Railway opened between Birkenhead Park and Wallasey
30.03.1888	Railway extended from Wallasey to New Brighton
?? 1890	Bus Service Seacombe-Telegraph Inn, Mount Pleasant Rd via Penkett Rd, Sandrock Rd. Later diverted to Mount Road corner
09.05.1891	Wallasey United Tramway & Omnibus Co. Ltd acquired tram and bus services in the town
01.06.1895	Seacombe branch of Wirral Railway opened
30.03.1901	Wallasey UDC acquired Wallasey United tramway undertaking
25.05.1901	(New) Seacombe & New Brighton Omnibus Co. Ltd formed
09.09.1901	Horse car line in Falkland Road closed. Cars ran both ways via Church St
28.10.1901	Horse car service diverted via Liscard Rd & Wheatland Lane in lieu of Church St etc.
01.12.1901	Horse cars diverted to loop terminus at Seacombe fewrry
02.12.1901	Horse cars diverted to run Seacombe-Molyneux Drive via Seabank Road temporarily; former route covered by (new) Seacombe & New Brighton Omnibus Co. temporarily
17.03.1902	Seacombe-New Brighton via Wheatland Lane & Rake Lane electric tramway opened
19.03.1902	Seacombe-New Brighton via King St. & Seabank Road electric tramway opened
07.05.1902	Seacombe-New Brighton via Church St. & Warren Drive electric tramway opened
09.1903	Birkenhead & Seacombe Omnibus Co. service between Seacombe &

	Charing Cross started
1907	Horse bus service R.&J. Evans Seacombe-St Lukes Church via Borough Rd & Poulton Rd
1907	Horse bus service diverted via Abbotsford St, Belle Vue Rd, Gladstone Rd in lieu of Borough Road
01.03.1907	Wallasey Village station opened
02.05.1907	Falkland Road tramway opened for inward Warren Drive cars
08.02.1908	Horse bus service extended from Poulton to Harrison Drive via Breck Rd
08.07.1910	Seacombe-St.Luke's Church via Poulton Road electric tramway opened
c20.07.1910	Horse bus service curtailed to run St. Lukes Church-Harrison Drive
14.09.1910	Horse bus service Liscard Village-Wallasey Village Stn via St Hilary Brow
07.02.1911	Poulton tramway extended to Grove Road (Warren Drive)
10.02.1911	All horse bus services ceased.
1919	Birkenhead & Seacombe Omnibus Co.'s service motorised but discontinued later in the year
03.04.1920	First Wallasey Corporation bus service – Seacombe-Harrison Drive via Manor Road started
19.03.1921	Seacombe-Charing Cross via Duke St Bridge joint service commenced. Company service via Four Bridges ceased
26.06.1921	Charing Cross-Harrison Drive joint summer service commenced
24.10.1921	Charing Cross-Liscard Village joint service commenced
11.08.1923	Charing Cross-Harrison Drive summer service withdrawn
01.12.1923	Seacombe-St Nicholas Road bus service commenced
09.04.1924	Liscard-Charing Cross service diverted via Gorsey Lane
09.06.1924	St. Nicholas Road bus service reduced to peak hours only
12.07.1924	Grove Road-Foreshore via Harrison Drive seasonal service commenced
01.09.1924	Seacombe-St. Nicholas Road service withdrawn in mornings
19.11.1924	Seacombe-Harrison Drive/St. Nicholas Road bus service suspended for road works
01.1925	Service resumed between Liscard and School Lane
13.04.1925	Seacombe-Harrison Drive bus services fully reinstated (but not St Nicholas Road)
04.1926	Liscard-Charing Cross permanently diverted via Torrington Rd in lieu of St Albans Road
04-12.05.1926	Services suspended during General Strike except skeleton services by volunteers
08.1926	Sunday morning tram services seasonally commenced on all routes from 10.15am
04.1927	Post boxes on cars introduced
05.06.1927	Sunday morning services commenced between Seacombe/Liscard and Charing Cross

28.08.1927	Sunday morning services to Charing Cross withdrawn
12.09.1927	Seacombe-Harrison Drive via Poulton limited stop bus service commenced
30.10.1927	Sunday morning bus services commenced:
	Seacombe-Hose Side Road via Borough Road, Liscard Road & Seaview Road
	Seacombe-Molyneux Drive via Seabank Road
	Seacombe-Harrison Drive via Wheatland Lane, Poulton Rd, Mill Lane, Marlowe Road, St.Hilary Brow & Wallasey Village
01.04.1928	Sunday morning Seacombe-Molyneux Drive bus service extended to New Brighton
01.04.1928	Seacombe-Moreton (Bermuda Road) and Liscard Village-Moreton (Bermuda Road)bus services commenced
16.05.1928	Moreton (Bermuda Road)-Liscard service extended to Queens Arms
27.05.1928	Seacombe-Hose Side Road Sunday morning bus service withdrawn after operation.
10.06.1928	Egremont Ferry-Albion Street bus service commenced
15.07.1928	Moreton (Bermuda Road)-Liscard (Queens Arms) service extended to New Brighton via Rake Lane
30.09.1928	Egremont Ferry-Albion Street Sunday service withdrawn
01.11.1928	Egremont Ferry-Hamilton Rd (Mount Rd) via St James Rd temporary service during road works
20.01.1929	Buses replaced trams on Seacombe-New Brighton via Seabank Road route
	All buses rerouted at Seacombe outward via Brighton St., inward via Demesne St
By 01.02.1929	Egremont Ferry-Albion Street reverted to normal route
25.03.1928	Seacombe-Harrison Drive via Poulton & Marlowe Road Sunday morning bus service withdrawn after operation
08.04.1929	Seacombe-Albion Street service commenced (weekdays only)
By 01.06.1929	Seacombe-Harrison Drive via Poulton became stopping service
26.06.1929	Egremont Ferry-Albion St resumed at peak hours only on reopening of ferry
08.1929	Egremont Ferry-Albion St resumed all day
21.10.1929	New Brighton-New Ferry via Charing Cross joint service commenced
01.01.1930	Egremont Ferry-Albion Street service reduced to peak hours only permanently
14.01.1930	New Brighton-New Ferry service rerouted via Cleveland St.& Argyle St
03.02.1930	New Brighton-Moreton (Bermuda Road) via Grove Road service commenced
05.1930	Seacombe-Gorse Crescent experimental bus service commenced

06.1930	Virginia Road, New Brighton first used as a terminus. Approach route via Belmont Road and Balmoral Road
07.06.1930	Grove Road-Foreshore service extended to Bathing station
by 16.07.30	Seacombe-Gorse Crescent service withdrawn
30.12.1930	Workmen's tickets at single fare for return journey introduced on all bus routes
01.01.1931	Route numbers 1-12 introduced
30.03.1931	Poulton and Warren Drive tram routes curtailed at Grove Road and linked as a circular route
	6 Seacombe-New Brighton via Church St, Rullerton Rd & Belvidere Road commenced
01.04.1931	4 Seacombe-Moreton Shore seasonal service commenced
07.1931	Virginia Road seasonal terminus reintroduced at weekends – Approach route via Rowson St & Wellington Rd
09.11.1931	13 Seacombe-Martins Lane (Serpentine Rd) via Trafalgar Rd peak hour service started
05.02.1933	Rake Lane tram service replaced by bus route 14 operating between Seacombe & New Brighton at peak hours and Liscard-New Brighton at other times. Circle cars terminated at Church Road, Seacombe
04.1933	Seacombe-Moreton Shore service renumbered from 4 to 4A
10.04.1933	New Seacombe Ferry terminal officially opened
14.05.1933	Route 14 ran through between Seacombe and New Brighton all day
06.1933	Virginia Road used as seasonal terminus throughout the week
30.11.1933	Final day of tramway operation in Wallasey
01.12.1933	New Bus Services commenced:
	13/15 Seacombe-Mill Lane circular via Martins Lane & Poulton (weekdays only)
	16 Seacombe-New Brighton via Church St & Warren Drive
	17 Seacombe-Grove Road or New Brighton via Poulton Rd & Oxton Rd.
	6 diverted via Brougham Road, Poulton Road & Oxton Road
18.03.1934	13 curtailed at Martins Lane and 15 at St. Luke's Church and run peak hours only
	6 rerouted via Borough Road in lieu of Brougham Road
13.06.1934	Tower Grounds-Red Noses promenade service commenced
30.06.1934	3 Seacombe-Harrison Drive via Poulton service withdrawn
29.09.1934	13/15 withdrawn
01.10.1934	6 Seacombe-Grove Road rerouted via Martins Lane in lieu of Poulton Road
	17 rerouted via Mill Lane in lieu of Oxton Road
24.12.1934	2 Harrison Drive terminus moved from Groveland Rd to Wallasey Village
01.04.1935	10 New Brighton-New Ferry rerouted via Bridge St & Chester St. in lieu

of Argyle St

Summer 1935	6 extended to New Brighton on Saturdays & Sundays
Summer 1936	18 number allocated to Grove Road-Bathing station service
	19 number allocated to New Brighton-Red Noses Promenade service
01.08.1936	Revised workmen's and children's fares came into effect
04.09.1936	Post boxes on buses discontinued
27.09.1936	New Brighton and Egremont ferry services suspended for winter months. 7 Egremont ferry-Albion Street suspended for winter
11.07.1937	9 New Brighton-Moreton via Grove Road diverted from Bermuda Road to Borrowdale Rd
1937-8	18/19 used for Football Specials (18 via Liscard Rd; 19 via Penkett Rd)
07.02.1938	8 New Brighton-Moreton diverted via Joan Avenue and Douglas Drive
06.03.1938	Diversion of 8 via Joan Avenue & Douglas Drive withdrawn
14.03.1938	Wirral railway lines electrified; through service New Brighton-Liverpool
20.08.1938	7 Egremont Ferry-Albion St. service withdrawn
01.11.1938	8 New Brighton-Moreton (Bermuda Road) extended to Hardie Avenue
20.05.1939	19 New Brighton-Red Noses promenade service extended to Wallasey Beach
	20 route number allocated to Grove Rd.-Wallasey Beach but not operated
24.09.1939	Reduced wartime services commenced- 4A, 8, 9, 18, 19 suspended
02.01.1940	8 reinstated- hourly service.
18.04.1940	4 works journeys Seacombe-Saughall Massie Three Lane Ends RAF camp introduced
	8 works journeys Liscard-Saughall Massie Three Lane Ends RAF camp introduced
06.1940	Saughall Massie works journeys extended from Liscard to New Brighton
30.01.1941	4, 8 works journeys curtailed at Saughall Rd (Hoylake Rd) for a time due to condition of road
01.06.1941	8 diverted from Bermuda Road to Borrowdale Road
Late 1941	4, 8 works journeys to Saughall Massie withdrawn
27.05.1943	Virginia Road, New Brighton permanently adopted as terminus at all times
01.04.1944	5 Seacombe-Albion St (Hotel Victoria) extended to New Brighton station 8 rerouted via Mount Pleasant Road & Seaview Road in lieu of Rake Lane 17 rerouted via Claremount Road, Sandy Lane and northern part of St.George's Rd
11.09.1944	3 Seacombe-Mount Pleasant Road-Liscard special late service commenced
06.08.1945	6 diverted to Promenade via Sandcliffe Road at summer weekends.
19.11.1945	4 extended to Saughall Massie via Acton Lane (4) and to Hardie Avenue (4B)

01.01.1946	17 rerouted via Wallasey Village instead of northern part of St.George's Road
01.04.1946	6 summer weekend service extended to New Brighton (Bathing Pool) via Sandcliffe Road
03.06.1946	Late services restored and special late service 3 withdrawn
08.06.1946	2 extended to Promenade (Harrison Drive) and circular journeys operated at summer weekends by linking services 1 & 2
08.09.1946	8 diverted via Seabank Road and Magazine Lane in lieu of part of Rowson St
2.12.1946	16 some early journeys operated via Kelvin Road and Birkenhead Road
26.01.1947	17 Early Sun journeys Harrison Drive-Seacombe via Wallasey Village & St Hilary Brow
03.02.1947	16 Kelvin Road journeys withdrawn except 5.15am ex Grasmere Drive
01.06.1947	6 weekend summer service extended from Bathing Pool to Virginia Road
	11 Liscard-Charing Cross extended to run New Brighton-Higher Tranmere (The Wiend)
	18 Grove Road-Bathing station renumbered 20
	18 New Brighton-Arrowe Park service commenced
19.07.1947	8A New Brighton-Saughall Massie weekend service commenced Summer Saturdays & Sundays
03.08.1947	5 Seacombe-New Brighton station summer Sunday service commenced
20.10.1947	6 diverted via Grosvenor Street & Westminster Road in lieu of Liscard Road
15.05.1948	8A reintroduced – to run Saturdays all year and Summer Sundays
16.05.1948	5 extended to Virginia Road on summer Sundays
20.06.1948	4/4B diverted via Brougham Road. Some peak hour buses continued to use Borough Road
03.10.1948	5 extension to Virginia Road & summer Sunday service withdrawn permanently
04.1949	2 summer extension to Derby Bathing Pool as required commenced
30.05.1949	10 extended from New Ferry to Bromborough Cross
	11 extended from Higher Tranmere to Gorsey Hey; through journeys diverted via Mill Lane & Poulton Rd. Liscard-Charing Cross journeys continued to use Woodstock Road and Oxton Road.
	12 Seacombe-Charing Cross extended to run New Brighton-Bebington station
	4 rerouted as Seacombe-Borrowdale Road via Castleway North & Birket Avenue
	4A rerouted as Seacombe-Saughall Massie via Moreton Shore
	4S allocated for Seacombe-Moreton Shore via Borough Rd. Terminus moved to Birkenhead Road

	8A rerouted via Moreton Shore in lieu of Reeds Lane
	9 New Brighton-Moreton Cross via Promenade & Birket Avenue weekend service commenced
01.08.1949	4A,8A rerouted via Hoylake Road & Saughall Road in lieu of Acton Lane
24.09.1949	9 withdrawn
23.01.1950	10, 11, 12 extended journeys withdrawn at certain times of the day
08.04.1950	6 summer weekend service ran to Derby Bathing Pool via Harrison Drive instead of New Brighton
29.05.1950	9 New Brighton-Birket Avenue weekend service commenced
27.08.1950	9 New Brighton-Birket Avenue weekend service withdrawn
09.1950	6 summer extension to Derby Bathing Pool permanently withdrawn
16.10.1950	4 diverted from Borrowdale Road to Town Meadow Lane loop (anti-clockwise)
	4B extended to Town Meadow Lane loop (clockwise)
21.10.1950	8A diverted via Reeds Lane in lieu of Pasture Road to Town Meadow Lane loop (clockwise)
10.02.1951	8A renumbered 7 and diverted via Danger Lane and Pasture Avenue to Town Meadow Lane loop (anti-clockwise)
01.04.1951	4, 4A, 4B, 5 renumbered 3, 4, 5, 15 respectively.
	First post-war fares increase
04.06.1951	9 Liscard-Charing Cross via Poulton Bridge joint service commenced and all route 11 journeys reverted to Woodstock Road & Oxton Road.
01.10.1951	18 New Brighton-Arrowe Park service withdrawn in winter
11.04.1952	18 extended to Woodchurch Estate (Ackers Road)
08.1952	Town Tour commenced
23.05.1953	13 New Brighton station-Tower Saturday evening service commenced
25.05.1953	7 became daily service New Brighton-Flaxhill via Bermuda Road. Route via Danger Lane abandoned
03.06.1953	21 New Brighton-Frankby Cemetery Saturday and Sunday service commenced
14.11.1953	21 Saturday service withdrawn for the winter
27.03.1954	13 Tower service withdrawn after operation this day
29.05.1954	21 Saturday service restored
31.07.1954	18 New Brighton-Ackers Road seasonal service extended to Orrets Meadow Road via Home Farm Road
	21 Saturday service withdrawn permanently
17.01.1955	13 Trafalgar Road-Central station joint peak hour service commenced, Mons to Fris
25.02.1956	13 Saturday service introduced
28.05.1955	21 New Brighton-Frankby Cemetery curtailed at Liscard
11.05.1956	11 withdrawn between The Wiend and Gorsey Hey

10.02.1958	2A Seacombe-Harrison Drive via Green Lane & Bayswater Road off-peak trips started
14.04.1958	22 Liscard-New Brighton via Mount Road off-peak service commenced
09.06.1958	3 & 7 diverted via Gardenside & Twickenham Drive
11.10.1958	22 Liscard-New Brighton via Mount Road service withdrawn
08.12.1958	First Leyland Atlantean in municipal service took the road in Wallasey
03.01.1960	Seacombe branch railway closed
02.05.1960	6 diverted via Mill Lane and Marlowe Road in lieu of Rullerton Road
	7 Moreton terminus revised as anti-clockwise loop via Town Meadow Lane
31.10.1960	22 Holland Road (Haydock Road)-Moreton (Town Meadow Lane - clockwise loop)via Martins Lane service commenced
	23 Seacombe-Mill Lane (Woodstock Road) via Line of Docks commenced
02.01.1961	6 limited stop journeys introduced – Seacombe-Broadway Avenue via Wheatland Lane, Liscard Road & Wallasey Road.
11.02.1961	23 Seacombe-Mill Lane (Woodstock Road) via Line of Docks withdrawn
24.04.1961	3/5 limited stop peak hour journeys commenced
31.07.1961	3/5 (and probably 6) limited stop peak hour journeys withdrawn
05.08.1961	19 extended from Wallasey Beach to Derby Bathing Pool
28.08.1961	10A Liscard-Birkenhead (Kings Square) peak hour service commenced
	13 Trafalgar Road-Central station curtailed at Kings Square
10 diverted north via Argyle St., Hamilton Sq. Stn, Canning St, Taylor St; south via Canning St, Hamilton St, Birkenhead (traffic management scheme).	
11.09.1961	22 revised as Holland Road-Leasowe Road (Wallasey Village) via Steel Av. & Rake Lane
31.03.1962	22 withdrawn
20.07.1962	8A/8B New Brighton-Moreton Shore via Liscard (8A) or via Promenade & Bayswater Rd (8B) to connect with Hovercraft service (BUA Ltd) Moreton-Rhyl 10.15am-6.45pm
10.09.1962	Seacombe night ferry service withdrawn. Bus service operated between Liscard and Kings Square via Liscard Rd, Wheatland Lane, Kelvin Rd, 4 Bridges, Canning St, Chester St 3 trips
	2A some journeys extended to Kingsway via Rolleston Drive
	Liscard (Queens Arms)-Molyneux Dr via Liscard Rd, Brougham Rd, King St, Seabank Rd
(augmenting 1 & 14).Route number?	
16.09.1962	8A/8B withdrawn
01.10.1962	14/17 diverted to New Brighton via Victoria Rd in lieu of Virginia Rd
12.11.1962	23 Gorsedale Road-Green Lane off-peak service commenced
11.1962	3 LSTown Meadow Lane-Seacombe limitd stop service reinstated 1 jny each way
09.12.1962	2A extension to Kingsway withdrawn

?09.12.1962   Liscard-Molyneux Drive via Brougham Road service withdrawn

c.1962   4S use of number discontinued

7.01.1963   2B Seacombe-Green Lane (Bayswater Rd) via Groveland Rd service commenced, off-peak M-F & Su pm); 2A operated at school times & Sats only

20.01.1963   Liscard-Kings Square night service withdrawn after operation this night

18.03.1963   6/15 one man operation off-peak commenced

29.03.1963   14/17 diversion via Victoria Rd ceased

13.05.1963   22 Martins Lane-New Brighton station shopping minibus service commenced

02.06.1963   Wirral Tour commenced

06.1963   12 summer service curtailed at Bebington Road (Mount Road), Higher Tranmere

09.09.1963   15 New Brighton Stn terminus altered to loop via Atherton St, Wellington Rd, Portland St. & Alexandra Road.

01.04.1964   23 diverted to Leasowe Estate (Ross Avenue) in lieu of Green Lane

13.07.1964   22 curtailed to run between Liscard & Kirkland Road only

?13.09.1964   12 summer extension to Bebington Road withdrawn

27.02.1965   6 Seacombe-Grove Road via Belvidere Rd withdrawn

        15 Seacombe-New Brighton station withdrawn

01.03.1965   1A Seacombe-Stoneby Drive peak hour service commenced

        8 diverted via Mount Road and Albion Street

        16A Seacombe-Grove Road via Wheatland Lane & Kingsway peak hour service commenced 17 curtailed off-peak to run between Balfour Road & New Brighton only

28.06.1965   1A extended to Hotel Victoria

03.07.1966   17 through service between Seacombe & New Brighton reinstated

        16 curtailed to run between Seacombe and Grove Road only

23.11.1966   14 Experimental one-man operation with double-decker vehicles with top deck closed off; extended to 1, 2, 3, 5 by January 1967

General revision of services in Wallasey:

11.02.1967   16A & 17 withdrawn

12.02.1967   2/2B withdrawn at peak hours and Saturdays & Sundays

        4 operated Monday to Friday peak hours, all day Saturdays & Sundays

        5/14 withdrawn Monday to Friday peak hours

        30/31 Liscard-Moreton (Borrowdale Road) circular service commenced

        A Gorsey Lane (Poulton Rd)-Victoria Rd.(Rowson St) via Marlowe Rd & Sandy La. 2Su

        B Hose Side Rd-Trafalgar Rd via Wallasey Village, Claremount Rd &

	Liscard 2Su
13.02.1967	22 extended to operate Wallasey Grove Rd Stn & Kirkland Rd via Sandy Lane, Belvidere Road, Trafalgar Road
	24/25 Saughall Massie-Moreton-Leasowe local services commenced
	26 Seacombe-Liscard via Poulton Rd & Torrington Rd peak hour service started
	28 Seacombe-Liscard off-peak express commenced
	32/33 Seacombe-Belvidere Rd-Mount Pleasant Rd-Seabank Rd-Seacombe peak hour service
?10.03.1967	28 withdrawn; 14 increased in frequency
13.03.1967	12 Seacombe-Charing Cross converted to one man operation and worked by Birkenhead Corporation buses only
03.04.1967	26 diverted via Marlowe Road and Wallasey Road
	Restriction point on Crosville buses moved from Leasowe Castle to Leasoweside
	B Church Service ceased
18.06.1967	2/2B diverted via Claremount Rd and Sandy Lane in lieu of St Hilary Brow
	2A school journey continues to run via St Hilary Brow
	24/25 revised as 24 Fender Lane-Saughall Massie
c.07.1967	10A, 13 curtailed at Bridge St. in lieu of St Mary's Gate. (after 26.6, before Aug)
02.10.1967	Some journeys on 11 diverted via Storeton Road & Mount Road as 11A; Birkenhead Corporation buses only
01.06.1968	10 diverted southbound via Hinson St & Argyle St in lieu of Haymarket
04.01.1969	30/31 withdrawn
05.01.1969	2 revised and extended to operate Seacombe-Grove Rd (Warren Dr). via Green Lane (2B no longer used)
	4 Seacombe-Saughall Massie: Sun am journeys diverted via Reeds Lane in lieu of Pasture Rd
	24 extended back to Moreton Cross via Danger Lane & Pasture Avenue
14.07.1969	22 diverted via Claremount Rd, Broadway, Perrin Rd & Wallasey Village
09.1969	18 Woodchurch-New Brighton summer pm & weekends withdrawn
01.12.1969	Wallasey transport undertaking absorbed by Merseyside Passenger Transport Executive

APPENDIX 7
PASSENGER & MILEAGE STATISTICS

Year Ended 31 Mar	Revenue £	Passengers Carried	Miles Run	Pass per Bus Mile	Average Fare per Passenger d
1921	9,174	811,853	118,214	6.87	2.71
1922	12,212	1,012,731	127,027	7.97	2.89
1923	12,882	1,073,207	141,399	7.59	2.88
1924	12,821	1,072,538	156,409	6.86	2.87
1925	11,228	945,126	141,599	6.67	2.85
1926	12,163	1,074,225	157,127	6.84	2.72
1927	19,611	1,832,036	221,191	8.28	2.57
1928	27,225	2,574,224	315,726	8.15	2.54
1929	53,540	5,621,658	748,480	7.51	2.29
1930	109,284	12,560,361	1,428,302	8.79	2.09
1931	116,933	13,372,607	1,573,300	8.50	2.10
1932	131,092	15,695,397	1,890,023	8.30	2.00
1933	136,137	17,169,274	1,990,001	8.63	1.90
1934	159,750	21,220,919	2,452,708	8.65	1.81
1935	174,616	25,170,923	2,932,626	8.58	1.66
1936	173,532	25,446,236	2,096,016	8.22	1.64
1937	171,693	25,587,024	3,120,472	8.20	1.61
1938	177,025	26,425,610	3,101,395	8.49	1.61
1939	172,971	26,316,499	3,076,602	8.55	1.58
1940	166,982	25,133,978	2,686,075	9.36	1.59
1941	151,492	22,592,733	2,116,369	10.50	1.61
1942	153,424	19,911,629	1,948,175	10.22	1.85
1943	175,123	22,129,830	1,964,738	11.26	1.90
1944	182,044	23,077,971	1,874,749	12.31	1.89
1945	196,700	25,024,570	1,974,454	12.67	1.89
1946	209,024	27,634,758	2,074,765	13.32	1.82
1947	243,244	32,027,743	2,641,971	12.12	1.82
1948	279,455	35,419,073	2,969,639	11.93	1.89
1949	286,147	36,398,742	3,122,400	11.66	1.89
1950	283,036	36,590,009	3,182,882	11.50	1.86
1951	267,233	34,735,285	2,977,568	11.67	1.85
1952	314,963	34,820,823	2,954,275	11.79	2.17
1953	355,294	30,920,055	2,955,092	10.46	2.76
1954	352,912	29,743,198	2,934,719	10.13	2.85

Year Ended 31 Mar	Revenue £	Passengers Carried	Miles Run	Pass per Bus Mile	Average Fare per Passenger d
1955	353,164	30,108,549	2,867,280	10.50	2.82
1956	374,439	30,364,462	2,896,993	10.48	2.96
1957	394,952	29,612,349	2,776,263	10.67	3.20
1958	381,308	28,496,520	2,763,962	10.31	3.21
1959	415,865	25,768,509	2,775,419	9.28	3.87
1960	419,881	26,124,250	2,787,521	9.37	3.86
1961	423,392	25,666,319	2,717,487	9.44	3.96
1962	446,328	24,758,523	2,688,562	9.21	4.33
1963	437,925	23,340,457	2,590,564	9.01	4.50
1964	464,046	22,077,734	2,548,511	8.66	5.04
1965	467,232	21,131,339	2,497,780	8.46	5.31
1966	462,646	18,987,291	2,301,215	8.25	5.85
1967	443,707	18,197,291	2,245,283	8.10	5.85
1968	401,810	14,045,078	1,999,364	7.02	6.87
1969	417,555	14,861,771	2,118,965	7.01	6.74
1969*	312,016	10,321,629	1,383,947	7.46	7.26

FINIS

Wallasey's pioneering first Atlantean entered service on 8 December 1958 after being one of four exhibits on the Leyland stand at the Earl's Court Commercial Motor Show of that year. Seen entering Lytham on the Southport to Blackpool Rally of 1995, restored to original condition. (© Ted Jones)